Y0-DNM-277

The Flowers of Albion

The Flowers of Albion

Arman Nabatiyan

iUniverse, Inc.
New York Lincoln Shanghai

The Flowers of Albion

Copyright © 2005 by Arman Nabatiyan

All rights reserved. No part of this book may be used or reproduced by any means, graphic, electronic, or mechanical, including photocopying, recording, taping or by any information storage retrieval system without the written permission of the publisher except in the case of brief quotations embodied in critical articles and reviews.

iUniverse books may be ordered through booksellers or by contacting:

iUniverse
2021 Pine Lake Road, Suite 100
Lincoln, NE 68512
www.iuniverse.com
1-800-Authors (1-800-288-4677)

ISBN-13: 978-0-595-36356-8 (pbk)
ISBN-13: 978-0-595-80793-2 (ebk)
ISBN-10: 0-595-36356-3 (pbk)
ISBN-10: 0-595-80793-3 (ebk)

Printed in the United States of America

To my many companions and colleagues at Cambridge for whose enduring wisdom, grace and friendship I remain forever grateful.

We live within love and yet run away.

—*Mowlana Jalaluddin Rumi*

Contents

Every Hour I am Alive

Every hour I am alive
My spirit will devoutly strive
To win your favour
And then your love to savour

Every moment that I breathe
My heart as well does seethe
With emotions to make you mine
Or else upon the alters of death resign

Every moment that my mind dreams
The essence of living seems
Like such a sweet and tender paradise
That life's love of life breeds avarice

Every second that my eyes perceive
The beauty that they cannot believe
I turn and look at your sweet face
And realise that beauty accompanies grace

Every burning light within my soul
Shines visions of you and keeps it whole
My spirit has no desires but one need
And your love is all upon which my longings feed
Thus as I live through you my every hope is freed.

After All These Hours

After all these hours their fated course have passed
And grain-by-grain time stands upon its height no more
After the seasons all perish and breathe their last
Dear love, do justice, remember well this score
My life, bearing no more than soul and heart
Surrenders all that is within its due
Yields up its full bounty and essential part
For that which in your beauteous eyes live true
So after deep death reclaims my spirit whole
Mock not the flowers that take my mortal place
Let them serve the lettered commission of my soul
And forever worship the bright glory of your face
As that burden bears such meritorious worth
Looking on you twice grants life a second birth.

Tresses Dark and Wild

Fairest maiden, of tresses dark and wild
In the mortal range you hold no compare
In grace and features with such Beauty styled
That heaven itself shines in thy sweet air

But this boyish heart is far too bold
For idolizing when Nature has intended none
Thus with boyish heart these words unfold
To tell the drama of the Moon and Sun:

In the night your essence shines like a star
That holds to soft perfection across the sky
In the morn your beauty streams ever far
With rays of warmth and calm that never die

Thus without reply, to a simple worship I am bound
Until your tender face in Love's temple be found.

Fair Show of Art

Life is the fair show of art
That hides deep within the mind
The soul is the substance of the heart
That none but the pure can find
So the quest continues onward and unseen
As thoughts deceive the plain vision of the eyes
Portraying all to be a beautiful scene
When in fact the world is only hardship and demise
This is the throne upon which all mortals stand
Believing that there is no remedy to toil
Nor can there be rest for the laboured hand
Until it is delivered to the eternal bed of soil
The drama of man has many colours and shades
Countless lives that every desire can satisfy
But in the end when the world decays
Nothing is heard but a noise of deafened cries
So then the birds all flee in silent flight
As then the blossoms lift their heads no more
All is betrayed, the earth resigns to the immortal night
Sans hope, sans dream, sans life forevermore.

Every Hour

Every hour that we share
I breathe in your air
Oh how it is delight
For me to call you fair

As there is darkness, there is light
As there is sunrise, there is night
But as your beauty shines
My love everything burns bright

The deepest of sorrow rescinds
The bird of sadness no longer pines
For as long lives your face
Loveliness is seen along your lines

Your features, your softest trace
Your kiss, your hands, your embrace
Those blue stars upon the sky
Are but slaves to your comely grace

Thus I dream your beauty, I live to die
Worshiping your glory, never to question why.

Tomorrow's Shade

Feel not tomorrow or tomorrow's shade
Nature's prime red or vernal green
After their golden hour will quickly fade
Thereafter will remain unseen
Hold not to time, count not its sand
For each hour a new custom brings
As then fate cannot hold on to your hand
Nor can destiny its proud songs sing
Rely not on fortune, it deceives
What one-day is loss in another will be won
Yes as each triumph returns what it receives
Loss and gain are a game once again begun
Think not on youth or waxen age
A fondness permeates each living day
Nor should regret over undone deeds be waged
For we live not forever, but quickly die away
We are born by some miracle unknown
United by birth, each to perish to death alone.

Innocence Falls Away

The gardens groan, innocence falls away
And we are friends to a drifting peace
No love, no unity can stay
Hatred itself seems to never cease

Upon the brighter day, the darker night
When the stars are banished from the sky
And gone is the hope of even light
I look around and still wonder why

Why, why, why threads cannot hold
Our mortal fabric as one kind
The story of our lives together told
The freedom of our hearts within one mind

Why love and brotherhood are ministered wrong
When in the end from this earth we all must leave
Why these beautiful nations, their people cannot hold strong
But rather chose to kill and forever grieve

Forever and forever, some things have no reply
But isn't it better to question them than to forever die?

Forever Free

Forever free, that term is a threat to need
Threatening myself for needing you
You who my hope does lead
To us wherein our love is true

Time holds its reins above the sky
The stars are but pilgrims to our dreams
The angels are attendants to our cry
Though life itself is nothing that it seems

Tomorrow naught, naught is today
Save the love and hope that we together told
Thousand days and years can pass away
But as we have love the world will not grow cold

Nay, this whole universe will not freeze
Not as long lives your lovely face
Not as long as our hearts our souls do please
We will live forever by your immortal grace

Eternity being no more than time
Sung through praises of your love in rhyme.

The world progresses, I let go of its rein
Time tumbles into the hand, never more its embers to regain.

In Your Eye

As there is light, light dwells in your eye
The perfect sweetness lives upon your face
An innocence that can never die
A pious hope that one cannot trace
Either happy to have or in regret to cry

Upon the garden there is one glow
One stem, one thorn, one aching rose
One display of beauty, one lovely show
Heedless to the summer time it grows
Until all its scarlet petals blow

One majesty, one shine, one great esteem
One regard above all high held regards
One word, one sky, one bright star, its gleam
A sort of poetry that all time retards
Leaving your love and beauty upon my dream.

Valentine's Plea

Sweet maiden, of flowing locks and golden face
Love's own affection holds to your grace
Yet a virtue more is found in your heart
It is the clemency of passion, sweet Eden's art
Thus be the lady of this Romantic day
This gentle soul do not shun away
But shine like the sun, glorious, profound
With angelic face and warm all around
In the temple of dream be my star alone
Before the summer rose, take up youth's throne
Ah, and be seated there, great notice I shall take
Until from that soft slumber my eyes never wake.

None Are Beautiful

None are beautiful as they are fair
Or like you who blends love with loveliness
Nor have they the charm or quality everywhere
As you combine purity with holiness
Thus I remain fixed to where I stare

There can be no motion upon that star of fire
For stars and suns rule their realms alone
Nor can there be an equal to desire
That would not place you upon life's highest throne
Forever sans lack of envy to admire

All the lovely features that you hold
From this world can never be fled
Nor can they grow dark or cold
Nor with internal eyes be considered dead
Which heaven to all else denies, forever bold.

Slender Daughter of Youth

Slender daughter of youth
Be wary of time's ruth
It has none, compassion naught
Of sympathy it has aught
Thus its cruel blade and hand
Will fall shade to shade upon the land
Driving all beauty to sleep
A slumber full of sorrow, ever deep
That the brake of innocence dies
Fled are the streams of sighs
The voice of reason fades
The madness of passion never degrades
The need of effort frays
None are the golden rays
Of tomorrow, there is no shine
Thus spirits to darkness resign
Wondering why this infinite scene
Bears the light of suffering as its sheen
Why all these mortal scapes must pass unheard
Why the essence of living seems absurd
All these countless musings they fall away
Darkness overtakes the richness of the day
Leaving nothing behind but times indifferent ruth
Oh be wary of this world, slender daughter of youth.

That Wondrous Shape

What is about that wondrous shape?
That makes me so strong admire
That luscious lip, that blessed nape
That glorious eye that sets the world on fire

What is it about that fair geometry?
That makes me divest a thousand looks
To the bosom of your beauty's maturity
Oh cupid's archery, my heart you have mistook!

That curve, that figure, that sinuous form
That slender grace, those gestures divine
Rally heaven's clouds into an ungentle storm
Which to no fit of calmness shall resign

What of those proportions or that smile
Drives the soul of man into a rage
What charm, what artful ruse, what wile
Causes man his sanity to blindly wage

Whatever traces or signs or symbols of romance
Breeds in you, it does not matter the least
Whatever sky or light or star of chance
That has made you also has my love increased

As nature its perfection in you portrays
It matters the least how you begot your beautiful ways.

After All the Pain

After all the pain, encumbrance and strife
After the sacrifices and hard burdens endured
Another hindrance appears before the stage of life
And once again the remedy of disappointment must be procured
There is only one cure; you and I know it well
That lives and breeds inside the wise heart
Its fame, its infamy shall forever dwell
In the minds of those who never let excellence depart
Always to excel with esteem, the grasp of truth
Never wanes or leaves those of steadfast will
To exploit and to challenge their intellect in youth
To never let their burning passion lie for a moment still
It is the secret of success, the potion and all
In stride to triumph one must surely exceed
The standards of the time, to preserve them, to never let them fall
Lest cruel time comes to make greatness bleed
Only this much needs to be enforced and said
The practice of baseness only to base products leads
And as our days are numbered few before we resign dead
It is better to contribute to higher vision than to attend to selfish greeds
Thus with all your strength, endeavour on and on
With truest devotion make your purest stride
Pursue the most meaningful things before they are gone
Else with the dust of regret the soul shall forever abide
O' for life is fast fleeting and then we die
Aim only for the profound or the world will leave you sans reply.

Like the Rose

The sunshine like the rose is grown
Upon the heat of your burning cheek
Paradise and beauty, they live alone
Only within eyes and sprits meek
But then the heart of kindness takes to the throne
A new brightness upon the face is born
An old love with its complexions teems
Bringing new strength to the rising moon
Lending eternal powers to love's unseen dreams

The season then passes from leaf to leaf
The blossom of youth buds in its prime
The complexions of tomorrow brings no relief
As we are then reminded of wasted time
Oh all these games played bear no ulterior belief
The reason of the mind scatters far and wide
Gentle madness softly settles in
Thereafter sadness takes to the mortal side
And lets the despair of life to eternal win

"Such are the tunes of joy that on and on do play"
"Until defeat comes to consume us," so the old men used to say.

The Days Go On

The days go on and on and on
Without an answer, with the quietest cry
The burdens burden themselves upon
This pain of life than can never die

So the hardship dwells within the breast
So the soul with fairest sleep is consoled
Through worry itself is never given rest
Until the living mind is buried whole

The conquests endure the triumphs smile
And all the while that fair humble sun
Points to the sands of time, its brief lapsing dial
When once again mortal hope is new begun

The efforts and defeats, the endless strife
Reinforce the thought of the void creation made
To the envious and victorious, to the scores of unheld life
That all the same with the tracing dust must fade

And so the hours all perish, nothing is left of us
The accords of ambition expire fast
Perhaps better it is to surrender without a fuss
Then to carry on in this parody that does not last
Alas the strength gives in, the darkness consumes the grief
As then we all escape into the black world of disbelief.

Consuming Fame

Fame—it consumes not the little child
Who occupies himself with busy deeds
Nor is it much effective in taming the Wild
Who would rather attend to their daily needs
Than to reach and drive and drink from fame's dish
Few are so brave and so bold
As to make Lady Fame their prized wish
As to pursue the dominion of men aged and old
More often yet, when those men of old are dead
She comes their way to give them their reward
Well after their feeling hearts and senses have fled
Fame comes to crown them as Her lord
When eyes and souls and lives are no more
That fickle Lady decided it is their due
Drawing out her precious glory from its store
Trading them who deserve their merits true
And yet still besetting those with uncertainty and strife
Who have not wooed her or tried at her enough
Making miserable and void their short life
For some measure or quantity of her eternal stuff

Though in truth we realize She eternal is not
It does not stop us from wanting of her a little and a lot.

Basest Greed

Affection is the basest greed
That carries with it the highest price
Many even claim that it is more a need
Than some pretty accessory that is nice
This is false, we live in the perjury of truth
Inside each person this falsity dwells
From old age, it is a creeping relic of youth
That yearly grows and yearly swells
It gives no rest neither to the heart nor mind
It is the servant beast that powers to destroy
Some call it a threat, an endangerment to humankind
Others cite it for its charm or its means to cloy
It does not cease till it reeks deep tragedy
And causes precious intellect to degrade
Some doomsayers declare it will forever live to be
Man's one vexing weakness that will never fade

The one labour, the one toil, the one demise
The does not relent till love full consumes our eyes.

Why Doth Thou Glow

Why doth thou glow the way thou glowest?
Doth not this lesser star die in thy envy?
Or that paler moon, why dost it glowest?
With the waning light of what it can't be
Why doth the sea with all its bright array
Try to compete with thee who has no compare
Or that morning sun why doth it turn today
When no flame like thee can even be as fair
O' why doth the bird perched on its throne
Sing songs of sorrow through its lip
Why doth it coo the tale of the man lived alone?
When from thy sweet eye all pleasure he can sip
Or that angel of the white heaven mead
Why doth she fly lonely across the sky?
When love and beauty to your heart lead
Trust is thus reborn, my soul can never die.

Nor can it rest until thee it finds
And all of worship to thy glow of beauty binds.

The Brief Hours

Were it not for these brief hours that remain
Before death's dark hand and sickness take
The love of you and life that I yearn to retain
The dream of your face from which I shall never wake
Were it not for this nightly shrouded sleep
In which I dwell in the higher thought of you
My soul would not rest so as your image to keep
My heart would pulse on, pulsing ever true
Were it not that your glory blossoms fair
I would rebuke that lofty heaven way
That teems with brightness, still is void of your stare
Being thus, that heaven shines with the blackest ray
As were it not for the pureness of your eyes
I would forsake this life, all in all
These brief hours and years, the less pleasured cries
So again unto your kinder hand destiny to fall

From everything of worth and life I would resign
If the ten thousand worth of your love would be mine.

Ode to Intellect

When the soft lamp of inspiration burns
And fair intellect brightly shows its way
Nothing to its former state returns
All thoughts of antiquity decay
The seasons turn from leaf to leaf
Time bends its hands over the unseen sky
The clouds darken upon the sun's relief
And the moon protests to never die
Oh fair Intellect, you are the queen of them all
Borne of this earth and this earth to inherit
To you I surrender everything until the evening fall
Still upon that hour you shall be the highest merit
That mortal man can achieve with his prodigious mind
If only true peace within himself he can find.

Whole Universe

Against the whole universe shown black
Against wide starless scopes that nothing mean
There lie beauties which nothing lack
All of them their worth from you must glean
You who embraces all that is profound
You who embodies perfections supreme
In you every token of glory is found
Which some less apt to truth would call a dream
A vision, a sight, a sweet reverie
Something unseen, desired and deeply yearned
You shall remain the light that will forever be
The loftiest worship ever upon the heavens to be burned
So brightly, the court of lovers loses its hold
Eden sinks below the solace of relief
Yet as there are your eyes, the winter is never cold
Nor can hatred ever enter love's belief
The cherubs fly to where the light rays fall
Out from the sun and the soft evening shore
The cosmos to a blackened end may fall
Yet as long lives with your heart, I shall survive forevermore

Peering deep into the mystery of your soul
Afterwards wanting nothing, life itself becoming whole.

Inconstant Ways

Man's heart dwells in inconstant ways
As such it shall always be, forever to see
His devotion with his faithfulness sways
Some call it fate's decree, other's nature's immutability
Such is spoken his soul's inbred song
Rehearsed 'Merry merry light as sherry'
Reciting verses as if they belong
'To either love, beauty or beauty's fairy'
A fickle seated, creed, yet they endure
Endless throes of pain, endless insults and disdain
The intents of their mind still keeping pure
As desires never ware, so too they shall not refrain
Imploring to woo love's kind and fair esteem
With hot desire like burning fire
Like a warm tempest blown upon their dream
Inciting them to aspire, oh sweet love to require
As thus is lived the many fine shades of youth
Begging its deepest need, imposing its dire greed
Believe me, this one thing along I know as truth:
For love men bleed, upon it they shall feed
Until the wings of heaven take them to the sky
And there before the court of love they all gently die.

The Hour Goes

The hour comes, it lapses, the hour goes
The rays call out the beacon of the morn
The evening falls, the night it shows
That the sequence of time is undying born
Oh that is the nature of wicked time
That mortals have lamented for ages through rhyme

The scythe upon the lotus shines
The stars glisten over the slumbering mind
The face of youth, its Vesper-like stare resigns
To a place that none innocence can find
Once endowed with a rattle then a cane
As then by accident, death draws out its chain

Hail to eternity, the clouds give life
To the tender leaves and buds of the spring
The cool air drives away warm summer's strife
As winter once more its sphere of darkness brings
Casting each within its slumbered shade
Wherein all must ever unwillingly fade

What frigid frost, hope thaws and revives
A bold vision is spread out upon an unheld dream
With that dream, a darling love survives
As then life perishes untouched, unseen
Who are we to question what must expire
Are we no more than actions of a game of self-desire?

The fashion of the young, the fashion of the old
It's about the words of trust well known
Worthy they are, so then let worth be told
Live true, be true else with regret you'll always groan

Crying and waiting, protesting loudly that life is absurd
Though in the end the suffered voice by none is heard.

Rays of the Moon

The rays of the moon like arrows fly
To where the heart turns its face
There the soul yields no reply
To the callings of loving grace
However much desire may implore
The will is strong and thus says "nevermore"

But even the thought to deny
Stirs sweet reason to not decline
The questions that beg to ask why
Sweet love to sadness must resign
Being mad, questions cannot impeach
The iron will be kept far from love's reach

For dreams are but a thrall
To this wakeless scene of deep
The soul wonders if there is any at all
Or whether any will wake from this sleep
Thus we look around, the stars are blind
Thus no true path will we ever find

The skies, the air, the ocean's shore
Nature, the deity of life supreme
With indifference suggests there is nothing more
That lies yonder this scope of unpurposed dream
So we wildly turn our eyes to pursue
Some great hope we believe as true

The days, the nights, the hours and the years
Without contempt lead us to visions far
Without rest, sweet hearts race with fears
Unknowing of the fate inscribed upon the fleeting star

But mortal men must be stronger, they cannot believe
That such signs of tragedy fortune will not relieve

Thus carries on the streams of tears
Like unbridled, incessant tides
Weary of the grief that life inheres
Of the deep honours it never hides
In face of all the conflict and misery
One thing gives scope to life, only love can set us free

Thus there is no use to refuse or deny
That sweet abuse of love that lets us fly
Oh to feel it and thus to never to die.

Must You

Oh must you die, die, die?
Gentlest flower, my beloved, my dear
How can you bear to see me cry, cry, cry
When my heart to yours is so near

My all, my darling, angel white
Those wings of yours are pure, so ever pure
So innocent, they are divine as light
Cast upon sweet eyes demure, demure

Oh princess queen, my everything
I worship the soft, soft word
That from your fairer voice does sing
And makes pain a thing absurd

Oh fly, fly, fly away
And take me to your golden height
Upon this earth no mortal can stay
After having perceived your glorious sight

Weep, weep, weep, nay grieve no more
For the sea of sorrow must fade
Much as the rose and moon are not at war
So shall the soul of love never taste death's shade

Oh time, oh time, oh ungrateful years
Human memory is but nothing at all
To the rebuke of the burning tear
That with your death must fall, fall, fall

With a melted hope I thus resign
To the dream of thought where you are again mine
And there too I contently die, die, die…

Every Hour That I Live

Every hour that I live, I am reborn
Into the fashion of things I know not
Every moment my soul breathes, it feels forlorn
One trace before the dawn, one step before the dust to rot

With every beat of eternity on which my essence thrives
I feel as a beggar to vast and lavish homes
Who himself along the shelter of the street survives
Yet never ceases to adore beauty where he roams

Every second that the stars their twilight shed
The skies glimmer with beams of golden white
The dreams upon those stars themselves seem dead
Oh ever glowing red before the steep fall of night

Every stroke of the clock that swiftly passes by
Lights up the visage of time, its shows unkind
Robbing innocence away, forcing hope to die
Upon the once bright and warm and cheerful mind

Every turn of the scythe and the season's blade
Brings change, oh wicked change to all
Lending tragedy to life, causing pride to fade
Until the notes of death upon all do fall

Every rise of the sun, every setting of the eve
A new story of sadness comes to tell
Shade to shade and from eye to eye we grieve
As against the madness of this world we rebel

There is no remedy to this game, time comes and goes
Against the scope of eternity, it smears our sorrows and our woes.

Never to Relent

I shall not relent, no, never
Not as long as these bones inhere their strength
To cry out their heart of love forever
To wail and pine their loss at length

Oh maiden, damsel, oh mistress dear
Know that my soul shall not surrender
And they who to it are sacred and near
No, cankerous time cannot be their offender

Hope is the defender, beauty is its form
Admiring eyes are its soft gilded grace
Passion is the thing that binds them warm
Romance lends fairness to every living face

The earth with its endless daylight shall shine
To keep the skies and stars and clouds above
Far from the table on which lover's dine
Far from the feast and fame of eternal love

Fate shall not stand in fortune's way
Much as April's musk shall not forsake the rose
Nor will the night be so bold to veil the glowing day
Nor the world so cruel to kill the dream that grows

For love is proud and vain, fiery blushed, unsatisfied
Raved with mad ravings that have no compare
Fed with the voice of gods, supremely defied
The legions that drink its milk die before its stare

Thus being crowned upon such a lofty throne
I lack all reason my feelings to repent

I will not fall to my knees or bow to make moan
As love is immortalised, there is nothing to which I relent

No lover! Be bold and never afraid
For those who love can never fade.

What Tears Can Be Shed

What tears can be shed?
For what cannot be restored
What use is there to weep for the dead?
Or cry for the years lost by the sword

Why wait the anguish of wretched time?
Or repent its scythe of misery
Can there be some benefit to moan its crime?
Or grieve its score of tragedy

Nay, it is written in the scenes of fate
That we must suffer mortal pain
To endure the toil, it is in our natural state
To forever bear discomfort and disdain

No night of heaven can we claim
No star of Eden can we defend
No life is lived out twice the same
No life is without its end

So we persist on, over and over again
Valiant, high-hearted, full of pride
Pretending to be more than mortal men
As then death takes us to its easeful side

What stilted heights, what vain pursuits, what glorious games
We chase the stars to their souls and leave them to die
What mad ecstasy, what wild plays, what unlasting fames
As upon this stage we are left forlorn to cry, cry, cry.

Sweet Moistened Lips

Those sweet moistened lips
They are a rarity, nay a casualty, a charity
Like the honey dew that the daisy sips
They are majesty, tyranny, a thievish courtesy

That heart, that soft sapient heart
It is fair, upon it all do stare
More graceful than graceful art
It shines bright both here and there and everywhere

Those eyes, those soft temperate eyes
They glow like brilliant spheres; within them love appears
To never decay into the troves of demise
They are so ever clear, none can fear, the beauty it inheres

Those tender cheeks, those strawberry cheeks
They blush divine like scarlet wine, they resign
Into the mouth that of your love fragrant speaks
That calls your face a shrine, its ruddy lobes to forever shine

Those hands, those soft curling hands
That equal burning palm, it is like soothing balm, so ever calm
It is the lush paradise spread across many lands
O' what a palm, what easeful balm, what placid calm

O' that skin, that pure and tender skin
It makes me profess, madness I confess
Its confederacy like a dream does win
The prophesy of life, oh yes, I love it more not less

Her throat, that throat, that sweet ardent throat
Causes me to hide, to subside along her beauty's side

To hear her lulling melody, her gilded and kindred note
Its like ambrosia for the ears, oh I hide, I hide, I hide!

O' that breast, that warm feeling breast
It is the opium of the mind when it cannot find
A pleasure on earth to give it gentle rest
O' my arms do wind, these lips to them forever bind

That waist, that worshipped and most magic waist
Like a goddess of mirth, it gives joyous birth
To every endearment that man bears lust to taste
What gravity, what worth, oh what a splendid earth!

O' that glow, that warm darling glow
It is red, it is wed, o' to my hunger that is fed
So glorious that the birds shall always sing this show
Until the earth and seas themselves are fled.

Glory of the Eve

The loveliest glory of the eve
Settles in slow and tepid haste
The sobbing eyes they dry and stop to grieve
The crown of beauty thrown to waste
For when the rays of dawn do rise
Fast fled is all sorrow and demise

The moon, the sun, the stars, the sky
The seasons of winter and spring
Contrast each other, no one knows why
The lapse of one the other does bring
But so it has been since the start of time
So it shall remain by the end of this rhyme

The dove then flies to a distant hill
Beneath the grass there lies a tryst
Over which scenes of love do spill
And fragrant flowers release their mist
Within that cove, that Avalon, pleasure is spread
In ways enjoyed by angels and the dead

The liquor of the morning runs pale
The larks gather by the open sea
Breast to breast their songs they exhale
In blithe joy and tepid unity
The rustle of the wind blows, all is sweet
When tender eyes on that soft vision meet

Along the summer meadow and verdant mead
Plush roses press their stems to the floor
Red, yellow, violet—all these colours lead
To the altar of time—beauty survives nevermore

For time is like a Satan, with sharp and waiting scythe
He stands to reap all that is too perfect or too blithe

Near the gentle and wavering stream
A babe is new born, an old man dies
The nymphs surround them both like a dream
Singing to them their soft and eternal lullabies
Unchanging, indeed, our existence is rife
Save for those who live, they have passion for strife

The clouds of the day then expire and flee
Eden falls from glory into the depths of night
The eyes, they weep again for what cannot be
Grieving in sadness the drowning of the light
Beauty is darkly palled, the tomorrows fade
No yesterdays live at all within times immortal shade.

Many Wonderings

Many and many wonderings have been spent
Questioning what this existence means
Many and many thoughts themselves have lent
Contemplating life's diverse scenes

Concluding no substance between it pervades
No single colour serves it just
Every degree combines within its shades
Everything resigns to it for it must

One ray the less, one ray the more
Upon this world has no consequence
Some call it a fable, some as truth's own lore
Some say it is an infinite and wayward sequence

That never dies though we must die
That knows not darkness though it palls
Every trace of being upon the earth or sky
Bringing death upon that which it falls

The weight of death is mere nothingness
When the scope of nothingness is bleak compared
To this wide universe which itself must regress
To a state that even hope leaves unrepaired

Oh what a dream it is, then let us wake
From this slumber innocent seeming
Or this drowsiness, let it our souls to take
Perhaps carry onward with this dreaming

To see where this open vision will lead
Or else resign amidst the blindness to be forever freed.

A Million Ways

In a million ways I protest my love
Knowing that still my voice is softest heard
By you to whom my adoration I wish to prove
With the elegance of a kind and loving word
For if hopes were prayers I would say amen
If prayers could restore hope into the hearts of men

Thus I continue on like a savage in his rage
Incapable of discerning between day and night
As if life was no more than an unspoken page
Whose contents are subdued to love's dying light
My eyes being subject to such simple grace
I desire nothing more than the beauty of your face

Oh what tenderness, the mind feels incarnate
Pondering the substance of time unheld, unseen, unknown
Praying for the truest virtue of the fairest state
Knowing that the canker feeds upon what beauty has shown
Realising this world is naught, I fear not death
For in your love I find life's new-blossomed breath

The will endures, uncertain of what may pass
Fortune is frequent prone to die upon its shade
Just as the gentle violet must grow amongst the grass
So too much youth upon its golden hour fade
Taking everything that in sweet existence lives
Save the belief that youth, love and beauty eternal gives

Faith, I suffer the lark's sad held grief
When I perceive the star of the warmest shine
Its loneliness compelling me to one thought, one relief
Either to die or to forever have you in these arms of mine

Oh what a modest touch, thus my revelling is like a dream
Where pride resides in you, lacking it does worthless seem.

Appeared As Gold

What once appeared as gold
In the eyes of youth
Their hue could not hold
So they died by truth

What once appeared divine
Without fault or blemish
In time it did resign
As something that none could relish

What once appeared perfect and supreme
By the inexperienced hand
Later emerged as a fabled dream
That only fools could understand

What once appeared pure and pristine
Innocent as the wakeless sun
After a while lost its lustre and it sheen
It then declined into days undone

What once appeared tender and tame
Gentle as the soft midnight rose
At closer view did not seem the same
Such are the faults of man, everybody knows

Being kind of heart, each time we stare
With selfish desire we inspect
Everything base we deem as fair
Always noting the good, ignoring the defect

Some say it is out of meekness, others greed
Others claim it is self-worship that we revere

Despite these arguments, it is the nature of our creed
To make things at first seem more than they appear

Thus we shall continue onward in this most unrighteous way
Mocking beauty, extolling things whose golden hue can never stay.

Where Love Presides

The heart resides where love presides
There all are free to pursue
Their passion with amorous strides
Until they win the heart that's true

Along the sky a gentle cry
From the winged cherub is heard
Its arrows are poised, its dreams cannot die
Its blood is untamed, its soul is stirred

Aside the fountain of youth, the gild lace of truth
Shines and embraces the waters pristine
The songs of the sirens, they fade uncouth
As the nymphs wake under the soft garden sheen

And so the sun glistens, so the bird listens
To the many tales of love untold
That sorrow related, on its own it christens
The word of heavy pain into lexicons old

The slender shine of fate, for none it does await
As then the warm summer with the moonlight grows
Into a pallor drawn and woeful state
Where only the unrelenting wind of desire blows

All is left alone, the dove is seated upon the throne
As then life in a deep silence decays
They who love, they are the first to groan
When love is void and empty from their days

Those wills that are strong, they do not long
For the things that by nature too quickly fade

The deep pleasures of love, some call them wrong
Others say it is a deception that from beauty was made

Yet the souls that thrive they do survive
When both their weak and hard faces fair
They nourish in their minds and keep alive
Preserving it here and there and everywhere

The lark flies again over the heads of men
Claiming that love, sweet love shall forever reign
Upon the warmest nights we seek, we shall find it then
There on our eyes, our breaths, our souls it shall sustain

Perchance the stars will lead us, the mind will defend
This endeavour of love that unto death can never end.

The Clock Ticks On

The clock ticks on, it is morn
Another dawn through the horizon breaks
Another sun through the east is born
Another howl of life from its slumber wakes
Awaking as if some sort of dream
Makes this life precious seem

A ray is thrown, its casts upon the clouds
Another crown of light brightly shines
Another mortal upon the surface crowds
Another creature to the ground of death resigns
Proving once again that there is no escape
That in the end death all will rape

The tide crests and crashes along the shore
Another moon shows itself upon the sky
Another night eclipses heaven's door
Another star upon its throne does gently die
Substance is eternal, form is not
Time forces all to one day rot

The tree gently sheds it summer leaf
Another flower blossoms upon the plain
Another bird sings his grief
Another darkness falls on the undying pain
The story of nature has no start or end
Yet its altering course all does amend

The seasons pass, they beset their fame
Another wind blows, grimly tossed
Another heart falls in love without shame
Another soul expires, a heart of love is never lost

Thus this fair and lovely game is played again
Beautiful pretending, though its poisons the souls of men

The dew and rain fill up the silent brook
Another fading year lapses onto its fate
Another set of eyes gaze with brave eternity's look
Another bold finality for those eyes awaits
Striving endlessly, surrendering their breath
Finding naught but this lone truth: all must yield to death.

Clouds of Life

Anon, anon, here draws the clouds of life
With its bitter tides and unseen shades
Fathering the pulse of warmth, its pains are rife
Even those that resist, they too will fade
So here comes forth the wide ebbing shore
Froth upon froth along the open Oceanside
Time seems as lost, yet in truth no nevermore
Within those grainy sands, an unchanging force resides
Immutable, though it pretends to be unseen
Inalterable, though it takes on unnumbered forms
A million shades, yet all of them are like a glory unclean
Death runs through valleys when misfortune storms
Oh happier are those who with spirit free
Hear the music of the wind and its call of romance
Those born enslaved, they wear the cloud of mystery
Unknowing of tomorrow, deaf to wild rhythms of chance
The days and years still advance one by one
And one by one the canker feeds
Upon the rose whose crown of youth is won
Before the summer's end, it dies upon the blossomed meads
Young but free, it dies, nay, it cannot endure
Nothing mortal can ever survive
The shine of nothingness, its gleam is too pure
To allow any being to remain alive
Defeat replenishes tears, it's like the new born jade
Whose glow of splendour impresses all
But after countless experience, the light is obscured in shade
Thereafter all of us before darkness fall

Unfeeling of the bleaker torments that us await
Sans comprehension, in silence we resign to that our infinite state.

Lucky Star

How privileged thou art, oh lucky star
Nested upon that high lattice sphere
How I wish I were what thou art
To exchange my mortal soul with thy starry tear
Oh ever bright heaven out yonder
How I wish I was blessèd as thou art blessed
Upon thy gentle air, nothing can look fonder
How if I were thee, my soul would have all its rest
Oh glimmered moon, how thou art fair
How I wish I had the trace of beauty that you own
Tranquillity would stream through my every stare
Oh how I wish thou and I lived far and alone
Ever peaceful sun, how you burn soft and bright
How I wish I could shine like thine ray
That from you doth burnst like brilliant light
How I wish I could live forever under your eternal day
Oh wondrous grass of the autumn field
How I wish I were the dust under thy feet
All the pleasures of the world through simplicity yield
How I wish my humbler parts thine could meet
Oh majestic sea, warm and tender are your tides
That timeless wash to and fro, bringing upon the face of change
The hours and the years, the stuff of ages upon you rides
How I wish my fate with your deathless grace I could exchange
This envy pains me so, life is immortalised
When the love of heart is sequestered without needs
As then quaint and clearly I realised
That my truer spirit through all of life breeds

Thereafter my love and soul were free
To all those things of nature that I did envy.

Hold Onto Love

I hold onto love
And think nothing of
What may come to pass tomorrow
Forget about the sorrow
For as we still have time
And this song its rhyme
The sun its shine
The stars their sign
You shall always have me
And I the soul of thee
Surrendered, here upon the hour
My love, you preside over my every power
My every cry, no heaven will not deny
Our love forever until we together die.

The Hours Call

The hours call
For us to fall
Into the days unseen
Youth's flower is always green
But as time declines
So too my heart resigns
To where hopes are more free
Whether or not they will live to be
It's a question unknown, I do not care
But as the sky glows so ever fair
I promise myself the dream
That my wide universe will redeem
All that henceforth stirs within my core
Will continue on sweetly as before
Forever to live, forever to be
Mortals are deceived in what they see
Upon the pleasure of the loveliest face
Or upon the splendour of eternal grace
Entreat nothingness, in me, virtue is not fled
No never until my whole world falls dead.

Worlds Turn Black

The worlds turn black
Never look back
To what once was or could have been
Deeds as those are worse than sin
For as there still is time
And truth to this rhyme
We can live for what tomorrow brings
Hope and freedom the new lark sings
So then lend me your mind
And to it a dream I'll bind
One bold whose vision is unseen
Whose fruits one can only later glean
As the noblest thing is to have belief
In yourself, seeking from the others no relief
These are the virtues that let man succeed
In humble ways far away from greed
Seek them and you will forever own
The happy throne, never to be alone
In a world half purposed—away from strife
The most beautiful thing is the true lived life.

Never To Fear

Never will we have to fear
Not as long as I have you, my dear
Today and tomorrow is the same
We shall together play the game
Of love and life and the living dance
Of passion, amourility and romance
We shall forever live to be free
Oh my love, you and me
The happiest creatures; one soul, one breath
Forever and ever well unto death
Until the sightless end of time draws near
My love, as we are together, never will be have to fear
Neither time nor time's cold hand
As I have you the whole world I understand
Never to wander or decay
With you my love, I shall always stay.

Those Who Admire

Your face is a prize to those who admire
The accents of a beauty great and rare
For them your eyes are orbs of fire
Forever burning, forever true, forever fair
Your heart, it is more than what words can relate
More than what a world can create, so modest, so demure
More glorious than glory's self made state
More righteous, more noble, more calm, more pure
And that soul, it is of a thing divine
That mortals with earnest mind can hardly understand
Those of steadfast pulse, they too resign
Their arms to yours, to embrace the warmth, hand in hand
Oh they who with a greater wisdom are bestowed
Worship you for things that passionate men would not
But if they with truer gazed were allowed
To stare at you, they would dearly envy our lot

For only those of us who deeper beauty appreciate
Know that you are more fair than fair, more great than great.

All These Days

All these days, they seem as lost
Youth has dragged on with it a fiendish cost
The blackest dross, no existence remains
But as there is your love, my heart it sustains
The soft beauty reflected in your light
As there is your warmth, there can be no night

The stars shine brightly all around
Inside the soul, a small hope is found
Rehearsing your name with graceful praise
Extolling the virtue of your loving days
O' what innocence, I resign away
To where your love within my soul can stay

Your gentleness from my mind can never depart
So indeed this love is bred deep within my heart
Despite the bliss of youth than cannot last
I hold remembrance for you, it dwells in the past
No the memories shall not fade, yet if they die
My love, this song shall live to multiply

In the minds of those fiery cheeked with youth
Who look to innocence with the impulse of desire
Who are too young to understand love's painful truth
Thus I turn to you and burn under your love's fairest fire!

The Days Draw Long

The days draw long, they depart
They leave empty my weakened heart
O' I care not for them, let them flee
Let bygones always bygones be
I will be more free when death comes to take
My spirit from my frame, no it will never wake
Therefore under the heavens I will lie
Wondering of the substance that makes up the sky
O' as I die, I die believing no more in fame
The darkness comes, it blots out my name
Yet still by spirit, I am the freest form under those stars!

There is No Rest

Upon the earth there is no rest
Pillowed high upon the mortal breast
Is the endless pang of death, its pain
Brings nothing but fears, misery and disdain
To the tender mind that yearns for love again
Time lends agony after having found love then
So the sad story onward plays
As here draws forth the shaded rays
Of times defeat, the warrior his hand does wage
With the blade of infamy, he sheds his rage
That warrior is us, so we live in despair
As onward again into this black siege we stare
Perceiving nothing but a darkness bleak
The heart resigns, the veins muster weak
As upon this depicted world, all against all decays
And nothing remains but the remembrance of fonder days.

As Youth Lives

As youth lives
And your face to it beauty gives
Forever yours I shall remain
Your love I shall uphold and sustain
For all of time, nothing shall transcend
The warm kindness that you lend
To me, my soul, all of my heart
I swear, my love, it shall not depart
Never from you, hope is not far
And we shall look to the symbolic star
For the eternal tracing of romance
Or for finer fate, or destiny, call it chance
Whatever the term, to you I resign
Within the depth of my wings I consider you mine
Until all of time does fade
And even shadows hide within their shade
The whole universe itself may decay
But as I have your love to your world I run away.

One Morning

One morning I did wake
Just as the sun, its rays did take
Away from the bright shining sky
Far and distant, I did not question why
Nature works in such extreme
Seeing all equal, holding no esteem
Neither for evil, nor for piety
Its laws are writ in immutability
For all to see and realize
That nature can bless and tyrannize
This is the way that Lady Fortune takes
The distinctions that the men of earth make
Mean nothing, as in the end we to dust will fade
Wandering about until in death's shade
We fall, our heads to never rise again
This is the way that morals go, even the best of men.

Gives Me Pleasure

She gives me pleasure
Beyond all measure
That is why I love hear dearly
And I will make love to her freely
For she is my friend
All my love I send
To the place that has no face
Receiving strokes of warm embrace
Till darkness traces
And beauty laces
The love that upon us shines
By the composure of these lines
She shall remain
The one I shall sustain
Inside my heart forever
Hand and hand we shall be together
As our souls immoral stay
But our bodies run away
Where you and I
Can never die
Our wings to fly
Above the bluest sky
Forevermore to be
The greatest lovers to see
O' love because she gives me pleasure.

We Have Time

As we have time
And in me burns this rhyme
I shall always try to woo thee
Despite what you may say to me
You shall forever remain
The dear beloved that I shall retain
Within the depth of my heart and soul
None can divide it, it remains whole
For you and your hand to take away
Your grace to brighten up the day
Upon which my eyes peer and in amazement gaze
Up at your beauty and most beautiful rays
Upon your gentlest cheek, your dimpled face
The rose of your youth, your loveliest embrace
Your hands, your fairness that is diamond bright
Clearer than the moon upon a cloudless night
Sweeter than the babe who in late evening wakes
And from his pious nurse, his suckled innocence takes
So then upon your glory I will feed
As your eyes tell stories, all of them I will read
Until time decays and there is nothing left to learn
Save your eternities that like all of brightness burn.

The Threescore Day

Upon the threescore day
You shall remain the Fay
Of all that I admire
I would set the world on fire
If that burning world can shine more bright
Than your sweet eye that glimmers darling light
Oh love, how you are like an angel in the sky
Whose loveliness leaves words without reply
Nor can the world's greatest written prose
Half of your fairness with blotted ink compose
The moonlight glows and so too does your face
My dear, you are the true queen of grace
That shall live to outlive undying death
So I shall resign to you my lapsing breath
If my hand with this heart you will receive
Forever with my soul in your love I will believe
Oh truth, oh hope, oh light, therefore I come to you
Only say that with your beauty you will love me true
My dear, upon that howl I will be free
To love all that your beauty will ever be.

Speak To Me

You speak to me
My soul does flee
To where yours cries
My spirit to there flies
There your beauty never dies

Though all hopes seem
To be not more than a dream
Born in the tenderness of the night
Under the warmth of the light
Where happiness is free and not contrite

There my spirit dwells
Where your fairness swells
Within the centre of my mind
Within me your voice is kind
To your love I shall always bind

Though nothing can forever stay
And all is meant to pass away
Yet with you near
There is nothing that I fear
Emboldened in every hour of every year

To love there can be no end
For to all your grace does lend
Humanity and the human state
Your nature's kindness does create
The salvation that one and all await

The sun upon it throne I shall cherish
Must as you amber glory will not perish

Your fairness shall remain
The one truth that I retain
Within my heart that you sustain

There is no need for time
Or the simple composing of this rhyme
If you are mind
All the stars do shine
Life upon sweet heaven does resign

I shall continue on to live
As long as your love to me you give
Enduring well past the mortal shade
When everything of earth must degrade
All save you and love that can never fade.

Every Hour

Every hour I am alive
Every hour that I strive
I look and aim to your beauty still
Oh heaven it overtakes my will
So be it then I am your slave
One perfection I shall save
The one glory, the one majesty
The one eternal truth that shall forever be
It's you my love, oh you alone
You who reigns the kingdom and the throne
Of this heart's love, it shall not leave
Its pining loss, it shall not grieve
As there is you, bliss is restored
Joy is kept within the dearer word
Of your love, your loving eyes
Those bare and starless skies
They mean nothing, dead is the sting of sorrow
I only look to you and the page of tomorrow
There a happier fate is writ
A brighter destiny, there my hopes are lit
Under the fairer light of your complexion
Its esteem, its soft reflection
To resign in your arms tonight
To kiss away your lips, fled is that light
My dear, amid the darkness I return to you
Forever this love and life to be held true—together.

The Lovely Day

The meadows, the banks, the lovely day
Cannot compare to you in any way
The brooks, the sky, the clearest stream
Before the face of you is a cloudy dream
The leas, the grass, the humid shore
Is as graceful as you nevermore
The stars, the sun, the nightingale's wing
Cannot flutter a more romantic song to sing
Than all the beauty that in you is seen
The angel above a greater perfection cannot wean
The hours, the years, the ages past
Against your immortality cannot last
For you are so glorious in your state
That none your fairness can imitate
The hands, the lips, the warmest breast
Will desire you until they are given rest
The brow, the arms, the admiring eyes
For all of eternity your tender love will prize
My dear, you are the greatest thing to ever be
Thus my heart and soul and mind all belong to thee.

Quickest To Fall

The caring and the most giving of all
The kindest of them will quickest fall
In this world where nothing is admired
Save the lust that satisfies what is desired
The tenderest who bears warm innocence
In his life will make the lesser difference
For what this world asks for and needs
Is a little avarice and a hunger that breeds
For that which we require the least
Still we are asked to be the beast
As well as the savage who heartless preys
On that which the purer mind turns away
That which makes dark the day and black the night
And blinds the eyes of truthful sight
Makes crooked the straight and the pious amends
To give up then righteousness for evil ends
Making putrid the soul, the spirit is foul and vile
When its whiter parts are betrayed and defiled
Oh I bid you, fair mortals of this earth
That human nature is instilled from birth
To take all that it can and then decay
This is the truth of which all men pursue the way
Forever, until the stars collapse and pall
Take heed, the kindest of them will quickest fall!

Draw Close and Celebrate

So let us draw close and celebrate
For your love my heart will always wait
Until the songs of passion in our breaths resume
And we the nectar of romance consume

Upon the meadows and the leas and the brooks and streams
Where the nightingale over the enchanted pond dreams
There we shall feed on the gentle play of light
Until love and destiny overtake our sight

Fond is the mind that does remember
The summer before the spell of December
But as there is hope, we in immortal summer shall live
As to every season, you living warmth do give

You are the sun, expectation is the fire
That fuels the impulse of desire
Thus my dear, I proclaim you to be
The one prevailing force that sets my spirit free

You are the flame, the stars, the elder of creation
The one longing, the one truth, the source of all admiration
Thus by my honour, I swear you are my queen
That shall outlive ages long-lived and unseen.

I Swear True

By my honour I swear true
That I love no one else but you
That you I consider my queen
Through all that thoughts may ween

I remember not yesterday or tomorrow
For in both of them remains the sadness of sorrow
I only look forward to the present time
In which you are held in these arms of mine

The world offers no solace or repose
The sun and moon their equal light impose
But as there is your beauty, there is no rest
To the words that describe your fairness as the best

In me you shall remain alone
As the grace who rules over my spirit's throne
Yet to this madness there can be no reward
Unless your kingdom upon me is forever restored

"Forever" that is a word I scarce use
For time can come and my heart abuse
But believe me there is nothing I fear
Save the loss of love when you are near.

One Divine Light

There is one divine light that I can see
And that beauty my love, is of thee
That glory all hold of time exceeds
The sun in envy of your fairness recedes
To the kingdom where darkness rules alone
And nothing is seen but your brilliant throne

Cast aside the shades, cast them far away
Upon your sheen of brilliance rises up the day
The cold shadows belong not on you
For through you face, warmth is felt as true
Across wide ages past, time shall come again
Gracing the immortality that you will have then

What gold, what prime, what gentle grace
Youth will endeavour your beauty to chase
Unawares that it cannot reach
The perfection that tender fame does teach
None can have you, you reside above
This plain and simple thing that mortals call love

That is why I long for you more and more each time I read
These verses upon your eyes, all the calls of love you plead.

Love Is Unfound

Love is unfound
Save where blushes are abound
With kisses of angel light
The stars of hope always burn bright
No, sweetness cannot perish
Not as long as we cherish
With eyes, hands, mouths and soul
This love we have in its whole
With a prayer tucked against the heart
That time shall not come to draw romance apart
Oh all things to passion belong
The least of which is this humble song
That exalts and esteems the worth
Of fair beauty that gives birth
To the embers of a blissful dream
Whose scenes of life more pleasant seem
That what can ever exist as real
Love gives to all an ethereal feel
A pride and joy that cannot fade
Not even when death draws forth its shade
A tender brow, a beloved's eye
Grants innocence to the gentle sky
The stars themselves do wander lone
Pondering on how love rules the mortal throne
As the rays fall down and themselves compose
Upon the shadow and petal of the rose
The sun sinks up and down
But upon passion's face there lies no frown
The warmest hour always survives
And as it does, love with it thrives

Bringing amourility's grace
To the wings of all who embrace
The fortune of youth in its prime
The glee of truth told in rhyme
For countless ages it shall endure
To keep the heart of those who love as pure
The mild throne sits, the sadness decays
For upon everywhere is born love's eternal rays
The flame burns on, the candle is lit
Its timeless chronicles shall not end with wit
Oh no, forevermore love shall be found
Where desire is everlasting and blushes are abound
Its strength resides where it can never die
Not as long as this world of lovers stare eye to eye.

To Save Our Fate

What force will come to save our fate?
Oh dear, what fortune will humanity await?
It does not matter, alas, all must end
As then finality all deeds will amend

Regardless of the course we take, doom hastens to fall
Upon the shadow and the crown of one and all
Absent is strength, from our graves we reach out
Only to find blindness and ruin spread all about

The stars collapse, the skies bleed stark demise
No trace of happiness endures to shine before the eyes
As amid the dross and defeat, there is nothing left to hold
As we remain in that infinite silence bleak and cold

Oh ode to fondness, to where has gone sweet and tender youth
Man's wide ambition is no longer aimed to golden truth
Yet still it stands pure and alive, listen well and take heed
To what from wisdom's timeless lips are decreed

Man's inner nature is no longer need
It is the custom of the day to toil for greed
For even things that we may desire lack
We still pursue them for there is no turning back

What has happened to the ancient day?
When man's strides were directed for loyalty's pay
Such reverence has ended, this innocence expired
The focus has shifted to the material idols desired

Labour without profit is labour in vain
Yet still some enslave themselves, becoming insane

Earning the thing that brings them need
Catering to the lust that only hardship breeds

O' to where has the modesty of effort fled
To what new horizons of dreams has this progression led?
Its outcome, although less positive seeming
Enforces difference that appears an optimistic dreaming

But then time must come to draw its shade
Each within their vault alongside their lifetime fade
Against the eternal hour, no labour can forever last
As this world in darkness is forever cast.

Uncertain Seeming

When life as uncertainty seem
And all its scenes appear as a dream
Plagued with doubt, effort rewarded with no relief
The hands denied their rest, the mind its belief
Of warm comfort. Innocence as well has resigned
To where trust under its shade has falsely died
When the praise of meaning is laid to rest
And with absurdity the eyes are dressed
After such bitter ills themselves have beset
And the motion of the stars with demise are set
I look to you my love, and deepest pain is allayed
Time's sequence with new wisdom is played
The wit of the world regains new height
And within it is found your darling light
Comforting the dolour, healing the lesion
Placing emollient remedy upon the region
Of the scarred and wounded heart, once torn
Which through the artistry of your love is newborn
Into a wide paradise all above the rest
Into the clouds of Eden, into heaven's nest
What beauty, what glory, what eminence
What sunshine, what power, what soft refulgence
O' the realms are unbound, so let us fly
And flee under the innocence of the sky
Never to question why, our passion to be free
There we belong, over the palm of destiny
Kept together, wing-to-wing, our soft-lit visions spread
Until the darkness of fate leaves us forever dead.

The Tenderest Creatures

When their eyes your eyes do meet
Just simply nod and gently greet
The sweet virtue of their face
With your hands every feature embrace
Thereafter all will be fine
If you return their smile with equal shine

Of their beauty, tell them true
"None can outlive the fairness of you"
If that does not win or please their mind
A simpler remedy you may find
Just take your two lips and give a kiss
And restore in them their inner bliss

If kisses leave them not to feel
The romance borne in you with zeal
Then touch their cheek and slow caress
Their blushing warmth and softly bless
The lone glory saved within their eyes
Make sure to tell them it is the World's Paradise

If still they say no, remind them of the light
That glows upon heaven's starry light
With rapt interest into their wide depths stare
Tell them the star you see has no compare
Neither in this universe nor in the long score of life
Absent of their grace, existence is darkest strife

If yet they reply no, turn to the moon
And say that its rays in envy swoon
For their beauty and that the night birds mainly cry
For the plights of they who sweet love deny

Weeping, tell them your heart still dreams today
And shall dream forever until their love is far away

Upon hearing that, these creatures tender
To love pure and true their souls will surrender
Else their sweetest souls would thereafter quickly die
And all the men upon this earth would cry, cry, cry.

Maiden Dear

Oh maiden dear
The whole world draws near
On account of your fame
And your beauty's name
The scent of your eyes puts the rose to shame
Its warmth never again will be the same
Your looks send the heart to take flight
Upon the lofty designs of the night
There the true worship of your face
Exceeds the stars that with the sky embrace
Exalting your lips as divine
Your hands as one of a kind
Your cheeks, a ruddy treasure
Your kiss, an Elysian pleasure
Every feature of your slender form
Sets passion into a raging storm
It sets the flame of desire
Into a tide of unceasing fire
Fantasy everywhere is abound
Where your sweet love is found
Dreams gently overtake the mind
Slumber all of sorrow does rescind
Sadness loses the lyric of song
Happiness makes the days seem long
Regret is washed away with merry tears
The prospect of tomorrow is void of fears
The wide scenes of amourility
Release our souls into the air liberty
For your soft love lights up the day
Like the glow of life that never fades away

Thus my strength and all with you abide
The majesty of hope shall never leave our side
As I take you by the hand and ask to dance
As we live forever upon our dream of sweet romance!

Lady Fortune

Lady Fortune, friendship, all
Never let me from your hands to fall
For within your palm I thrive
Lacking your grace none can survive
With your blessing I can always fly
To heights unseen, without it I sorely die

Princess Beauty, maiden chaste
These long days are but spend in waste
If they feed not off the glory of your eyes
Which is brighter than the diamonds of the skies
The meadows and the meads, they appear pristine
But compared to your light, absent is the glowing sheen

This, the breath of life does dwell
Where the heart does fall and swell
Desiring the dreams of yore
The sweet fondness of days before
Being those gracious days denied
The heart resigns to where tears have dried

Dried, but still the tears do not end
The ways of fate heaven never does amend
The stars with their motions, the planets in their way
Take the course of destiny and turn it away
The bleakness is eminent, death we must face
Thereafter all the sorrows of this would we embrace.

Be It Always Known

My beloved dear, be it always known
Your beauty rules my realm alone
And the aspects of your lovely trace
Lend to this savage world some grace
Thus being to such glory bound
All treasures are unearthed from the ground

But cries cogency do not lack
If they plead to never turn back
To the darker scapes of yesterday
Yet if they were absent of your lovely ray
Then there was no virtue to be had
In those scores of yesteryear, if they were sad

The light of morn gives birth
To the sweet prospect of mirth
For in that light your fairness can be seen
Once beheld, a greater perfection no one can wean
Void of blemish, your essence is ever true
That is why mortal spirits fall in love with you

That art of love being so divine
It is like a symbol, a starry sign
To the feeling and affectionate heart
Whose passions never far depart
Form the depths that stir life wild
Driving it to where dreams are all but mild

What zeal, what power, what splendid charm
To take pleasure in that does the world no harm
But the soul, surely it cannot remain chaste
If your feral love it has embraced

Thus the spirit will be chastised to the core
Torn between loving and pursuing it nevermore

Such are the plights of romance
Unsteady, uncertain as a wayward dance
That none but those of maddened mind
To some degree appealing find
Thus angels of pure heart retire
To where your beauty burns like eternal fire

Thereon all happiness is throned bright
And the kingdom never tastes the fall of night
The hours of hope, they are not in vain
The promise of love bears no disdain
Against the truce of time we to unite
To touch the stars and bid farewell to that darling night!

Comely Lass

Comely maid,
Of sinuous curves and complexion sweet
My hunger raves, let our bodies meet
And in the feast of corporeal embrace
With my fingers your gentle parts I shall trace
Until in your voice I hear the cry of joy
Shrilling aloud; unabashed, unashamed and never coy
With my palms your heat I shall caress
With my eyes your soul I will undress
Like the pent oratory of Romance
I will lull you into an amorous trance
A dreamy state of fantasy-laden mind
Where carnal pleasures their fulfilment find
As with my brow I shall soothe thine sigh
And with nectarous lips proceed to your thigh
The spirit melts there and never again uplifts
From that playful rest of wanton gifts
O' maid, hold me again, I wish to feel once more
The touch of your Ladyship, Love's pleasant chore
Thus I desire naught else but to dine
On your sweet skin, shall it all be mine?

Morning Sun

The morning sun rises up again
Sweet love, as you remember when
Time had no effect on mortal men
When the mind of youth was free
Let us return there, oh amen, amen

The eye catches glimpse of heaven's door
The soul sings out "nevermore, nevermore"
But that eye being foolish to its core
Cries out in innocence "forevermore, forevermore"

The redolence of hopes fonder place
Grants to every dream a living face
Yet if that dream is vacant of your grace
I will none of it, fie to this world's embrace

Upon the sky, love spreads forth its shine
Saying that no star is divine
It saves its power, its most holy sign
For they who to her with sweet love resign

Perfection is most beautiful when it is blind
And life most desirable when fate is kind
But as the truth of darkness impales the mind
That no one true happiness can find

So we live in the glory of dear lies
So we thrive when delusion is the prize
When darling dream nothing denies
Some say we are all fools, otherwise

So we take this wisdom close to heart
Hand in hand from this world to depart

Until our souls are no longer apart
Oh we fly to where death is no king
And sweet love is one and all takes part.

True Spirits Long

True spirits long
The beautiful song
Of lovers in their prime
Such odes have no need for rhyme
As we sing them louder day by day
To never fade, for such things we pray

A worship divine
A warm starry sign
Neither of them can depart
The altar of the soul nor heart
Thus with laughter we fly away
Unto the brighter and yet brighter day

A friendship sweet
Darling eyes that meet
In happiness draw near
Thus they are held forever dear
Oh shy blushes may burn meek
Save when kisses grow upon the cheek

The wildest mind
Its glory does find
When upon the sky to stare
Dreams appear most ever fair
Like honey moonlight, desire softly glows
As then sweet hope with the tempest blows

From the slow awake
The dream of death does take
The kind prospects of life then turn
To where desires never cease to yearn

Oh the hunger of love is never fed
Until the mortal frame itself falls dead

Such gentle peace
Can never cease
As long as lovers swear
This old world to forbear
Thus true spirits shall always long
To be set free by this love's beautiful song.

Old Man Cried

The old man cried
And so he died
Though deep inside
A trace of youth he did hide

Yet he nothing but loneliness he found
For emptiness everywhere teemed abound
It is like poison, stealthy and lacking sound
When it strikes it consumes all who are around

Such is the sadness of tomorrow
So it must be endured in sorrow
A day of life each morning we borrow
By night it frails and frays like the summer yarrow

So where is the budded vernal due
That is to crown the cheeks of me and you
When will the spring of life flourish new
When will sweet paradise be lived and true

Toil, tragedy and hardest woe
That is the substance of this show
That each mortal can never forgo
It calls our names, thus let us go

The portrait of the sun is black
There is no use looking back
Onto what can never turn away its track
Time is the betrayer, all virtues it does lack

So where has gone the beauty of the mind
Or the art of life, where does it bind

In the modern world none can find
Their purpose as they walk blind

It stakes us out, tenderness awaits
The innocence of unlived fates
As in oblivion the angels states
There is a heaven, but closed are its gates

It dwells like pain within the heart
A sense of grief that can never depart
Thus each man plays his destined part
Until death comes and breaks the stage apart

So onward with the performed game
Everyone plays it well nigh the same
Within the scripture of each person's name
Fate is not more just, so dies the mortal fame

The days are over, here comes the long shade
Death's pall for the breath of one and all has paid
Humankind but of dust is made
From dust to dust, then all does fade

The veil draws near, gone is the light
As we resign unto the dream of the eternal night
Nothing anymore remains white
Done is the power, gone are we unto that gentle night.

Harp Softly Plays

The harp softly plays
Under the warmest days
Of summer and youth, prime and jolly
The fever of the rays
Blends in gentle ways
That is void and lacking of the winter holly

Oh woe to the evergreen
Or to the pallor of the cloudy scene
Thus passion runs fast to summer
As truest love is never dim
Therefore mortals look not grim
If a happy heart to them is a comer

The lark does thrum his flute
And the pond pipes its reeds like a flute
Oh everywhere is a cheerful face
When romance does run
And hope is new begun
Dreams become the friends of highest grace

Hail! Oh glory to the wings of esteem
As the moon with its train of stars does gleam
The bower as well sheds a yon tender light
When the boughs of sunset shine
And red burning love is mine
Oh there can be no shade of darkness to the night

The heavy songs of sadness bruise
When the wanting mind does abuse
The scarlet throne and kingdom of the rose
The flowers blossom with no leisure

If deepest yearning lends a seizure
To those ears inured to the heart's romantic prose

The year passes with the latest season
The brain lacking purposed reason
Sets the pulse of life on fire
For beauty is only fair
When into your eyes I stare
And feel the eternal flame of desire!

Dream of Life

The dream of life does never wane
Not as long as your love you sustain
Keeping our heart above everything
Nothing else can for passion sing
Save for your love, my love—eye to eye
As together we to eternal heaven fly

Thus I see a star shine through the bough
When it teems, of one beauty alone I know
And that is of you, there is no point denying
That sometimes your love compels me to shying
Half kindled by the warmth that you exhale
Ah as when I see you, all other spirits fail

A heart may fail, but a soul is not sworn to death
Not as long as inside me stirs some loving breath
Your complexion I shall always desire
Your face shall serve as my internal fire
Lighting up the contrast of a world shown black
Beautifying a beauty that does nothing lack

Sparing naught, all of loveliness is of one kind
My love, when your vision appears within the mind
All the shades of darkness seem no more as night
For all of Being lives under the darling light
Forever granting blessing to all that I see
Long live that grace, may your glory forever be

As a monument standing against the force of time
Reminding all of the beauty preserved in this rhyme.

My Darling Love

My darling love
I do not think above
Anything but the thought of you
Thus it shall always remain true
As your fair beauty is near
I worship you my love, my dear

Oh sister bride
Take to my side
And I shall proclaim you as a goddess divine
These words shall serve as an eternal sign
To the virtue and strength of poetic power
With your love all of life seems but an hour

Oh sweetest maid
This world shall never fade
Not as long as you and I are one
Upon such times life is new begun
The banners of triumph hold to prevail
As symbols to a love that can never fail

My angel white
Your glorious sight
Makes all the heavens gleam
Like a warm and gentle dream
Whose contents can never expire or flee
Not as long as we are united by destiny

Oh fairest child
Your loveliness is wild
My adoring praise shall survive
Through untold ages so as to keep alive

The truth about your beauty profound
That nowhere save on your face is found

Oh tender girl
The skies do whirl
With the stars of faith and romance
That beg our fates to share this dance
Oh together we to fly so high above
As I think on nothing but you, my greatest love.

This Parting

This parting brings me rue
I cannot at the least bid adieu
Not to you who owns my soul
When you are near, I feel as whole
I sense as though nothing I lack
There is no regret, no turning back

No need for desire in this fleeting world
When your beauty upon the sky is pearled
Nay, heaven itself cannot look divine
If it must compare with your brilliant shine
The stars hung upon the cloudy night
All retreat after perceiving your tender light

They all resign and most rightly so
For what force holds equal to your lovely glow?
Oh what a gentle show, I desire it best
When the garb of innocence from you is undressed
That perfumed touch; to me it is so dear
That is why when you are close, I have no fear

What need is there for apprehension or for dread
This earth is no more than a mad escape for the dead
With only one truth that upon it survives
One rose of youth that with your face revives
Oh one truth, one solemn truth, it is your love
Having found this wisdom, nothing else I think of

Philosophies, philosophies, they are ever unkind
When your bright complexion teems within my mind
Oh never to rescind the fancies that fairer gain
Within that Eden lot, your shall never wane

Thus I love you beyond what any word can express
But if only words had strength these feeling to suppress!

Oh they cannot—as I die! To say farewell
It makes the heart swoon, my veins they dwell
On the thought of leaving you—oh away, away!
This parting brings me rue, I can no longer stay
The cold dust welcomes me with grief as again I cry
Without you, my soul, it fleets—I die, I die!

Carmine Tryst

Under the solemn carmine tryst
Inside where the dank air is kissed
Rises the antique musk of woodbine
That mingles with the little rays of sunshine

As the leaves of the nightshade gently grow
Along the mead where the soft fairies glow
Under the hawthorn moon and its warm array
That tries to conceal the treasures of the unborn day

Oh hail to those pleasures! The songs uplift
Out through the hearts of the sweet birds who sift
Through the leafy chambers of the bough, they prize it most
When their eyes catch glimpse of love from coast to coast

As then the lovers walk away hand in hand
Through eclipsing eyes, each other they understand
Romance's stronger wing compels them to fly
Thereafter they believe hope can never die

Mortals are intrigued with the unseen
As are wild lilacs for pastures green
Upon the stream, the beck, the garden of delight
Like untamed children, into the sky they take flight

Oh happy is the star that never dies
Brave is the warrior who never cries
Over the tragic fate of life which all share
Though beautiful seeming, is far from fair

The flowers sway to and fro, from side to side
Heaven is compelled to make the clouds its bride

As the sea serenades the lovely shore
With songs of passion forevermore

The roses and the daisies draw strength from the ground
Serving as the canker's feed, there man's weakness is found
As he cannot outlive the days allotted him
So he expires, disconcerted though less grim

For the reaper leaves his scythe in every place
A reminder of what's to come, imprinted on every face
Thus father time is called names, considered bold
For quick depriving some of youth's finer hours of gold

The tower and the palace then fall to decay
As time ticks, its passing all shall betray
Bringing ruin to what cannot be won
As life's pursuits are then new begun

Another babe is born, an old man retires
Unto the eternal grave of his desires
Forfeiting lust, fame and fortune's greed
Being made of dust, what use has he for need

Thus the earth, the tryst and the musky care all sink
Along with the madness of heaven's teary drink
Each day the tale is retold, describing the lives of men
So it shall endure, unpurposed to the end, again and again

For life is a fable whose flattery
Resides in the nature of its immutability.

Soft Voices

Under the gentlest night
There glows the tenderest light
And all around the heavens shine
With your grace and love that is mine

The verdant summer and the garden field
Their true harvest of beauty yield
To you who is the master and the queen
Of all that is unlived and unseen

The bulbous lily and the enfolded rose
Along the plain where the mandrake grows
With the violet and the daisy wake
Before the lifting sun comes their pleasure to take

Upon the rolling pasture there softly lies
An angel who his little tears cries
Pining the loss of innocence, to him it is grief
Pity him for your love is his one relief

The seas, the shores, the trumpets ring
With a tune of sadness, the sirens sing
Uncertain of what with tomorrow will come
But as there is your love, all of life is martyrdom

So then let death come to bear
On what with my eyes I behold as fair
Forever this shall be my decree
As I live, you shall always be a part of me

So be true and unite with my soul
Upon that hour we shall be as whole

Whatever this madness let it be undone
Upon a newer page of destiny our hopes are won

A happier fortune, a kinder fate
Oh such jealous dreams themselves instate
As on our knees we fall to steadfast pray
For righteous love to never fade away

Thus I yearn our promises to be
The one immortal source of all sanctity
As the moonlit drops trickle and brighten your face
And we draw close together, by perfection to embrace

All this in my ears, the soft voiced starless fairy spoke
Through out the muted night, as from this vision I awoke.

No Cure

There is no cure, there is no repair
Not as you wander everywhere
At your beauty I shall forever stare
Resolved that your face has no compare

Did I mention that you are fair and bold?
Beyond what any mortal can grasp or hold
Your everlasting features shall not grow old
This through the mouths of prophets I've been told

Nor shall the winter grow cold when you are near
The summer blossoms are tenfold more dear
When your constancy flows through every year
And seasons fade without a shading tear

Nor shall I ever fear the darkness of the night
As there is your warmth, love is the light
That drives me away from the shades of fright
As you are close, the sky is blue and white

Thus I feel not contrite when all the howls are fled
And all of life's richness from the veins are bled
Still my heart and soul shall be kindly fed
With the image of you until the whole world is dead

Yet even when those flames and ashes bleakly fall
Still with the one standing pulse you shall remain my all.

Deeply Craved

You men, you who women deeply crave
And call lust the most natural desire
You who for blissful satisfaction's rave
Should know that pleasure is like a fleeting fire

Ho! You maiden and you comely maids
Who hold similar yearning, yet better contained
You who I have oft seen faint for amorous shades
Know that in man's heart a place for you is retained

So what need is there for such disguised business
Our aims will be better suited with a united trust
Such common deeds in time will regress
Until we mutual cave in to that great natural lust

Fairest parties, hold each other hand in hand
And with a vow of passion prepare to embrace
The timeless laws of romance that pervade this Land
That shine clear through each and every loving face

These are the ways of our modest creed
We feign to hate what in truth we love the most
Calling tender affection the basest need
Praising the unworthy, prone to scorn the more beautiful host

This game goes on and on and naught decays
Until the soul of humankind does perish
And no remembrance remains upon the trace of mortal days
As then all within their time each other cherish

So the game plays on, as such this play shall always be
Mortals, as they live, never relish their true fated destiny.

Love Onward Streams

As love onward streams
So do my dreams
Until they yours do meet
Upon that hour to call them sweet
Life is nothing that it seems

Unless upon the brighter eye
Upon the cheek of the tearful cry
Your soft voice is heard
Gentle fears become absurd
To the fonder realm of hope I fly

Your beauty leads my direction
There is nothing of you I question
For as your fairness does hold
Warmth can never grow cold
Everything is seen from your reflection

How lovely is that face
Whose deepest heart does trace
Nature's most eternal state
Which cannot be subdue to fate
How youth and holiness you embrace

Your tender innocence
Makes all the difference
In this world and the next
Here or there to not be vexed
If you shall be with me hence

Life will not retire
Of its burning fire

Or its passion flamed red
Romance can never be dead
As you are the reason of its desire

The white moon will not resign
Nor the stars their faithful shine
The halo of the brilliant day
Will continue on its way
When you are in these arms of mine

Oh when you are ever near
The orb of heaven is ever clear
It does not wander in the shade
Nor does darkness come to raid
The remembrance of the rosy year

Every day and every night
Every blessed ray of light
Upon the hours will surrender fair
With every power, everywhere
When your love is seen in full delight

Everything itself will prove
In this ageless game of love
As all decays with time
Save what is writ within this rhyme
For you are all that I can ever think of

Eternal to live, eternal to fall
Before the pangs of death come to pall
But as your soul my soul does chose
There is nothing of life that I can lose
Within it you are my truth, my love, my all.

Salvation of One Kind

There is only salvation of one kind
It lives constantly within my mind
Your pure vision I conceive
Thereafter in eternity I believe
As your beauty I embrace
Worshipping the glory of your face
You know that love as this can never die
Never, never darling as we stare eye to eye

Oh what eyes, they are like the paradise
That emotions live in, breeding avarice
Yet your fairness is so bright
That as it lends dimension to the night
Granting relief to the depth of shade
Below your grace, naught of this world can fade
Realising this, I can never be satisfied
With anything less than your beauty being deified

Oh your loveliness is so supreme
That some are apt to call it as a dream
More so I adore that generous shine
Those charities of love that never decline
Forget the world, I have no desire
Other than to see you burn like starry fire
Heaven allowing this wish, I seek nothing more
Than to be united with you along heaven's door

There our souls shall forever be
The freest born by their own decree
Immortally, no force can separate
The emotions of this, our human state

Oh we shall conquer all that we need
Upon the harvest of love to eternally feed
Darling, hope will not hunger, desire shall be provided for
As romance lifts us to the sky, wing to wing—forevermore

Together like two stars or a distant sun
That longs for its partner now many years undone
Amourility is the song of the nightingale
When sadness overtakes the heart impaled
Deeply wounded, oh sweetest love, yet how you repair
Every hurting pain with your complexion fair
That is why to your tender arms I shall resign
Never fearing death, knowing you shall be forever mine.

Nothing Lasts Forever

Though nothing lasts forever
And all things to their end must fall
Still I feel we can be together
Even after time itself does pall
For truly I believe love can transcend
Beyond the reach of what petty hours lend

Trust is a thing buried in the night
That youth's callowness cannot understand
Even against the darkness, it shines like light
Ultimately leading itself into the searcher's hand
If the pursuant is strong, so will be the heart
As when passion is gained, it can never depart

So then intellect is drowsed, slumber falls deep
Dreams take over when realities deny
The comfort of hope oft remains in that sleep
When this world of pain offers no soft reply
So thus love must die and with it the mind
Resigns to whatever finality that it can find

Draping darkness everywhere, causing all to fade
Save you and love, them none can ever own
As we remain side by side upon love's eternal throne.

To Believe Love's Myth

Who would bear to believe love's myth
When forward draws its jagged scythe
Imposing death with its blade
Forcing all into hatred's shade
Blinding hope's eyes with mutiny
Making love's season appear as eternity
Oh who would forbear the troubles and the strife?
For that warm deceptive feeling of life
That proud passion, that lively burn
Which compels those who lack it to hotly yearn
For the features of its high grace
For the virtues of its soft embrace
Nay, its esteem brings ingratitude
Yet those who scorn it live in destitute
And they who try to stay afar
In the end sustain the heaviest scar
Embossed upon the condemned heart
That tried from sweet love to live apart
No, such efforts are destined to fail
No one these seas alone can sail
Or bear these hardships on the breast
Or endure the pains without loving rest
None can do it, none can survive
Without affection nothing stays alive
Although its fashion is no more than scorn
All mortals with it are innately born
So be the kinder soldier and resign.
To these warring plains of love divine
Hour after hour, there can be no fight
For love instils us with raging might

Take its strength and fly away
Seek out the warmer climes of its day
Hoist up the flag and the soft anthem sing
For Love to one and all triumph shall bring
The conquest prevails night through night
Its victory wanes brighter and bright
Until its mystery this world consumes
And its great dream in all people resumes.

Love to Wane

Never let the love to wane
Never let the heart to twain
That red pulsing desire
Let it burn like brightest fire
The sweetness of the face
Let it the soul to embrace
The kindness of the mind
Let it a gentleness find
As well as the grace of the hand
Let it to trace life and understand
The fondness of the stare
For it pervades everywhere
That warmest innocence
Let it to make all the difference
The affection, the smile, the tender charm
Let it to rescind away all harm
As then the skies of high romance
With the stars will elope and dance
The blue glory of the sea
Will resound with waves of majesty
The fantasy, the jubilee, the azure light
Upon the airy wings of love will take flight
The candle blazed against the eve
Will not let the teary eyes to grieve
Nor will heaven be darkly swept
With the cries that lovers have wept
Oh indeed when love is set free
Time will not oppose fair destiny
The whisper of the wind will remain soft
The golden hue upon the clouds will stay aloft

And everywhere a pleasant song will be heard
Without an uttered tune or infant word
Oh most truly life will appear as a dream
Where your comely love upon it to gleam
Thereon there can be no hate
As then all for sweet love await!

The Seasons Pass

The seasons pass one by one
My beloved is all that remains upon my mind
Is the fragrance of love, everywhere it's won
Its beauty one and all can find
That is why I look to you, in you it teems
That sweet perfume of remembrance
That darling scent, it always seems
To be true to the strength of innocence
Certainly your being is so divine
That none, I believe, can recall a face
Whose splendid majesty does resign
To the art of such love and perfect grace
Oh ever warm is that fair magic light
That kindles up your skin like paradise
Like an Eden planted in the east of Night
Like a glory visible only to admiring eyes
Oh and how they are so brightly seen!
Like a scarlet rose caught on brilliant fire
Like a minstrel playing his song serene
Like Love's dream burning with the star of desire
Thus I shall dwell within that lofty sky
Where your supreme beauty does reside
I shall speak to angels, but never question why
Why one of their kind upon the earth does abide
That sweet cherub is you, oh holy maid
All the burning in my heart speaks one word
That timeless phrase is your name, it shall not fade
Until death comes to take me and it is no longer heard
Against such long lengths of time you shall be prized
The changeless ways of nature shall never amend

Neither the way I love you nor how I worship your eyes
As both my prayers and thoughts to you alone I send
Knowing that blushes are prime in youth
I go to the verdant garden and sit along the stream
Reciting the praise of your beauty, all of them are truth
As I speak and stare and think and forever dream

Forever entranced by your soft vision that arrives
Here ends the rhyme, yet my soul with yours survives.

Brings Me Rue

This parting brings me rue
My heart, it cannot bid adieu
To say good-bye, it rends me whole
And besets agony onto my soul
To speak the very word "farewell"
To your face, it makes my spirit swell
With such an intense and burning fire
That lost is the passion of desire
For this beautiful world and life
Both living and longing appear as rife
When your loveliness does starkly lack
When your fairness is seen as black
Thereon destiny affords no scope
To the mind that burns with hope
Oh woe to such piteous, pious zeal
It compels the purest maidens to sadly weal
Yet the vestal hearted, they revel
Hearing the rustlings of autumn's spell
Of queenly summer and her array of prime
Of youth that is abound with unrelished time
Of kisses and cheeks, brightly shown
Of romantic arms upon each other thrown
With the airs of sweetness that rescind
All the troubles and burdens of the mind
Oh what charm, what fond remembrance
When dreams and love mingle with innocence
Held up proud and high like the nadir shine
Until the winds of paradise all resign
Oh until then, never to say goodbye
Never to whisper of the end, never to cry

As I hold you softly hand in hand
As we together fly to our eternal land
There my all, each other we shall understand
O' let us fly, let us fly yonder to that emerald land.

As Love Breeds

As love breeds
My heart reads
Of this madness and the siege and its laws
Of lovelorn desolation, my eyes recognise
That your warmth can immortalise
The brave passion that in me is sunk
Whose sentiments from your soul's potion are drunk
So then I resign to the scene of your perfection
Warmly basking it the night's reflection
Steadfast holding on to what is true
My dear, that precious thing is only you
Who spreads wild contagion from side to side
Indeed your artistry is like a bride
That I fancy for myself to take
Or else from this dream to never wake.

Tender Rosy Grace

Loveliest born of tender rosy grace
Quiet child of summer and sweet rhyme
Gentle daughter of Eden's garden with verdant face
That the stars lose hold of their show of time
When the fair wind of our hands run through the boughs
Lighting up with the fragrant breath of the vernal stream
Of buds and blossoms, of nature's holy shows
Hung aloft the verge where there shines the dream
The divine hope of the mind, it cannot flee
The emerald leaves, the poppies, the white citadel
Nor can autumn a cold autumn be
When stores of warm love of your eyes tell
The branch of the laurel, it is too thin
To hear the music piped through these sensual ears
Relating of regrets whose deaths leave memory to win
The defending power by which the destined melody steers
Leaving your years of youth untouched, I will stare deep
Until my eyes feel tired and feed no more
But such a day cannot come, no resigning sleep
Can beg my soul to move from your spirit's care
Thus hear the lute and the chimes of summer ring
Everywhere that the sweet breath of childhood greets
The dew of innocence upon the brow, its fondness brings
Recited tales of old joys and love's lost defeats
So be my empress and we shall trace the sign
That gleams for us past the darkness of the even clouds
The prophecy of romance, it is forever yours and mine
No it can never die for it is too proud
Oh too, too proud to ever bid wide adieu
So open up stalls the of night and let the moon rays in

Its hawthorn crow, it dances without rue
Shun away its heart, to see it thus content is pleasured sin!
Stand aside this life, here now the vesper orbs look bright
As if by some envious plot, they these hours can take
No, they can never, our hold, it is too tight
Our love is too strong from this dream to ever wake
Lend me your hand, with an aerial ferry we will fly
Up to that sky where such dreams cannot shatter
Heaven will lead us there, desire shall keep us nigh
There thoughts of love and death do not matter
Everlasting sung, now these cries among the orchards and sweet meadow spread
This love shall burn immortal, till like fabled scenes our hearts fall dead.

Few Words of Justice

There are few words of justice to describe
The hard unfeeling pangs of love
Nor can the mind to philosophy subscribe
When its thoughts are spread over and everywhere
No voice, no law, no ordinance divine
No mouth of gentle sport can compel
The eyes to happiness resign
When the heart is full cast in sorrow's deepening spell
No bird, no dream, no vision of the unmet year
The sadness of old can rescind
Neither warmth nor the touch of sweetness dear
Can cause the grieving soul solace to find
The incense of memory does cogency lack
Tears only bear the power to obey
The remorse of time whose eyes turn back
And never from that broken scene look away
Thus regret makes slaves out of us all
Enterprising life for the things not had, unseen
Blinding the inner truth, causing its grace to fall
For matters undesired, betrayed, obscene
So the performance with the drama ends
Dragging feet and arms in heated rage
The bright star of heaven nothing amends
As this bitter story replays age through age
There is no comfort to be had in hope's belief
As only death grants to all the world's relief.
When the seasons betimes reveal the frost of night
When the hours of the months return to decay
When after this wide world is full dry of light
Dear heart, remember me is this way

Describe these words upon the talus of life
That I loved you best beyond the worth of things
Admired and prized you beyond the ken of strife
Which being true in cause, of love so often brings
So after all of these have lost their strength
And the power of movement stirs the veins no more
Be content to see my mortal frame stretched
Mark how it did love, how time did mock it to its core
But feel no grief, love is the greater part of me
That shall outlive it all, even into long eternity.

Men Pursue You

Lady Fame, men pursue you, though they are blind
To that mad, crazed rage of your stare
The consequence of your pursuit strong sieges the mind
Into the darkest corners that the blind call fair
The weaker of spirit are apt to heed your call
Just as a piper summons his lambs to dance
The intellect, he never before your alter will fall
For he knows your graces are all a game of chance
That some win by gamble, some by fortune's draw
Some by the circumstances over which they have no control
Some by the triumphant blows of destiny's law
Altogether by a fickle force that plays an indifferent role
Crowning some with need, others the feed of misfortune taste
Still others suffer denial for the whole of their life
Some make worthwhile sacrifice, others their simple pleasures waste
Dying unknown, enduring countless and needless strife

Feeling the cold knife of betrayal as then into silence they fade
From a world where the truest pursuits are the fewest made
Oh fame, dear fame, your envied ways are fierce and ever cruel
Yet nonetheless they have and shall forever rule.

Arman Nabatiyan

Ode to Sleep

Dreams are no more than a wonderland
That piously take the thoughts at hand
With a twist of luck they lead them away
And once again begins the new born day

Fancy is no more than a darling ray of light
That carries the soul through the passage of night
Whispering to it the soft words of relief
As reason departs from the reality of belief

That is what makes the daydream sweet
When drifting summer thoughts each other meet
Whole new worlds of fantasy are fashioned and made
Unchanging seemingly, though in fact they quickly fade

So I take my wings, the mind is flown
To where the zephyr with the vernal song is blown
There the fields give blossom to nothing save mirth
There old hope to new hopes lends eternal birth

The sunset falls, there shines the skies
With its stars of slumber and lullabies
How calm, how peaceful, how serene
This earth has different charms under the nightly scene

Gentle is the music, tender is the glow
All mortals when they die to heaven go
So let us then to this warm paradise resign
To the cradle of sleep that is both yours and mine

Hand in hand our minds these dreamy slumbers take
Fleeing to a realm from which they can never wake.

Sorrow of Our Time

Such is the sorrow of our time
We trade abuse for ignorance
And persecute the things we least understand
Such is the nature of our dominance
By these rules alone we reign over our land

Such is the sadness of the modern day
Where men exert their breath for their own promotion
They madly toil to satisfy the innate greed
Modesty, they are blind to such a notion
It is the common practice to perceive wants as need

Such is the curse of the living world
Affairs are chased without the aim of their end
Efforts put forth leading to progress made
The earth abruptly changes, vices themselves amend
As then all the exhaustion to silence does fade

Such is the valour of mortal bravery
Enduring the plights of darkness and defeat
Tending newborn hope in an unslept dream
Fighting on when it is easier to retreat
Remaining certain when all does uncertain seem

For we are the creed that prevails above uncertainty
Yet this game persists unchanged throughout the scores of history.

This Sweet Life

What can this sweet life be worth?
If it is not for living
If happiness is not for giving
Then better it is to die than to suffer birth

Through the eyes a light is seen
As if hope gleams without cause
And hatred rules destiny's laws
Then the whole world is ever unclean

Polished are the white grains of time
Though there is nothing left to youth
Save the stark reality of truth
For not even wisdom ends hope in rhyme

The sun with cosmic brightness revives
Though the stars to darkness resign
Telling of a forgotten age that is not mine
Only nothingness against the night survives

Naught is the strength of human reason
But as the mind retains a power
It conjures up an unimagined hour
That will save it from death's treason

Another ray of the morn is shed
But with no purpose it is carried
We are like coloured fairies
Living out a fable that is dead

The long silence draws its robes to pass
Are we like servants to its hand?

Whose infinity we naught understand
But in the end still retire to, alas

The curtain falls, here comes the shade
That none look onto with greeted cheer
Consuming all, each in his own year
Until all to a wide nothingness does fade

How we are the players of this great game
Whose burden of consequence does fall
Until the blinding blackness comes to pall
And once again this play resumes to its start the same

So it has been, so it shall remain to be
Until the all in all decays to wide eternity.

The Days Pass

So the days pass, yellow turns the grass
There is no looking back to youth
For inside it lies no truth
Thus these words are as morass

The things unseen, they have a golden sheen
But when at closer range they are inspected
Even the rose with a canker is infected
Being disfigured, beauty has no right to preen

The times of old, that old men behold
Through reverent eyes ancient days are esteem
Some would call them most supreme
When in fact they are better spoken of, better told

The glories of yesterday, they cannot stay
The lark flies here and there to sing
This wisdom into the ears of all to bring:
Within the heart innocence dies away

Time is not a slave to the hour, it wields the power
To give life, to glorify, to ruin or bring on decay
It bears the art to ruin the immortal way
Placing death upon the blossomed flower

The wide human shore is corrupted to the core
Base in heart thus its affections resign
To where the soul can in ease recline
There to pine its wretched nature nevermore

The dream of tomorrow is strewn with sorrow
The stars of the skies with dust awake

The softer slumber of the eyes they take
Never to desire the yon morrow

As none remain to think or feel either love or pain
Or even live to see that bright tomorrow save in disdain.

That Cruel Way

No, no, turn not to that cruel way
A darker day there awaits, flee from it
From the orchard leave; upon that meadow stay
In deepest love and peace we shall together sit
Not wondering what the cloud of tomorrow will bring
Giving no heed to what lulling songs the lark does sing
For we have passion, the wings of passion are more free
Than all these buds and blossoms and flowers combined
As they to the short weeks of death are resigned
Yet in faith we live by laws of eternity

Thus nothing can come between this shared love
Neither the stars, the mountains nor the moon
Have strength to climb our thoughts or fly above
That soft realm of sorrow upon which maidens swoon
For it is more pleasant along the April mead
Lend me your eyes; to there our eyes shall lead
Being freed from the cold chains of yesterday
Hope awaits us at its bright cheery door
Youth shall kiss our heads
Anoint our brows forevermore
Like little children we shall fly wide and away

This course of time and fate drags wild
The doves hear our tale of madness and coo in delight
In shear amazement of how life in sadness has been styled
How still the fashion of love believes not in night
Thus drowsily the wise owl turns to sleep
Though he never dies, his spirit is for us to keep
That inward substance, it is held inside
The flame of the beloved, it burns most true

Yet it has never burned until it sets eyes on you
Then the streams of sadness shall forever hide

Until the brooks with the morning star rise again
And within my fading tears I find your beauty then.

Friend to Sadness

Be not a friend to sadness, its sullen drink
Shall feed the appetite and thirst till sorrows high
Leave this world and its lonely sun to sink
The faithful moon to perish without cool reply
So the stars they die without a spoken word
Their garish lips pressed against sweet summer tasted
The sunken veil of midnight, its flow wasted
Then the darkness passes over the sky unheard
While all along the nightingale sings
Of the deep pain that loves solitude brings

It is a destitute too harsh for the heart to endure
Mortal veins, they stretch, lacking strength to abide
The fragrance of youth caressed, it is too pure
Thus the glow of warm solitude takes to the side
Where the wreaths and laurels of spring shine bright
And the sylvan woodbine dresses not the noble bark
For the brink of paradise, it is too far, too stark
Being so dark and obscure, everything passes into night
The breath is clouded, all is fading, and all must go
The pulse is crowded with blossoms of resplendent show

The fairies and the angels, wing to wing they gather
To relate the soft stories of broken love
Like elves upon a fabled knoll, their tongues chatter
With rhymes that no invention can climb above
Much as the rose can never be true cankered by the weed
So shall love in the eye of its beloved always flourish
Being kept near, true lovers its fine shall nourish
Until that flame becomes a fair innate need

With these silver brooks espied the autumn plains devour
The righteousness of love's wide and unflown hour

There flies the Eden realm, its dominions green
Hold back neither the splendid magic nor the charm
Of redemption that with downcast gaze is seen
But in truth it veers, it causes no dreaded harm
Through ancient woes through velvet buds are born again
Page against page, these wondrous chronicles are blind
To the true score and depth of life that none can find
That bliss being hidden, death reveals it, all shall find it then
And now the thunder comes, it dwells inside us like a dream
Rupturing the soul apart, sorrow is no more than love's esteem

And so it has been, so this shall remain to be
The one outstanding truth of life until all eternity.

Ode to Mortality

The drowsy light, the bright burning torch
The soft lamp of morning, the carols of the eve
The embers of time, they fall, they scorch
Sandy dreams fill the eyes, while old passions grieve
That fond book of yesterday, its page untold
Lies dormant within the bud of summer cold
The voice of the lark, its song does warmly breed
Bringing in fresh joy to the unmet hour
Of happiness smeared upon the rosy bower
No, the plague of hope bears no ripening seed
Thus we sink further in, waiting for the dawn to alight
The scores of darkness that shall always remain as night

The howl, the scream, the cry, the sobbing tear
It looks across the sea, there the blazon of fate
Smiles happily upon itself in woe strewn drear
As the chariot of death does most patient wait
For the downy feathers of the soul, its wings to fall
Thereon innocence shall lose its shame and all
The portrait and the art, life will speak of seasons past
The zephyr blows, there thrusts the vernal wind
The trumpets sound, Eve's children have thus sinned
Now the gold shine of yesterday expires; it can never last
Love's daughter thereafter leaves and dwells with truth
And in laughter all are blinded within the depths of youth

So the canker builds up a mound, serving as its throne
That none with strengthened hand can break away
A monument to endless time, its glory lives alone
Feeding on the pleasures of fame till they die away
The carnage of nature then arrives rocking back and forth

Inventing this world anew, raging from the south to the north
The bitter hold of ambition, its point, its dire pain
Leaves the human mind to believe in immortality
To fancy its true shape, oh its fashion is dark disdain
As then our names are blotted to naught unto eternity
The wreckage of defeat, the hard wilderness, the bloody rage
All shall carry on until time consumes this unreal stage.

Little Bird Sat

A little bird sat on my shoulder
He cried, "Your burden is like a boulder
"That dear Sisyphus could not rid, as hard as he tried
"Until into the chronicles of eternity he died
"I tell you brother, this show of life never ends
"Fate is that cruel thing that sorrow always lends
"Until sadness comes and mingles in its pain
"And leaves purpose to lie in shameful disdain
"Oh the grace and horror of this mortal play
"Shall neither cease tomorrow nor today
"Weak is the trace of hope, most feeble is dream
"If we try to impose a reality that does not seem
"To be congruent with perfection in its truest
"Or if we feign to be an insubstantial purist
"When all catches up, we will be brought to its knees
"In hundredfold ways of miserable degrees
"By the need of it, we shall conquer the undone
"And the drama will be then once more begun
"Until the philosopher with his muse brings ruin to all
"As one by one to his piping tunes of truth we fall."
These were the words that the little bird spoke
As then his wings did fade and his voice broke
Everything torn asunder, life could be heard no more
As the world in the darkest silence fell forevermore.

Forest and Wilderness

Against the forest and the wilderness glades
Far past the willow tree and grassy blades
Lives this maiden in a cave whom no one admits
Behind her leafy screen, in beautiful pose she sits
Though she is fair, I confess most like a queen
Still no mortal eyes save mine her loveliness have seen
Until this one day I passed by
And all her sorrows to me she did cry…
"I am Diana, I sit in loneliness
"From day to night, sunk in my own emptiness
"Shielded from the cruel fists of this world
"My own hands in innocence lay curled
"Wondering why this life is so filled with hate
"Each time I think to leave, I hesitate
"To enter out onto the merciless scene
"That for no one is peaceful or serene
"I sometimes consider what everything is worth
"When no equality pervades over the moral birth
"When the fabric of mankind is so fiercely torn
"And its skin of kindness so deeply worn
"That oft I feel it is better to forsake
"Rather than in corrupt affairs partake
"Sometimes I think it is the better good
"To abandon the pious shrouds that never would
"To surrender far away from an evil place
"Never to look back with a regretting face
"Yet when with such thoughts my mind teems
"I resign myself to sleep and fonder dreams
"There innocence can always stay alive
"And humankind for its betterment can strive

"Against such seas of grief I turn away
"Finding solace in the vision of the undreamt day
"Oh to turn away, such are the words that kill
"The hearts of men, their passion, their truest will
"Such is my sadness, so I then will turn
"From the life starved, fled and fading, nothing can forever stay."
All this spoke the maiden, as she buries back her face
Unto that cave of darkness, as she dies upon youth's blackened grace.

Glorious Angel

O' glorious angel, hear this story told
Of a love outrageous as it is bold
It is of a traveller who came up far
Out from a land, he was led by a star
A vision and a yearning that inside him did dwell
An emotion that day to day did increasing swell
So he followed his heart wherever it led
He pursued that direction toward which his chambers bled
His journey lasted through many days and nights
Ranging from the deepest depths to the highest heights
Until at last he arrived into a quiet town
Whereon he at once took off his traveller's gown
And immediately began his quest to find
A great Love that appeared perfect in his mind
Place to place he went and probed ever deep
But everywhere he looked the people were asleep
Not in a slumber, but a dream like trance
They whispered to him "Love is but fortune's chance"
Undismayed this traveller carried on
He knew that love did not only reside in Avalon
He came across a stone, there he sat to rest his feet
As then little fays drew forth his personage to greet
Their sight invoked in our traveller a surprise
But nonetheless their sweet visage delighted his eyes
They surrounded him with a warm embrace
And peered into his soft glowing face
They danced and sang and asked him what he sought
He replied, "That which I desire cannot be bought
"Neither with money, nor jewels, nor precious gems
"Nor with the grace nor glory of regal diadems

"For what I seek is something pure and true
"More golden than the gold of brightest hue
"A perfection so rare and great, I call it Love
"That lies neither on earth nor in the heaven above
"Neither on the seas nor over the ebbing shore
"As it is found within my heart and no place more
"And now I look to see if there is another heart
"Whose content from mine own is not far apart
"Thus the pulses of my soul led me to this place
"But I have yet to find my maiden of perfect grace"
After they heard his plight, the fays gathered ear to ear
Reciting to each other the words that each one did hear
Rehearsing the plaintive anthem and the woe
The rue, the mystery, the sadness and the sorrow
Then the eldest Fay stood out from the crowd
And to the man warmly cried her voice aloud
"Dear Sir, you must come to understand
"That this love you seek can be found upon no land
"It is a virtue as rare as it is blind
"Which is the scape of darkness none can find
"Therefore your pursuit to us seems in vain
"Whose fruits shall yield bitter pangs of disdain
"It is better that you drink this potion here
"To ascend to heaven, there your Love is near
"Upon an instant, there you shall plainly see
"Fulfilment in every page of your destiny
The traveller then pressed the liquor to this lip
And began its lovely bream to softly sip
As then he slowly upward ascended
To an ideal realm that he had always intended
Disdained, he expired and perished away
Upon this earth his soul could no longer stay

As then in the new Country his eyes did wake
And in his lofty slumber a lover he did take
Alas, he took her in his arms, though cold as stone
True love is found only upon death's dark throne.

Seldom Seen Tower

Upon a far and seldom seen tower
Near the purple brakes of an enchanted land
Stood a bird a top a lovely tower
Singing out all his thoughts at hand
While all around the sky was sunny and still
The cerulean scape was with silence bred
There hung drapes of blue over the distant hill
A perfect backdrop to all that this bird said…
"This scene may seem haled now, young and fair
"Unblemished without any unsightful feature
"But be assured time shall bring disrepair
"To all of Beauty, whether a landscape or a mortal creature
"The scarlet shades of the night will draw
"To fall upon the lilac of lavender bream
"The posy too will yield to the unchanging law
"Of savage Nature, of life that perishes with the morning gleam
"As time bears the virtue and the crafted art
"To break down marble temples, to make glories fade
"To rob the season of its kiss, to cripple the loving heart
"To curse the blessedness of hope that only death can degrade
"Worse than these it strives with wretched soul
"To lend ruin to the mind of innocence
"It suffers to destroy the things that are whole
"Conquering with defeat the pride of excellence
"The leaves, the trees, the brooks, the meads
"Every substance of this earth, kind and unkind
"To the fate of stark finality leads
"The wind of love as well will be driven blind
"The pureness of the soft rosy stem
"The white reflection of the darling gentle moon

"The cries of spring, the joys of summer's diadem
"Must yield to the scythe, each in its age will swoon
"More wretched than this, man who is cunning and shrewd
"Who labours to build monuments of eternal state
"He denies himself the thought that nature can be so crude
"As to bring to ruin the immortality of our destined fate
"That the deities above him would not be as cruel
"So disrespectful, so hard as to full sweep away
"The treasures of the world's grace, the trade of the fool
"He rather believes the works of man are to forever stay
"No, no, time's power shall bring all to decay
"A life full lived is one happy and true
"The wiser mortal makes the most of each day
"Never to look back, o' may this truth forever live in you"

All this the bold declared as from the world he fled
Enjoying every minute he lived until he fell dead.

The Little Boy

There was once a little boy, with time he swiftly grew
Out of his babe-like guises, thereafter he was a man
Whose wisdom yearly waxed, soon everything he knew
Except how the great continent of love to understand
Years passed by but without hopes at avail
For the man's prudence did starkly lack
The comprehension of love, soon he bewailed
His fortune in a world that seemed dark and black
Day after day in secluded destitute
This man endured his pervading plight
In between he never accepted of his solitude
He believed stars make dreams come true at night
So then he gently pressed down his head
And to the deepest slumber resigned
His thoughts teemed, though his sense was like the dead
But inside his heart a wild glory shined
As his breath carried on, a vision to him came
Of an old man, imp-like, who before him proudly stood
Who cried to himself "Love is a game, love is a game
"That in the end does more harm than good"
But then our man realising what the other had spoke
Was intrigued to approach him and enquire
About the story of love, of its chains and its yoke
Of its nature, why it burns within the mind like fire
Quiet and restless he stepped forth and aside
Toward the old man without uttering a word
While within him many musings flourished wide
Nothing was voiced, but still the old man everything heard:
"My dear sir, my lord, do forgive my approach
"But I wish to ask you of some things

"Regarding the nature of love, its hard reproach
"Its fond enchantment of which the nightingale sings
"All my short life I have lived alone
"Devoted to the higher causes of life
"With madness I have toiled for the scholar's throne
"Yet lacking love, my living has seemed most rife
"Thus now I draw near, your eminence beseeching
"Asking if I can provide some remedy for my infirmed heart
"If indeed there is some cure that is far reaching
"That can quell my malady and make my illness depart
"Oh turn not away, I impeach you, I implore
"To have pity on this, my most pitiful state
"To have compassion for the soul that rages to its core
"My spirit is desirous, these ears for your wise words await
"Dear fellow" said the man, "I hear you well
"And understand how life for you has no worth
"How your visions are unseen, how they in darkness dwell
"How the light of love has fled from your earth
"But in truth, there is no holy power that I inhere
"Nor fortitude of the mind, nor strength of the breath
"That can restore the paradise which is so dear
"Namely the Eden of love, before the falling drape of death
"There is no word, no song, no truth at all
"That can be offered for your pain to console
"No ballad, no verse, no profound wisdom tall
"Can another mortal advise to make you whole
"For life in its manifold aspects is full and bright
"Each deserving of exploration, a searching will
"Like a lens to comb across the stars of night
"Finding richness in each, a beauty that never lies still
"A deep loveliness; fulfilment does not come cheap
"But is deep and requires of its every denizen sacrifice

"Bliss and levity, the field of contentment one can only reap
"If one beholds the world with wide gazing eyes
"O' I apologise but for such reasons I must decline
"Any help or aid that I am able to provide
"For in truth it is you who to love and life must resign
"Through personal efforts alone such things in all reside

The young man walked away, he pondered and he found
That an absurd solitude within him teemed abound
Thereafter he turned away and all of life embraced
Thereafter every happiness upon him was graced
The message is simple, a life without ambitious desire
Is coloured without colours, is fated to expire
Seek your fortunes in many ends, you will discover then
That you will never look back on life with regret again
Thus be it said, thus be it known
Forever upon the scenes of heaven to be shown
Never has been heard a flowery tale as this
The poem ends here, now go seek your destiny of bliss.

Sweetly Sung Rhyme

Once I had heard a rhyme sweetly sung
Its uttered phrases a fond remembrance brung
Each little verse was spoken forth from a bird
And all its gentle notes as such were heard:
"Many have come to live and as well have lapsed to death
"Whilst living, exhausting their hearts for what they prized
"Resigning to attrition the life inside their breaths
"For a crown of glory, later looked on with demise
"Over the years, nothing came out from them save scorn
"That scorn slowly became a depthless passion of emptiness
"Realising that all is a game, they regretted being born
"They traded the life worth living for common laurels of nothingness
"Oh what an exchange it was, they denied themselves all
"For the sake of contrived needs less true and bold
"Though in the end, they did nothing but fall
"Into the bleak oblivion of age with nothing left to hold
"Nothing to show for at all; in this way time is the cruellest foe
"When with its arts it demonstrates that its arrow cannot reverse
"Upon such hours, youth becomes the hated object of woe
"Old age holds as the pounding hammer, as the wretched curse
"Robbing gold moments away, there is little left to do
"But to pine one's own blindness and ill fortune
"Understanding that fate nothing else can pursue
"As when death is neigh, all things must surely end soon
"This is the plight that is played out day after day
"In those that lust overtakes need and desire
"In the souls of those where greed carries reason away
"And leaves nothing behind but that soul to burn in wanting fire

"Such are the visions and the dreams, heavy filled with hardest sorrow
"With sadness these tales endure through yesterday, today and well after tomorrow"

All this the bird declared as then he abruptly and upward fled
To heaven where human cries are heard by none but the dead.

I Envisaged You

I envisaged you to be like a queen
Much to my surprise I noted difference
In every aspect you differed from what I did ween
So afterwards my dear I wrote this song hence...
"Love is never what it seems to appear
"It has a thousand faces and none are true
"It beguiles the hearts of men from year to year
"But still these selfsame hearts this strange thing pursue
"It deceives us most when we want it best
"It disguises the marks from which it is made
"And gives to the labour of hope no sign of rest
"Until the workings of the mind to dust do fade
"Ah what an actor it is, the greatest muse
"That plays the part of dreams though it has none
"It is the stage upon which all men abuse
"Their will of passion until it is worn and done
"What a charlatan, love is the schemer of schemes
"That draws out life's plan with brightest rays
"Compelling perfidy into the tenderest dreams
"Driving innocence to naught until it all at once decays
"Oh I cannot overstate it enough, love is a game
"That feeds on the weak and lonely who silent dwell in pain
"And in the end it offers them naught but shame
"Trading their high expectations with deeds of miserable disdain
"To everyone out there, be warned, take heed one and all
"Love tries to place its venomed fangs into every heart
"Leading one to stray, from their destined course to fall
"Ultimately causing the soul of life and love from them to depart
Thus be it writ, this is all I have to say, indeed all is said
Love shall forever stake the hearts of men until all men to it fall dead

And that is why my dear, I refuse to fall prey
Realising love chases on, I shall forever from it flee away.

The Soft Petaled Flowers

The soft petaled flowers preen
The gentle moonlights lean
Over the frosty windowsill
Upon the zenith of a hill
While little birds all around
Sing songs with sweetest sound
Until a fabled love did enter near
Then their heartstrings thrummed ever dear
All night and day they played
And with warbled voice this tale portrayed:
"There was once a little girl who steadfast grew
"And at the age of ripeness, she her true love knew
"With which she wished to elope
"Or so her dreams were bent on that hope
"Until one morning she awoke
"And her former heart of passion helpless broke
"Right out of its mould, what could anyone do?
"How could one persuade her truer passion to pursue?
"Nor could even any one try her spirit to redeem
"She persisted to keep her whims as her desired dream
"Until with days and years she matured old
"And with new eyes came to behold
"This drama of life and its truth of worth
"From that moment on it was like a reborn birth
"For her and her deep felt need
"From that hour she a new life did lead
"Of piety, kindness and reserve
"Yea, her purer sentiments she did preserve

"As chants of devotion to her new faith she cried
"Forsaking love until her spirit died."

Thus played that tune of sadness from the beaks of the bird
Without a melody, still the sorrow was forever heard
This being the moral, that often in life
People change abruptly only to bring themselves strife
The mortal mind of man, it fickle be
This is the fate it suffers all throughout history.

To Gracefully See

All around I look and to gracefully see
To find the wondrous sight of a beauty
That I feel that I have known since birth
She to me, everything and all is worth
As every evening I cry out to the night
This little song in prayer of her darling light...
"Oh Evolina, how I love you dear
"Every moment that I dream that you are near
"Suffering cannot stand, all hatreds fall
"The world against our love can impose no wall
"Nor can the withered grasp of time impeach
"All the prospect of romance within our reach
"The majesty of truth will not fray
"As long as affection true enamours our day
"As long as sentiment retains its fruitful hand
"We shall be sustained to walk from land to land
"Immortally, against the stars, age through age
"We shall be the actors to endure upon life's stage
"To make alive the dreams of love's sweetest life
"Even though passion often proves to be most rife
"Still we shall prevail above the hardship and the labour
"Every moment of togetherness, them to savour
"Every warm embrace, every artistry of the heart
"Every sun, every flame, every burning to never depart
"As long as hope persists, every kindled trace
"Shall remind me of the kindred memory of your face
"Every aster, every cloud, every sidereal glow
"Every moon that glistens and trickles through the dusky bough
"Maiden you should know that the nightingale is but a sign
"Who symbolises how you are but fair and fine

"Its voice is but a slave to what emotions cannot speak
"Or if they could, their hard strength would grow weak
"For you are more than what a tongue can explicate
"Beyond what soft lips with a kiss can relate
"So with these rehearsing words my efforts I will seal
"Until your vision returns again so as my soul to heal"
"Come to me my love" this last verse I recited
Earnestly each night until she with my dreams united.

Man Who Abruptly Cried

There was a man who yesterday abruptly cried
"The cause of my sorrow has forever died"
So I gathered that a new friend he had found
And in that former sea, his sadness he had drowned
So I approached this man, blatantly I said"
"Indeed Sir, now surely you have lost your head
"For making remarks such as the one you had made
"Don't you know sorrow is a thing that can never fade?
"Perhaps" he softly spoke "that once this would be true
"But I am no longer inclined to believe you
"For now I see the world in a different way
"Love has changed my eyes, carried my heart away
"To a fonder realm, for a maiden I have found
"In the former sea of darkness, all my woes are drowned
"Be it known, she is the kindest, most compassionate creature
"Whose truth and honour are second only to her lovely features
"As she is the most beautiful upon which my eyes have fed
"Objectively I think that none like her can be ever bred
"Overlooking nothing, she is perfect in her form
"And when she speaks, her intellect rages like a storm
"All the angels of the sky hold her in envy
"For all the things she is and they can never be
"Her faultless virtues and qualities of esteem
"Are like the things people conjure up in a dream
"However glad I am, she has agreed to take my side
"Forever as my wife, I hold up my Pricilla in pride"
This my fellow man said as he walked away
Nodding contently, so ever blissful and gay
Blind to the darkest secret that before him so clearly shown
This woman that he loved, every man of the town has known

Alas, often the things in life we are most anxious to embrace
In the end turn out to have the ugliest of face.

An Old Love

Let me of an old love tell
Whose story I'm sure will spell
The plight of passion to its full degree
Therefore come and all, you as well will see
How the sweet and charming Piper of romance
When he plays, all to his tune dance:
There was once a little boy in a town
Who lived in a world where no love was found
Neither here, there nor anywhere
Could one gaze to ever find love's stare
When a passing traveller of love would speak
This boy's intelligence would grow weak
As utterly he did not know
About love's pageant or love's show
For all the folks that he ever knew
No affection in their hearts did brew
And when it came time to wed
Each would chose a random head
With which to breed new scion again
Both unemotive woman and passive men
But that little boy was different from them all
For he was much receptive to passion's call
Yet alas he felt lonely and forsaken
In a town where love was for granted taken
Unbridled, that little boy set out to seek
The emotion that within him burned meek
Relentless, he strove both day and night
Until this pretty girl appeared before his sight
"Pardon me, dear thing, I wish to implore
"If whether you think love is truly real or a bore

After a long pause of pondering the blond girl said
"I think true love is a hope that has long been dead
So this boy grew and ventured further out
Until an old lady before him stirred about
"Pardon madam, I was wondering if you could tell me
"If true love is a thing that I'll ever live to see?"
"Many years I've lived," the old lady cried
"And never did one love true until they died
At that point the little boy released a sigh
As he desired true love before his time to die
The old lady went on "There is no need to despair
"As long as your heart is pure and your intentions fair
"You will win, conquer and prevail above
"This magic thing you desire and call love"
As he walked away, the boy a bit happier felt
As his heart of sorrow began to thaw and melt
"Oh joyous jubilee, maybe not all is lost
"Perhaps I'll court true love, though high its cost"
Then our little boy ran into a recessed glade
Where the sirens' song of passion all around did raid
But since the ears of the boy where callow and young
He was impervious to the rueful songs that they sung
Within moments by himself he silently realised
This was not the kind of love he truly prized
And as love in this place was not found
Undiscouraged, he merely turned himself around
So he carried on to find his meed
But then all at once his spirit was freed
As from his dreary slumber he did wake
And romance his soul to paradise did take
The bells and lutes and lyres then warmly played
Over all the plains on which the boy had stayed

Like an angel from the earth he ascended
And all of his labours of love were thus ended
For when this world denies the pure hearted, heaven has a place
Of refuge for each and every neglected face
When hardship grips the tree of life to shake
Fate comes the fallen fruit to take
Out from this world so to plant its seed
In every other realm where there is a need
Even today the cries of romance ring loud and tall
And if you are wise you will heed its call
Oh indeed in the end all will turn black
Save the bright soul of those who return back
To the call of destiny like that little boy!

One Fine and Mighty Day

Upon one fine and mighty day
A lad born poor into great fortune came
All at once his former fate gave way
To lavish riches, life became a lavish game
Soon after all of his past misfortunes he forgot
As new-found wealth greeted his fattened plate
With it, a whole new ethic he adopted, he begot
The praise of the rich, condemning the beggar's fate
Despite that he was once in the beggar's place
All of his former allegiances and fond remembrance
Faded as prosperity lent colour to his face
Dissolving his young naïve charm of innocence
Alas, it was not long at all before
That little lad grew to be a man
As he waxed old, he pledged to nevermore
The plight of the poor to ever understand
Buildings were erected, his enterprise climbed high
But inside nothing but toil and labour teemed
He opposed his own comrades till they did outward cry
And not a sigh of compassion from his eyes gleamed
Yes his heart was cold, miserable and unkind
He felt no trace of sympathy for his brother
Only his sole welfare was on his mind
And thus there was no room for another
More and more cold-blooded grew his veins
Until one day as on his deathbed he laid to rest
He remembered back to his youthful pains
And regret began to pang through his breast…
"Oh my, oh my, how I have done society harm
"By becoming one of them that I once despised

"How greed and avarice have a splendid charm
"Yet only after being attained are their venoms realised
"So now I have committed injustice with grief
"As the call of my people fell on death ears
"And now that I am to die, life affords me no relief
"No solace at all for those long betrayed years
"I can do nothing but think back on the times
"When I had power to make a difference
"Before corruption crept into my worldly crimes
"And cankered the sweet flower of its innocence
"Oh woe to those heavy scores of eternity
"It hurts the most when there is no turning back
"When eyes must confront time's immutability
"And know that before it they must fade back
"There is not much more of a will left in me
"Thus with the last abiding strength that remains
"In a solemn oath of truth I dear decree
"That compassion is the thing that man sustains
"That generosity is the thing that keeps us alive
"And binds the soul of good to those who it deserved
"It is the uniting bond with which we can survive
"With which our heritage of warmth can be preserved
"Take heed, be the wiser, ye who read this
"Come not to make the same mistake I made
"The most prudent understand that the truest bliss
"It is one that is shared and to all is paid"

And thus with that last and quick fading breath
That rich fellow gave orders to his men
For his wealth to be parcelled to the poor after his death
As once he died, that rich man was once more poor again

And that is the way all men go, save their spirits they alone flee
To a higher realm that has no need for wealth, there they are forever free.

Why Evil Breeds

Oft I used to ask myself why evil breeds
Why it consumed the inside of man's heart
Why the sentiment of hatred so strongly seethes
In the societies of mankind spread wide and apart
I pondered and pondered, querying the unquestioned
All the while I felt perplexed, unsatisfied
The circumstance of doubt, it passed unmentioned
Though in truth, it gripped me from the inside
I searched high and low, here and there
In quest, in hot pursuit of a sound reply
Instead I found injustice scattered everywhere
Intermixed with hardship and oppression's cry
Then all at once, an old man appeared
Elfin like with a trollish appearance
He drew close, told his story before he disappeared
Thereafter his wisdom in my life made all the difference:
"I see that you are troubled and quite bewildered
"In search of a vision that is seldom found
"And thus your burden has made you beleaguered
"But be assured my answers shall your soul astound…
"There was once an evil demon that lived up high
"Within the dominions of life's perfection
"No sorrows did he have, he looked down from the sky
"Staring at the mortals below yet with dejection
"For this was a time that mortals dwelled in united peace
"Sans enmity for others of their kind
"They lived in a happiness that could not cease
"The thought of war and strife never entered their mind
"In sweet harmony they shared all they had
"Like a harvest of paradise, each mouth and soul was fed

"With the richness of delight, with joys good and never bad
"With treasures of grace, indeed jealousy there was long dead
"These mortals, yea, quite unique they were
"They overlooked the weakness and flaws of all they saw
"Only the good of things their hearts did stir
"For that reason they decreed goodness as the universal law
"But that demon, seeing how they lived in placid bliss
"Was quite enraged at their good fortune found
"So he conceived to deliver them a bitter kiss
"With which to destroy their Eden-like ground
"Thus he set to work and designed a window pane
"That when looked through gave a distorted view
"In every good thing it made the dire parts reign
"To the beholder former things acquired a wretched skew
"In every way it amplified the poorer aspects and features
"This glass, the kinder virtues of all things, it concealed and hid
"It made the loveliest flowers and birds seem like the basest creatures
"And once perceived this fiendish vision could never be rid
"From the eyes of those who were so brave
"As to boldly peer through that pristine glass
"For afterwards nothing their soul could save
"Their spirits over warmth and compassion would pass
"Thus that demon, in his wicked sense of charity
"Threw down that lucid glass to the world below
"Into the centre of a wealthy kingdom, a pious society
"In which every citizen all the ways of sin did forgo
"A young lad quickly found it, attracted by its gleaming rays
"Each beam that it reflected intrigued his psyche more
"Cautiously he approached it, muttering silent praise
"That poor fool, the youth never know what fate holds in store
"With valorous effort and stride, he lifted it and looked around
"Perceiving his once precious world with novel sight

"Shocked and amazed he was at what he found
"For all that he saw appeared blemished and contrite
"So astonish this lad was that he immediately ran
"To his sovereign, his king, to relate to him his find
"When he arrived to his majesty he forthright began
"To tell his story of how mankind through this object shone unkind
"The king was aroused and piqued by what he heard
"He abruptly took up the glass from the young lad's hand
"What he first thought was impossible and absurd
"Before him materialised, he too began evil to understand
"This king, he considered the glass his most prized possession
"He applied it to all he had, as well his councillors and noblemen
"He examined them close, inside their hearts he found imperfection
"So outraged by this corruption, he ordered to behead them
"He then looked and inspected his wife, the fair queen
"And then the lovely princess and the prince to be
"In each he saw disfigurement, a dishonourable sheen
"A glory lacking lustre, as he bid them to death by royal decree
"Oh with wrathful intrigue the king fast set out
"Unto a journey extending from day to night
"High and low he searched his dominion about
"For something that could retain a pious light
"Exhausted and weary, with all his energies expanded
"He concluded no such thing ever has or could exist
"But then he looked up above to the glow of heaven suspended
"He schemed to apply his glass to God, this temptation he could not resist!
"With his royal might, he ordered for a contraption to be built
"That could greatly hoist his cherished glass up above
"Yet all the while, inside he sensed a doubtful guilt
"For the misdeed he was to undertake with such brazen love
"Still he ignored his inner voice, cleared his doubt and carried on

"With his intended plan, indeed his design was almost set in place
"When all at once the glass shattered from before the heights of Avalon
"Like powered dust, the fallen pieces settled into the eyes of every mortal face
"Oh those poor and guileless eyes, from that time forward
"Man has had no choice but to behold both sides
"Both the good and bad, though the good before the bad is lowered
"Oh shamefully forever on the impulse of hatred within man resides
"Now that I have revealed all that I have seen and know
"Surely you can understand why evil lives within our creed
"Upon the countenance of this wide and unjust mortal show
"Do you see to where the contempt of one king does lead?
"Now we must suffer for his sake, relinquish our former state of bliss
"Yea, forsake all that once made our kind flourish and thrive
"Now death, envy and jealously throw to us their kiss
"Making a savage jungle of life in which only the strongest survive
"But not all is without hope, this much I must say
"For when man is made to suffer and from that suffering is forced to cry
"Upon such an hour, upon such a rare but enlightening day
"Man will be redeemed, the blinded vision of the embedded glass will thereafter die."

All this the old man spoke as he walked even further away
Saying as he left "Keep your heart pure and you shall have your day
"Oh forever, forever, that warm happy day once more to take
"And we from this black dream of hatred to forever wake."

On the Windowsill

Once upon a time when on the windowsill I leaned
When the banter of my thoughts newer thoughts weaned
I gazed out the glassy pane and there perceived
A maiden whose vast loveliness could not be believed
She sat all alone, in soft contemplation sunk
As the pale moon shined on her as her, making me all drunk
I espied her and quaffed her beautiful rays
And then gently resigned to the remembrance of fonder days
As in a tender dream, all these words to her I spoke
And thereafter from that unfulfilled dream never woke...
"My lady, my maiden, how you are ever fair
"More prized than anything beheld by human stare
"Even though in solitude you are perched out far
"Still in that seclusion you appear as the brightest star
"Whose blessed excellence so warmly glows
"That the bud of summer in your reflection grows
"Your face, the sweet composure of your hands
"Drive me to wander through many faraway lands
"Through the desert and the rocks of a mountainous shore
"Through fables and tales and mysteries of yore
"Every unscaled surface I have climbed
"Every unversed word I have put in rhyme
"To woo and coo, to relish your kind favour
"Your heart to win, your loving soul to savour
"Every ocean and sea I will transverse
"Every lost moment of time I shall reverse
"If somehow I could rewrite the history of fate
"I would assign you from birth to my own destined state
"I would soar through the skies over and over
"Moulding those dear orbs into a shape of a clover

"That has granted me the fortune of your eyes
"Heaven itself at such displays of posterity cries
"If indeed life was the game that could be so easily won
"My revels would be ended, with you my purpose done
"My pursuits satisfied, my longings no more denied
"My esteemed desire not broken off by callus pride
"Everything that I admire in you is found
"My every hope and promise to you is bound
"Yet as all this speech rests unheard within the night
"Darkness surrounds, there is no prospect for hope's light
"All of the aspirations of the unfolding tomorrow
"Die away unsung with the lyre of heavy sorrow
"The birds, the angels, the glimmer of the day
"Flee the world in swiftness, leaving the shadows to stay
"My deep blackened soul perishes unknown without name
"When your love is unheld, untouched and expired is the fame
"Of my true longed being, everything then must fade
"When your vision is not near, when death's legions raid
"The pangs afflicted, the pains, the strong hurtful throes
"All upon the unlived hour so blindly close
"The earth dies unseen yet a new day is begun
"And I remain to thee faithful as the Eastern sun"
These phrases I cried out as my innocent head
From the window lattice in lovelorn siege fell quietly dead.

Warm Summer Air

Upon the lank and warm summer air
Within some kingdom below an enchanted lair
There sat a maiden along a wooden bench
Planked with despair as her hands did wrench
Along with her sweet teary eyes
That left nothing in their paths but supple cries
Oh what demise! That gentle dame declared out her plight
Under the moonlit remembrance of the night…
"There can be for me neither today nor tomorrow
"For as I live my heart blends in bitter sorrow
"Over the handsome love that I once did prize
"Among cankers and cold worms now he lies
"Under a blanket of hard pressed dust
"Below the stones and sand of earth's red black crust
"His spirit from his frame did depart, his soul expired
"A week ago, upon an early eve, after he retired
"Returning to bed so as his head to lay with his chest
"To give his weary limbs slumber's gentle rest
"But suddenly he awoke by a disturbance, or so it seemed
"Being fearless, he slipped deeper into his dream
"And out came father death ringing his knell
"And my brave beloved until his knees he fell
"Begging the old man for his life to be spared
"Or youth's grain of justice upon him he fared
"But death was brazen and did not heed
"To the beseeching of my lover's plead
"With a heavy hand, father time smote
"Blotting out all that in Life's book was wrote
"With a single stroke he did effectively smite
"The tenderness of my lover's resting night

"As there within his gentle sleep he remained
"A stiff posture unto all eternity sustained
"Drowsed there forever, he never awoke again
"That is why I grieve him as the bravest of men
"For those who try to battle with death's rule
"Wage vain pursuits, in the end they are the fool
"For living out the days they have, though being blind
"To man's immutable need to return unto his kind
"This is the mortal way, none can pervade
"To conquer over death as they alas must fade"

Thus spoke the maiden as she departed to the bed
Where her bold lover's once laid to rest his head
Feeling weary, towards the starless sky she turned
Amid the silence, closing her eyes, she too returned
Unto that indifferent world that shall always be
Our one and destined realm of finality.

A Man Whose Lips Related

There was once a man whose lips related
A story whose message the world await
For indeed its content salvation could bring
If all people heeded to the words he did sing…
"My dear mortals of this earth, listen all
"Nothing lasts forever, man too must one day fall
"And as for this time given in between, spend it best
"On those things prized by you, give them no rest
"For the passion of the true-lived heart
"Can satisfy, imparting fulfilment that will never depart
"And those who try their dogmas upon you to beset
"Deny their authority, this you shall never regret
"Never let them have control or the upper hand
"Tell them there is no true owner to our Land
"This wide world we share, in it each has a right
"To strive for the things he loves and for those things to fight
"Never obey or be subservient to their view
"Else they will try to subject and tame you
"With a structure of reality that for them is real
"For which you may no hint of affection feel
"As the purposelessness of our being is innate
"Save for the purposes we for ourselves instate
"Therefore be strong and in yourself always believe
"And if the world presses down hard, yourself relieve
"With the comfort of the thought that life nothing means
"And all our endeavours are meant to be as dreamy scenes
"To entertain, to enliven, perhaps to obscure
"The aimless void of existence for which there is no cure
"For dust we are, from bleak nothingness we were born
"To nothingness to return, so this is played out from morn to morn

"And so it shall continue, undying and without end
"Until the drape of death comes our eyes to send
"To the black pit of drifting silence, blinding our sight
"Killing the mind in silence, drowning love in the eternity of night."
So spoke all this the man as his voice passed into the shade
Into that same darkness wherein all do fade.

Many Sorrows

Many sorrows have been told
The affairs of time as evidence hold
As to how love can come to wound and sting
The selfsame heart that of love once used to sing
Passion pricks the eyes with indifference
It blinds the very soul of innocence
When romance throws itself upon young days
Thereafter the concern for tomorrow itself betrays
Love holds out neither meek nor kind
If desire plagues the yearning of the mind
Obsession must surrender and release
Before time comes to withdraw its cherished lease
Allowing darkness its sense of void to retain
And the forlorn sentiment to always remain
Upon the destined sky lit up at night
With dreams and hope and destiny's light
Ah what a plague it is to be born
When Love heaps upon us scorn
And ardent strides lead to no end
Save all the patient virtue can amend
Torrid fantasies fetch naught but pain
Besetting harmony with grave disdain
What a treason love is, what a gentle ruse
Heed this dear friends, never let its sweetness abuse
Your souls or your spirits or the essence of your heart
Better that it should flee and far away depart
Than to bring ruin and tearful demise
To all that is sacred and precious to your eyes
Thus if you are wise and wish to prudent be
Then take note to what I advise, it is clear to see

All those who give in to love shall not be found
Save lying agonised upon the dregs of the ground
Serving as surplus proof to the deeds of love untrue
Which countless nights of rationalising cannot undo
Do yourself the favour and kindly spare
To have this malady of love as your fare
For those who do, I swear they always say
"Love is the cruellest thing to fall upon your way
"Never can one turn away if it comes to kiss
"And with its venom makes the world appear as bliss"
I cannot bear it more, thus I take flight
With wings of Reason, away from the path lit by love's light.

Flowery Tale of Love

Let me this most flowery tale of love relate:
Affection is its trade, this tale seeds
Itself in every heart that breeds
Desire and longing in its eternal state
Thus the roses and the lilacs pursue
The harder thorn of emotion that pricks untrue
Cankering the soil with rue and festering grass
Blinding innocence from the sharp eyes of truth
Relinquishing hope, allowing dreams to pass
To where the throes of happiness skulk ruth
That sweet harmony, as it is to the mind denied
It drives the soul to grieve the sorrow it cannot hide

The poppies fall from the grave, the bird sings
Its softer trill under the warm sunshine
The darker shades of day below its feet resign
The reign of destiny its heavy cask brings
Inside it rings a most dreadful cry
Echoing the prophesy that "tomorrow must die"
Man is fearful of such words so he shuts his ears
Failing to believe that soft ditty heard
To him there can be no death in mortal years
If man lives not out his days foolishly or absurd
Being self-assured, he then retires to sleep
Drowsily he sinks, never to wake from a depth so deep

Unbroken, the morn is entranced in ancient grace
The luminous patch scatters far and away
Oh what becomes of the unlived day?
When we are taken in by the dust sans any trace
The wishful part of us merrily supposes

The soul lives on; so what becomes of the roses?
The flowers, cats and stars, they too yearn for paradise
But Eden was not made or fashioned for their kind
Thus their lots are fated for bleak demise
They lack virtue, we are heirs of the creative mind
And each new story and substance the mind creates
Our sullen fears of the unknown it strong sedates

These fables are weaved, back to back, end to end
And nothing from their strings shake out
Beauty is lost, glorious truth is nowhere about
Time with its poisoned fangs comes to mend
The fabric of harmony that does manifest
The charm of life that with tragedy is dressed
So the days, weeks and hours continue to expire
Until at last the sun veers to its final draw
And the earth is consumed, the world in its fire
Repents nothing as it is subdue to nature's law
This is the tale that carries on, neither love nor strength can cure
This hard deception of life to which we are all inure

The story carries on, where is joy to be found
On the plains of happiness, are they green?
Are the fields wide and clear enough to be seen?
Space and time, they are majestic and abound
The glory of existence, it shines not as bright
Fearful of the truth, we seek solace in the night
Upon dark and brief hours, the stars are not so cruel
To bind our fearful hands with restive hold
The one who believes he's free is the greatest fool
Overtly unaware of death's blade, poised and cold

The woes wear on, some brand them as unjust, unfair
But sanity is not inclined to heed what passions declare

Madness cries out to the faculty of reason
Despair grips it, he desires to make sense
Out of this scheme of life that reeks offence
The smell of bondage is like the chain of treason
Fortune is heaped with so many foul sins
That the birth of the babe with crime begins
Uncommitted wrongs, so the journey flies
Out unto the truest scenes of ruffled peace
The young and tender man, he with his spirit cries
Protesting the fierce stab of life that does never cease
Thus he perishes in silent pain, like all the best of men
His rebellion, above all, dies and is never heard of again.

Here, Inside Me

Here, inside me a story bleeds
A rueful tale whose contents like this reads
There was a man who once lived all alone
Being alone he lived on the highest throne
Though the rest of the world by him was unseen
Perhaps beyond the realm of what he could ever ween
To all kinds of happiness and mirth he was blind
Though he was content within his made-up mind
Beauty and fairness he did scorn
Loveliness he claimed was never ever born
So like a hermit from day to day he lived
As the years through the hourglass sieved
Until one day he awoke and realised
From within his own depth and with his own eyes
The truth materialised, its rays did glow
He understood that his life teemed with woe
When emptily life is held to onward pass
When left to wither and turn brown, to die like grass
No, the life of meaning with brightness shines
With tender verse and warm romantic lines
With sweet roses, songs, and the prettiest flowers
With the moon, the sun, the stars, their gentlest powers
As often solitude wears the disguise of peace
But once fulfilled it quickly draws to cease
Tranquillity of such nature cannot endure
For man requires company, to this no one is not inure
Nor can it ever be otherwise lest sadness take away
The soul of thee like the man that died that day

The poor chap, he did live alone
Ruling the kingdom of his world that had no throne.

When the Rose Must Fall

Once long ago sat under a hazel tree
As before my presence I did see
A maiden with a complexion of radiant flair
That transfixed, upon it I did everlasting stare
With the desire that her countenance serene
Would continue with its bright glowing sheen
As my eyes yearned their humbler sight to lead
To where she reclined amid the lush verdant mead
Oh how my lips wished to convey a loving word
But only grave silence from my mouth was heard
Though my heart wished deep passions to relate
Instead in cold hesitation did it patiently await
Perhaps tarrying for the proper moment to be shown
Yet in between remaining all alone
Woe to the heart that hides in shame
It shall conquer naught but a disdainful name
The bashful minded taste defeat
When from their true emotions they retreat
Then regret creeps in to emplace its crown
Replacing the prospect of happiness with a rueful frown
The deferred sentiment can only gain
Nothing but sorrow, hardship and pain
Oh what agony, as I remember the scene
Where she, that glorious beauty, did lovely lean
Along the silent brook and river bed
Where my mortal hungers upon her vision fed
Oh forever I shall pine my fair fortunes last
Remitted with mistakes of highest cost
What errors, what blunders, what vain dreaming done
What ignominy, what proud triumphs shunned

I tell you all this as I sit here aged and old
Without grasp or strength of anything to hold
Never the master of my fate, the day expires
With it perishes my endless human desires
Everything lapses in the night, much as the rose to its shade
As then the all in all once more does fall and fade
Upon the hour, there will be nothing left to see
Except the world of yesterday that never again can be
As I sit here forlorn under this frayed hazel tree
Of a once youth and love and now cold death and eternity
Dear friends, if one thing I must bid, this I do
Always cherish your days and live them true
I say this final prayer and then resign
To where love flees from these wanting arms of mine
Oh does not this world in deepest darkness shine?

A Bird's Parable of Love

Love burns in me like a fire
A chariot, like a swift blaze of desire
A desire that shall never die
Not unless my soul from me does fly

Softly I heard the little nightingale sing
As a pang of sadness through its heart did sting
A sting that carried on from year to year
Until before its eyes, nothing short of death did appear

Then I heard ramblings from the lips of a crow
Who in his loneliness sat high upon a bough
A bough whose tender branch then did break
And a martyr of that lonely crow did make

Thus spoke the dove as he lied
Over the olive tree of his pride
A prickly pride whose consequence did lead
For our dear friend unto death to bleed

These echoes softly murmured from the mouth
Of the darling sparrow as he headed south
A south that ended up to be
For him a grave unto cold eternity

Two swans exchanged these verses as they flew
Recessed deep in the pond of summer dew
A dew whose drops are never tasted
Save by them whose heart with love is wasted

Thrice played Love's tune upon the tongue
Of a skylark when he was passionately young

Young and brave, such birds are often bold
Until death resigns them to grow decrepitly old

So sang the blue jay of warm romance
As from branch to branch he did haply prance
Oh what a prance, its stole the cuckoo's fame
Leaving nothing to the bluebird but a pleasant name

Such is the sorrow and the rue
With which the pheasants daily coo
A coo that marks a grieving loss
Of the pure heart of love filled with dross....

And so played the story on and on
From sky to sea and to bright Avalon
Oh Avalon, foreshame, that thing of love we prize
After it is lost and gone, still we hear its cries
Sung upon the lips of bird after bird
Until its tale of sadness by one and all is heard.

Tale of Narcissus

Oh Narcissus, narcissus, your story reads
Like a tale of sorrow and mystery
That from the dolour-laden heart bleeds
With songs of hardest pain and misery

Oh beautiful son of sweet nymph Europe
Beloved of mortal and immortal men
Darling boy whose soul thrived without hope
It stings the tongue to recite your plight again…

If only your pride had not been so bold
As to that sweet maiden Echo to disdain
Her love for you was so true, it was untold
That a lady of the antique world could so pure remain

But those charms, those boyish charms
They did not move your pulse to stir
Or your arms to surround her arms
Or your world to surrender to the world of her

Self-indulgent boy, you were deaf to the cries
Which that tender maiden nightly sang
The world is unjust, though grief never dies
The spirit flies, thus her tears the death knell had rung

And the sounds of her pining soft fled away
All except the faint whisper of her gentle sigh
A woeful sigh that carried day through day
An echo reminding all that love can never die

Oh most baleful fate, here lies the tragedy
Nemesis in her rage did command a curse

A most hateful law, a most dreaded decree
That the indulgent boy should his plight forever rehearse

So one day as Narcissus passed by a stream
He fell in love with his own reflection
Admiring his face as if it were some pleasant dream
That was so true, it bore no imperfection

Thus he admired and admired for many a day
That face, that complexion which lacked all scorn
Until time and hunger his beauty did betray
And his death brought forth a new flower to be born

A comely thing it was, it bears his prized name
And stands among the ponds as an ageless sign
To the sadness of love, to sad love's fame
That ends never, never until we all to death resign.

Leander's Tale

Oh fair Hero, oh brave but poor Leander
A greater story of love none can recall
Mythology shall forevermore serve as their defender
Never letting their fame from memory to fall...

Hero was a priestess to Aphrodite's clan
She a vestal maiden was, full of innocence
Pure hearted too, she foreswore every man
To please the gods and thereby make a difference

But maturity is the blemish of youth
And as her soul was fresh, gentle and kind
And as she was tender in her signs of truth
One can say that to truth she was blind

Or rather all men are blind to the ways of fate
Not even the boldest gods can prophesise
What tides the shores of tomorrow await
What new fortunes will greet unborn eyes

So thus unripe Hero made her vow
Against the throes of maturity she forsook love
But this selfsame oath would come to make her bow
Before the altar of romance that she dreamt not of

For in Abydos lay Leander's abode
He as much as she a sweetness bore
The oracle for him as well forebode
That one day Love would doom him evermore

So the days passed until upon some isle
Upon the seldom hour our two angels met

And quickly fell in love between the while
But solemn swore to keep the affair most secret

As by decree, Hero was banned from being wed
As by nature Leander's love for her did burn
Thus faithful Leander each night was led
To the tower where Hero for his arms did yearn

Oh jealously! Each night Hero lit a flame
That allowed Leander to swim across the Hellespont
Guided by Hero's rays, Leander blessed her name
As he dutifully arrived to their arranged spot

Then at dawn the lovers would sadly part away
And Leander once more would traverse the sea
Yet not without the promise that by the close of day
He once more with her would united be

But dear friends, herein lies the brunt of tragedy
The betrayal of fortune that evades none
For harshness would soon beset their destiny
Leaving their hopes shattered, their dreams undone

For upon one ill-fated and stormy night
Leander boldly tried the Hellespont to cross
But the raging winds blew out the guiding light
And Hero's heart then filled with darkest dross

Oh poor Leander, confused, amongst the tides he drowned
By morning his slender body washed upon the shore
When Hero's searching eyes that heavy scene they found
She swore to live on nevermore, nevermore!

Her world was torn asunder, her heart was twain
Her once beauteous spheres filled with lamenting cries

As this priestess her spirit could no longer retain
She thrust herself from the tower toward dark demise

Her body fell into the sand, crested by Leander's side
Hand in hand, against each other they were pressed
Immortally their souls in heaven reside
For a story of more woeful love cannot be confessed

Oh Hero, sweet Hero, look for Leander no more
The light of life in its time burns then expires
Thereon each mortal man washes upon death's shore
He perishes, he dies, gone are the loves, forever fled the desires

Thus the sorrows endure unkind, untrue
Forever ancient, reborn, in the life of man, forever new.

Jason's Tale

Now here begins the tale of Jason, proud and strong
King of righteous Iolcus, Aeson's son
The story of his life can be told like a song
That liked all others with an act of injustice was began

Ever-wicked Pelius, he was the half brother
Of Aeson who held rightful claim to the throne
Kinsmen they were, but shared not the blood of the other
So Aeson was disposed, thereafter Pelius ruled alone

Now Aeson, being a wise man realised
That his son Jason bore perilous jeopardy
As the oracle to Pelius had prophesised
That a one sandaled man would usurp his liberty

So Aeson sent Jason to Chiron when he was young
Like all other heroes to be educated
In the arts of warfare, with the strings of valour to be hung
His life to learning for many years was dedicated

Until at last the day arrived when Jason was grown
And he had ambition enough to reclaim his land
The seeds of manhood in him were sown
He was sworn to return and make his regal demand

Yet his journey was neither smooth nor straight
For the goddess Hero decided him to test
She stood by a river and asked for his manly gait
To deliver her across from east to west

The prophecy was fulfilled, with one sandal he arrived
To Iolcus, but the challenges were now set to truly start

It was a time of festival, Pelius refused with him to strive
So instead he set him tasks, deeds most odious to the heart

The first was a golden fleece that hung from a tree
In Colchis, guarded by a snake that never slept
Jason began to wonder about his course of destiny
Yet the Oracle encouraged him on despite where it was kept

The Thessation warriors an expedition formed
In whom the Argonauts were the crew
Of the ship Argo that many hardships stormed
Until this boat of heroes to Colchis drew

There Hera and Aphrodite with her charms they schemed
To make Medea, second daughter to Aietes the King
Aietes the Greek-hater, for Jason's death he dreamed
So he too commanded Jason to also do an impossible thing

The hero was required to yoke bulls that fire breathed
To plough and sow a field with dragon's teeth
To slay the armed men that at once would seethe
From that selfsame soil that life had bequeathed

With the skill of Medea's magic arts
Jason completed these tasks within a day
But corrupt and base was Aietes's heart
For he refused the Golden Fleece to give away

So secretly Jason and Medea, his newfound lover
Planed to attack the Argonauts for their villainous pride
With magic dust, the eyes of the sleepless snake she covered
Jason then seized the fleece with unbroken stride!

O' but if only all tales were to end so fairy-like
Indeed not, for their return to Thessaly

Caused a storm of rage in the mind of Pelius to strike
That he sought to rescind his promise and decree

But Jason and Medea were too clever for his kind
For when King Pelius's back was vulnerably turned
They counselled his daughters to act with malice blind
To murder their father, to have his remains burned

The disgrace of Aeson's death was now avenged
But far was this story from a happy end
Though dishonour with dishonour was revenged
The messenger of mirth, no blessing to Jason did he send

Thereafter he and his Media led an unsettled life in Greece
Before long, noble Jason deserted her for a woman more fair
But as Medea was not content to accept her fate in peace
She killed her lover's rival and Jason's children for whom she cared

Jason himself died when the Argos fell on his head
Afterwards the gods raised the ship up to the sky
And crowned a constellation out of our hero fallen dead
His soul appears near the zodiac for all mortals to wonder why

Oh why oh why must all sweet things end in tragedy?
Why are the fists of fate so fiercely tight?
Why must the softest tunes of life subside in elegy?
Or the fairest rays of morn to end in night?

This is the nature of the drama of our formidable stage
That none can evade, that all with fortitude must bear
This is the show without end, welcome youth, welcome age
These million colours of life that like Jason await your stare.

Arman Nabatiyan

Achilles the Warrior

Great Achilles, he a noble mortal was born
Son of Thetis and Peleus the King
A warrior by blood, poor Troy did mourn
The anger that into their city he did bring

Somewhat uncertain was the nature of his birth
Both Zeus and Poseidon desired a son
From beautiful Thetis, Prometheus said they lacked worth
So a scheme by those two gods was begun

Quickly thereafter Thetis was arranged
With some lowly earth mortal to be wed
She became gravid, her vows she exchanged
And prayed to have a son that could not fall dead

A boy she was granted, various means she tried
To have the newborn babe immortalised
She pined and wept, along the river Styx she cried
Dipping her babe into the tears before drying her eyes

Oh for now a great soldier had been forged and made
Whose only weakness was the heel that she did hold
Still Thetis was confident that her boy would never fade
Neither in strength nor fame in the minds of young and old

The years passed, agile Achilles gained skill
From the hands of Chiron in whom warfare was mastery
And on occasion they together climbed a rugged hill
To end wild games, to increase noble Achilles's ferocity

Little Achilles grew, his courage was renowned
Day and night he shot arrows high into the open air

In perfection they landed back on the ground
Everywhere he aimed, his shots were found precisely there

But then a dark cloud lifted over the Grecian plain
As countless legions were summoned up for crusade
Against Trojan dishonour and disdain
Young men were at will to fall before death's blade

Oh but not he, not Achilles, his mother would let not
For him to partake in the battle where he was sorely needed
Against all throes of prophecy she schemed a plot
To sent Achilles to Skyros isle, in woman garb seeded

But as there is no force that can fortune's reins overtake
His dear mother's design was destined for doom
As when Odysseus his trip to Skyros did make
He exposed Achilles with his arms of gloom

Unmasked, Achilles had no choice and for Troy set sail
There he quarrelled with wretched Agamemnon
Whilst poor and misled Iphigenia, white and pale
Was wed to fire only, sacrificed to Avalon

But fair Artemis was not pleased, in his tent Achilles stayed
Refusing to fight the Trojans despite persuasion
But once Patracles was forced to taste death's bitter shade
Achilles was roused to action and made quick invasion

With Hephaistos's armour he entered the fray
He came up against Hector, his savage soul he slew
Defeating him, he dragged him round for twelve a day
Until the Trojans gave rites to the coldest man they knew

Achilles began to savour the glory of the conquest's rage
Despite the truths Xanthus whispered in his ears

Achilles thought himself beyond the reach of mortal age
And so he endeavoured on, unmoved by all tangible fears

After killing hundreds, proud Achilles stood
Beneath the Trojan walls all content and gay
Then on the sudden tasted Paris poisoned wood
Guided by Apollo, the arrow slew Achilles once glorious day

Such mortal wounds, they are most dear
For they aim straight to where man is weak
Life throws many arrows and some cut near
The very virtues that we boast of and exulting speak

It is the universal hardship that we all share
We are all as fallible as Achilles' kind
The proud flourish neither here nor there
Only their stories of defeat are left behind

Thus Achilles bowed out, never to see the world again
A hero he was to great Alexander nothing less, nothing more
A myth, a worshipped legend before the eyes of all fearless men
Who lust for immortality, but die before the tragedies of war.

Allegory of Aesop's Fables

When the rooster with the lion does speak
The whole universe itself grows weak
As when an old man musters up a word to say
To the world he preaches, none would dare betray
For pearls that are uttered from the wisest lip
To the last drop, like dew, they are sweetly sipped

Thus the hare and the fox walked together
Thinking that their time of friendship was forever
It was not until the eagle over the serpent swept
And the hare in the cave of death eternal slept
The lesson of this story being plainly told
Befriend those with whom you shall grow old

Then the tortoise with the falcon flew
To heights that he never dreamt or knew
As then the fox became the lion's thrall
Thereafter leaving him and losing all
The moral is simple, never desire beyond need
Else you will bring on your own ruin with greed

Once a most thirsted goat walked down his path
Before he was engaged with the wolf's sly wrath
The hawk and the pigeon made an accord of peace
Though soon after their shared harmony abruptly ceased
It has been once told, let it be told again
Look before you leap else you will regret it then

As next the dove and the ant sat together near
Counselling each other of approaching fear
Then the raven and the swan their places exchanged
In vain, as a glorious death was for both was arranged

Though every mortal seeks his lot of fate to escape
In the end the curtain of death over all will drape

All in all, the lesson of these tales to be learned
Is to live out your life without being spurned
With temptation or regret, they are the same
In equal measure they shall blot out your fame
Which each mortal thinks he forever has
Until death comes to take this life away, alas!

Allegory of Life

The lion's paw, its shadow is a scythe
That culls the mortal coil when life is blithe
Its teeth are drawn red and filled with dross
As then its power unleashes from its bitter jaws...
How youth once seemed soft and fair
Before truth beset itself upon the stare
Of fond remembrance, here the tiger leaps
As the wolf pursues its prey of hope, a modest sheep
So the stench of mortal death everywhere is felt
Its dark and coldest touch fall upon the winter veldt
Pressing forth, now here the jaguar comes
To impose on its victims their fate of martyrdom
The hours draw late, these vicissitudes endured
Invoke into the flesh a dream that cannot be cured
Oh treason! That is why we age yet wish to never die
Then the panther creeps forth as before its claws we cry
We endeavour on, winning from defeat's wicked dream
Of grief and emptiness the pervade with a gleam
Across this wide expanse of eternity
But then the jackal strikes, gone is all that can ever be
Gone is the beauty; blown away is life's gentle light
As now everything shines better in the pitch of night
The leopards run in, there again begins the chase
As for things unseen, we with our efforts race
To the imperilled paths, these nimble strides of play
Carry on until ambition itself in finality does decay
The vultures assemble, there falls the curtain of fate
Crying out prophesies of darkness that we all await
But then the lion of the yesteryear stumbles in
He is too aged, worn hands and knees naught can win

All the strivings of the man's breath are in vain
In this fierce world that begs of all to go insane
For humble conquerings that in the end are nothing worth
But then the sun rises, this whole pageantry is given new birth
The pulse subsides then dies thereafter; the exotic din is heard no more
As then our names fall like torn corpses before the alter of death
forevermore.

Servant to Time

All the world is but a servant to time
And we are the faithful players that forgo
Many hours and sweet pleasures unmet
But change gives surface to hope
Memory reminds us of the perfection of dream
As with a weakened breast we wildly chase
That scene of youth that cannot be again
Thus we escape to where the mind believes it is free
And there pine our sadness of the darkened world
Sans ears, sans the blood of pitied love
The tears carry on crestfallen, dismayed
Destroyed, the plights are heard by the unborn womb
And are relived a thousand score without contempt
Unbecoming, the truce is shattered, the cries are heard again and again.

Dream-Like Comfort

These days with dream-like comfort
Will this comfort even arise again?
Will men rage against graves of silence when memory
Serves to strike the flame of fondness after death?
When old age reminds youth that time passes once
Like a forward arrow that pierces and tears the flesh of the heart
When kindness dreams of tomorrow, but tomorrow is gone
The joy of the prime moment is fled far and fast
Oh who ever stops to think what this world is worth?
Naught, nothing at all, the perished seem to say
The golden rays of reverence fly out
To where the embrace of darkness is eminent
Unfolding, unrelenting, unyielding of the bitter tides
The human shores, they are only washed with the ebb
Not with the waters of goodness but hard defeat
Thus the mind takes to the crypt and sleeps below the stone
Of the eternal moment sans tomorrow or the grace of the past
Inside our depths rocks overturn with passion
The leaves blow soft, the winds whistle wildly
And in our comfort we are taken away, taken away
Oh forever silenced in our sweet womb of joy.

This World's Content Must Fade

To feel that this world's content must fade
That it will never return, there never is return
After we thrust ourselves beyond the unseen brink
Nothing but cold solitude remains
Just as if we were never born
Plunged into the sea of immaterial silence
But dear friends still keep forever strong
The soul of humankind is worth far more than that
Be kind, be true, be fair
Let not the wild hours of youth to die in vain
Oh be bold, life requires such heraldry
That sometimes against the wretched throes of this stage
It is the tactless that with surety thrive
Be not a beast, but the faithful pilgrim of nature
Let brotherhood stir your blood, fraternity be your dream
Solidarity to be the thing that redeems all that purpose is worth living for
Be sacred in mind, the pureness of heart will follow
And thereafter the chains of time shall enslave you never, nevermore!

Truth of This World

To where has the truth of this world fled?
Where is its justice, where is its pride?
Where hides the truce that can amend a million wrongs?
Of the unfeeling heart whose faults committed
Deny love its most noble and righteous due
Oh world! Where is your virtue, where is your strength?
Where lies the crown that can sustain the soul of innocence?
That can preserve the mind of gentle dreams
Where is the power, where burns the sweeter light?
That can keep passion alive for ages untold
That keeps the candle of midnight as a child to eternity
To forever burn in those wondrous skies of no end
Of no tomorrow, no yesterday, no regret, no tears of parting
Oh farewell, farewell unkind world! Where is your grace?
Why does your greatness fail to stop these unseen views?
For that kindness we die, for that compassion we are slaves eternal
Oh for that mercy, for that precious drop of rarest mercy
We are bondmen in a land we know nothing of
More soldiers against a rage and siege of blind nothingness
Youth yields to the cruel scythe of time, nothing remains of us
But a mark of dust unto the chronicles of a glory swept away
An age decayed, a time forgotten, a score lost, a fondness faded
So we take to our place, seating ourselves upon a throne that hardly exists
That hardly exists in the mind that believes, man must believe is true
Oh but to where has the truth of the world fled?
The earth declines, the worlds perish, inside we are all dead.

Everything Disappears Away

How everything disappears away
Into nothingness we are born again, let them disappear
With a wink, all the hardest hours are gone
All the brief weeks and years, they expire, they flee
Without a word, all of them bid farewell, a long goodbye
The moments of yesterday, the fond harvest of youth
Like a most happy dream, everything fast decays
So quick, so soon, so unexpected, so undesired
There is no looking back, no forward scope of tomorrow
We remain in the forever footsteps of today
In wide regret of deeds undone and burdens bore
Of torments suffered, of bitter grief endured
So our spirits sink into the darker womb of eternity
Where they can find solace within the coves of solitude, endless solitude
Where refuge awaits the deafened harmony of the mind
Oh how the pain lingers, the pulse aches from the inside
With the red flow of agony, the veins rupture apart
Unheard, the heart melts and dies in dismay
The lot of purest stars, they set with disbelief
At the thought of what the tides of destiny can behold
What cruel designs, love is the impulse of the soul
That breeds the inculpable and everlasting disease
My bones are consumed by the drier dust
Nothing remains of life but the hope of brightest levity
An optimistic bliss, it too must lapse and die
The moon dissolves, the blackness of the earth fades
One light alone is seen, it is the vision of the unknown
I reach for it, it burns, the world and I both die with it
Together yet disunited with what can never be

The skylark stirs; the composure of the day is morn
As once more I stand poised upon the human shore
Of time and love and gravity—I resign to it
Withered away, oh withered away
My soul, it lapses from this mortal play
Tasting only the bleakest of hate and finality
I resign all enfeebled, all unsung, all unfelt
Through my eyes as if never born or alive at all.

Deathless Men

We, the deathless men of this earth
Are too blind to our errors and call them strengths
We trump forth proud and uncivil in heart
Heralding our prized attributes in bloodless sport
When in fact weakness reigns and holds out to the feed of worms
What merit is there then for the face of cheer
That must look into this scope of bleakness, yet still smile
There breaks out the jaws of the mortal chords
We think too much on our features that fools call fair
When indeed all such rites belong to the agency of death
Unguided, we let our better powers to decay
To fester in the sands of unwaking time and hate
Whose shores sombre tides shall not return back
To the frail looking glass of tomorrow or black yesterday
For when all the sands have bled their final grace
We shall still cry and grieve the virtues we bear the least
Praising the greater valour that we do not have at all
That is altogether void from the scene of existence
Like misguided prey, we exalt the faults that dim truth's light
Oh the soul grows wearing and faint and exhausted
After having endured all these absurd labours
The bones and the once burning will surrender to the toil of the flesh
To seek the flame and fortune of those stars evermore blazing
The mind grows despondent of the games, it has slept too long
The dreams have expired since, nothing around the dark earth
remains
Except the softer promise of hope that too must fade
The prospects dim, the rays shatter the night, the world decays
Upon the stellar heights and sidereal plains a silent anthem plays
Under the fists of cruelty and passion nothing has changed

Against the fiercest rage, the torments carry on unabated
Unscathed, the rebelling arm of men takes up the reins again
To lead out into the veldts of the unknown, the darkened eyes to look around
The lorn and anguished soul to find peace at all.

Beyond the Scope of Man

It is beyond the scope of man to say
What all these dreams and sleeps are worth?
After the tired scene has been played endless times
When the ropes of life refuse to rehearse their part
When time denies recital to the evening bird
What is left of these hopes and spires of paradise?
Do not the towers crumble and the aspirations fray
To what harbour or seashore do admirations ebb?
Upon what strong rock do visions fall back?
Those sidereal heights, how do their shapes expire?
The landscape is but an uncurbed bourn
It is the bane that devours the ministry of the mind
When the brain yearns to believe in things eternal
What cruel jests, what carnage, what wreckage, what ruin, what despair
What blinded aims, what false benisons of mirth
What leisure bereft, what lowly hours of dismay
The tongue is parched, the soul startled, the spirit raped
The colour of the night like some jealous phantom fades
With it our pinions flee, life is but an intrepid casualty
Sans contempt, with the dust of midnight our eyes are worn
In mutiny we lapse into the cold fit of darkness once more
Forsaken, alone, resentful, unforgiving in the million warmth of youth
Forever drowsed, forever faithfully to that black slumber
In blind distaste we fade believing in the truths of the endless dream
Until tomorrow's face dies, with it we perish, and all things are carried away
Let us toast the good fortune of those who have none
Let us praise the benison of those who are cursed
To delight in the mirth of those who live by sorrow

And having done so
Let us exalt the god that renounces all gods—all!

Tides of Fate

O' what the tides of fate make of man
They wet him with the cold blasts of the sea
And transform cowards out of hardened men
Those men of fear-emboldened spirits
Are destined to endure the most
For this world and life are sometimes no more than fear
Dressed up in the incessant barbs and arrows of time
Which hold up like costumes of defeat and mockery
To those fools who cast away fortune's gown
And instead chase the garb of love and innocence
Of fragrant dreams that carry the soul away
To realms unseen and ever unfound
Thus the mind is a traveller of inconstant grace
Wayward in every step that pushes to, fro and back to naught
Tragedy is ever unrelenting of love's mortal pain
The inner pulse makes gentleness expire
As we are brought back to the state of the carrion
Emaciated, forsaken of all burning cause
With earnest face, we try to resign to ancient days undone
But even there the custom is unkind and the chains unfading
Thus we are drawn into the unforgiving race
Of sudden death sans the shine of fruitful fame
Of yore sans those blind rays of sweet redolence
We retire with doleful songs left unsung on the lips
The palate is made bitter with what it is forced to taste
The rains purge the seasons of rebirth
Gone are the second ways not taken
As then all in solitude decays
Save the memory of an existence pursued without light.

Jagged Sword of Time

The jagged sword of time
The wrinkles of age, they mean nothing
Its cruelties, its wicked bounds of youthfulness
Like some rage-born parasite suckles the blood
Of the pensive paramour perched below the tree
Pondering why the stream carries away the mournful tears
Of the lover who the kiss of his beloved has not tasted
But forgoes to release her unto the reign of death
Below the bower of hope, the limber years are shed
Like the strength of Hercules deflowered from the immortal throne
The breath draws stale, the only repose is the soul's probing beauty
That stems out from the gravid bed of paradise
And stares all around in glorious zeal
Of flowers and perfumes and the heart's gentle musk
All of these are tokens to the cosmic sky
That sans contempt harbours the sweetest stars
Whose garish lights upon this Universe bear no equal
Save what is stored within your face, it alone has one compare
And Queen Beauty is it, she is your priestess
Who worships your sole blush like a prize of sanctity
Daughter Love is penitent, she marvels at your graceful sight
And thus shall forever remain a servant to your mien's majesty
A thrall to a scene that teems with such holy fortitude
That all things in compare appear as a barren wilderness, a score of waste
For your hazel eyes, they are like the inner torch of an angel
That burns through the clearest part of heaven unbound
The rose is only red, its scarlet complexion gleams
It blazes in envy for of the beauty it cannot have
Its cashmere skin frays when it looks upon yours

The twilight of the sky casts across the shores of the human earth
In admiration of all that your warmth embraces
Oh dear angel, do not then deny this one sweet pleasure that I plead
It is your arms, hold me in your arms, let love's shelter grow
And this life will be the happiest life by mortal creatures lived
Undying sans any rest, we shall be free
To enrapture each other's eyes unto eternity.

Life Unlived

What is the world of the life unlived?
Or the full-lived life that throughout was dead
What is the purpose of this grand arduous scheme?
All hopes are shattered strong and prayers are answered mainly
If the reply of fate is to toil in labour
Until darkness blows out our eyes
Until the weakness consumes, we onto death
What is the aim, what foul ambition can supplant our work
Our strides of nothingness, they to nowhere lead
Though we amuse ourselves with the pride of conquering
It is a deceiving smile, we beguile to amuse
The fancy of the mind that truthful dreams cannot tame
Therefore we riot on, out to where the lone nomads breed
To make kings and fools and paradise of whims
It is an unrighteous evil that the greedy soul plays
Coercing the mortal heart to the impulses of desire
Compelling it to the thrusts of want and misery
While all around the sunshine and the seas decay
And nothing remains of time's wide and sandy shore
The stars burn out, the ray of splendour dies
Fled is the music of old tranquillity
Gone and bled are the hours that make jealous life sweet
Perished are the calm days, expired are the tearless nights of joy
Passed is the revelling, nothing but death is sustained
As amid a thousand quandaries I let my mind to drift and flee
Wondering what of this life is worth to be gained
Whether it is better to die in youth or age or altogether never be
The lease of warmth expires without a cry and I think no more on it.

Open Hearted Dream

Oh open hearted dream
That I can withstand every defeat in life
Save having you withdrawn far away
Save having the brilliant vision of you paled and darkened
For while fate bears many throes of encumbrance
The thought of deliverance true redeems the soul
The gravid trust of the heart slow decays
When the hold of your palm is held within the hand
Regal time itself becomes a slave to the glass
That is the keeper of grains of mortality
Unatoned, unrepented, the mind wanders on
Unbruised, unscathed, the pulse of admiration bleeds
And drowns the seas and fills the skies with mysteries
It cleaves the strength of that lithe star
Which glows ever bright, unaware of the black universe
Those scapes of worlds that spin without end or purpose
Implore nothing of human pain, neither sense nor satisfaction
Nor the ingratitude that lends madness to the reasoned mind
Can make the agent of suffering to perish and die
Passion then journeys the road unknown and blind
Before the rocks of hope, it stumbles and falls
Unpacified, cursing the vile accidents of birth
That thread through existence, making sorrow manifest
Lending to privation an unfading cape of infinity
The lamp of morning then rises to its rank
Its rays, they shower the earnest thought of mirth
For levity is the phantom that can liberate
The illuminated power of love and its unquenched yearning
Therefore the hours blend with the composure of the dusk
Making new babes born from its embers of vitality

The old dusk draws against the brink of the eve
The scythe resigns to the depths of the unmarked grave
While all around a supernal loneliness pervades
Love in that mind wherein the soft and brightest dream
Teems and thrives eternal!

Amazement of the Sky

The amazement of the sky is gone
For she has taken it and has left no trace at all
To remain upon this shallow earth as a memory
As a token, a gift, a solemn cry
To the world's loss and grieving pain
Which haunts the midnight ease and freedom
Of the unshackled soul that desires love
And would forsake the pleasures of the dark existence
To preserve the sweetness shared within her eyes
Oh the nightingale pines the night in vain
As its limbs are unsensing of the dullard pangs
No time, no hope, no gentleness can redeem
The innocent of its signs, oh fairness dies
And wails the agony of the unspoken word
That pierces through the untouched climes and morning brink
Of horizons unseen, unfelt, unembraced—there is no joy
When the infancy of the mind must face the truth
Of this life's law of proud and blind inhumanity
Thus cruelty makes savages out of us all
Thus the mortal palate is smite with rebuke
Of golden youth lacking bright salvation
The lamp then blows out, hope's decorum is lost
And nothing but the bounty of autumn overtakes the summer light
Of happiness sans the grave monuments of injury
Of the enlivened breath absent of the palsy shakes of weakness
That stake the flesh to resign to the tombs of wild extinction
The commission of death is but too strong and we are but slaves
To an unrelenting struggle of demise
The torch of conflict is but a pageant and metaphor
To the records of despised scenes that we must endure

Until love and valour condemn the stark hate
And make free men out of our passions once again
By mutiny, the star of romance is cleared
Its blood runs twain, its scar is but a symbol to destiny
With wide pinions I fly and in that higher realm flee
To where the dolorous moments follow not the hours of tomorrow
Uncast, I obey the shades of purest dream alone
As then life and solitude combine
And rive to make fame known to my undying self
Of beauty pressed against the garland of love's liberty
Of life and that glorious love lacking defeat and all finality.

The Heifer

Those heifers grazing along the meadows
If they only knew the blind end for which they race to feed
They would not act with such aggression against their brothers
Nor display brazen contempt for their kind and fraternity
They are like civic creatures, only meant for the leading
By tyrant characters, they are not designed to lead
They are fashioned to be selfish and the world's traitor
When the circumstances allow it, they jump to the ready
Glorifying and exulting the most base and wretched
And vile and loathsome and deplorable things of all
It is their nature to dignify the wicked
And bring to supremacy he who defiles and transgress the most
And harshly exploits the vulnerable and the weak
Brings on the cold bonds of the oppressed to shatter like dust
Before the force and thrust of man's indifference
The cruelty and the chains, they slay compassion
And drive the warmth of the soul to flee to places far and alien
The wrath of hatred then begins to show its strength
In this fierce game where all against all is waged
Until some madness emerges out as victor to the manifold defeats
That we set against ourselves in sport, malign gestures of apathy
The conquests begin to bleed out, the plains are staid
All around the wild hunger of the earth becomes sated
It is better that we leave and forever at that
Never to look back and pine the injustice of this world
Lest we be washed away in tears forever
Our day will come, the dawn is the harvester of each
Who dwells in the prosperity of dream
If not to die by the blade of the human hand
Then by the restless slaughter of time

The reaper comes, cleaving ingratitude, the hours draw too short
And altogether against that meadowed scene
These vain passions and pursuits are left behind forgotten and unsung.

These Trees

These trees that loll and dangle peacefully
Which the warm summer current breezes through
The gentle light of the morn upon the season's foliage
Scattering across the leaves with lustrous shine
What will become of them when the blade of time ripens
And draws to take out emerald vitality from the stem
And of those boughs and the soft cheerful birds upon them
What fortune will lead after Winter brings on its pallor
When with his cold breath he extinguishes all in finality
What sweet songs will then thrum from the abyss of life?
Nay, there is no hope for redemption at all
The tempests cool the soft petals of the flowers
Yet even their oblivion cannot escape the dust
Which the bee and the human share alike
The nectar of sweetness is sprawled everywhere
But its commission delays to bring fortitude
To the mind that lacks the inward sense of peace and levity
To the heart that lacks cause to rejoice on its own account of life
Blindness sheathes the many viable hopes inside
Which are denied the proper flame to burn and raise forth their light
Oh that splendid dew, that lucid stream, that glow of paradise
All those temporal luxuries that extol me
Are but tokens to what death must take away
I must prepare to resign these mortal fortunes
And subscribe myself to a life of simplicity sans regret
The day, it opens wide—those blue chasms I will miss
As to the vaults of heaven I fly, looking down once more
Forever free, forever beautiful—oh forever to die!

Darling Roads of Life

These darling roads of life
They are so severely torn with grief
So stricken and diseased, there is no hope of redemption
Deliverance is something blind and strewn far away
The perils hang like tendrils from the sky
Coiling and enrapturing around the mortal nape
Like a serpent that hungers to extinguish strength
Draining the blood of its youth, colour and prime
Supplanting hardship where once happiness thrived bright
This world is loaded with sorrows and despair, nothing less
Dreams are made to be shattered, the fates they weave
The thread of life always too short and haggard
Old, worn, the fabric drawn from the caldron of dismay
For time eternal, the pattern is left to bask in emptiness
Forlorn, in the loneliness of age it ripens
Only to later give birth to the harvest of pain
Such is the mortal lot; its sheaves are rebuked by all who count them
Misfortune is the substance that never departs the soul
But forces it to decay, making it yield to nightly darkness
Without scope, without face, the mind runs wild
The stars flee in madness, everything collapses and resigns
To the raven depths of the earth which none desire to see
Against all hazards, yearning to disobey the art
And the delirium of death that afflicts the human heart the most
And fashions tragedy of its warm and true affection
The days retire; unsung woe is born again
Without a sign, the streams trace the well of the eyes
Bidding a watery farewell to this ancient shore
To the rueful brink of wide existence, which insofar as compassion
relates

Ministers the everlasting defeats of humanity without a coming end
So we surrender, without protest, without a word
Admiring the darkness as it falls, falls, falls.

Every Anguish Felt

Every anguish felt cries out
Like a soft little bird in agony
Whose amber breast is beaten and torn
By this cruel world which leaves innocence bloodstained
There is no escape, against the confederacy none can win
The shades fall, the campaign of hopes is lost
Everything to the dark drapes retire
Destroyed, the moon wanes to some unseen brink
Of desire and warmth sans paradise
Of man's visions and the fellowship of dream
That lends a brighter hue to the shattered heart
Which skulks in the demise of its broken pieces
Its chambers drown in the flood of sad litany
Slanderous fate the draws in its chariot of dawn
Pretending that the drapes of time are vain and feeble
When in fact their bitter grasps are the rule of the realm
What then remains to this stage but hard disdain?
Oh absurdity of breath! Oh disparaging force of life!
It would be nobler not to make such a monkey fool of the soul
Whose essence is so pure that it flies
To the supernal heights which only Beauty is heir to
Which glory can only ravish with the distant stare
Staid! She only glistens but is denied the fame
Or the supreme practice of adoration, she must die unknown
That federation belongs to the likes of the olive tree
Whose crown endures against the trellis of defeat
Whose strength cannot be surpassed nor divorced from its abode
It stands to call out the unparsed title of eternity
And all that everlasting timelessness embraces
Thereon, the birds scatter away from the leafy boughs

The bays dry of their verdant sheen
As in darkness, not even a single cry more is heard
Save the laughter of this great game that endeavours on
The tears fall, they are swept away, I die
Below the shades of the morn, thinking on nothing
But the dream that brought them forth.

These Limber Pains

How can I express all these limber pains?
The thirst of sorrow goes unslaked
As it tries to fend away the fears of tomorrow
And all the bitter cries and aches of yesterday
The fret, the anguish and the unquenching rage
All storm together unabated, unalloyed
The heart sinks down within some surrendered trench
Dreaming thoughts of brooks and ponds and happy days
Light glowing rays, softly scattered here and there
Upon every place that the mind is gentle and undismayed
A flow rises up only to fall down onto its knees again
Undespaired, unbroken, not hating of itself
For hope never rests upon its laurels
Nor does wicked time vouchsafe anything less than treason
The swift weeks and years of life promise only gratitude
Memory swears the barren commission of regret
As then everything darkens in forgetfulness
And we, the proud and mortal villains of this stage
Carry on with our heads high in vanity
Forgetting too soon the things we swore we could not forget
There is no profit to nature, so we must soberly resign
To this bright fleer of life that abruptly decays
Without a word, without utterance, without opposing complaint
We restless fade into the darkness from which all things are born
Allying ourselves to the blackness of the night
That holds incumbent to the fortunes that may never chance to be
Oh faith, man holds too strong to his reins of authority
The society of the sun must pall along with the moon and stars
Leaving nothing behind but a lonely trace against the sky
Of desire, love and immortality

Our bones bear not the custom to atone
The riotous licence that creeps twixt the strides of fame
Therefore we strive in delusion, letting the defects to lustre on
While all around it twains our schemes with tragedy
Lacing death everywhere, there is no joy to preach sweetness with
So then the deceit flees, our hands are left empty again
Reclining into the every undeclined depths of eternity
There our pains conceive themselves as free
But indeed are even more condemned to an unending state
Without physic, without defence we die under the courtesy of heaven
Under its brilliant host, its charity, under its unlit scapes
We perish away unknown.

Stars of Night

Those stars of night
They who look down, they who glower on us
They who behold and perceive our every moral corruption
The deflowering of our age, the lechery of our hours
They softly stare upon the night watch, what do they think
What judgements do they hold against us
With what crimes do they charge us for our villainy
Our dehumanised wants, our decadence
They gaze deep and see the fruits gleaned from the trees
The cherries ripe, the apples red, the nectar sweet
Our machines rage against the boarders of the earth
Do they believe our foulness is inbred in nature?
Like some innate part inseparable of substance
Do they think our dreams are conjured up by demons?
Or our strides are plotted out like schemes of farce?
Conceived by some unholy element that lacks eyes to see
What force of god can have fangs and be so cruel?
What creature of this world can bear thirst and lust
And with unsatisfied hunger still be incarnate
For eternal power to die and never be satiated
For all that the will of greed has gathered and begot
Still for our own promotion we toil and leave the rest unredeemed
The rose to wither upon its soil, the sun to fade upon its mighty throne
Death in its cask of darkness, life in its stillbirth of prime
Everything to wage and siege in tragic enmity and hatred
Against its own brother, its own love, in tyranny against its own kind
Until everything unto eternity is devoured, consumed and perishes without word
And no ray of fortitude remains to guide us the least

Save those burning stars whose hearts are not fled, who shall forever lead
Our souls into a realm, unseen, unknown, untested yet divine
Oh but what do those stars think of us?
Do we at all merit the prayer of their cry?
Or for these wretched hands do we deserve to die?

The Blades

The blades, they come to me
The spear of love, it is the edge that hurts the most
Not even the strongest of will can stave it off
Thus it thrusts in, digging in the flesh, making the heart bleed
Making the soul shed its tears of paradise forever
The mind is consumed and everywhere madness dwells
When thoughts try to impose reason to the whims of passion
Such things cannot be, they are the fool's trade
Such ways are what unwilling men portray as truth
So time is lost in the brotherhood of sweet remembrance
No proof to desire exists, though it burns brightly everywhere
In every realm, in every dominion that hope breathes free
And is not constrained by the laws of the hourglass
The veins throb with unrest, an uneasiness settles warmly in
Where the aches of yesterday have not yet died and are still ripe
Love is profane when it milked for more and more
Like the rose whose petals are pressed for crimson dye
Or the honeybee for its feed, the sky for its azure brightness
The clouds for their dew, the streams for their innocence
The hours of youth for their richness, old age for the wisdom it provides
The summer land for the vernal bounty of its scene
The stars for their beauty, the worship of gods for being divine
All these in excess spoil the very gentle budded flower
Whose prized and graceful treasure is picked
Elected alone, thus the fonder face of a once beloved fades
The coloured anthems, the serenades, the scriptures all decay
Upon the trace of dust, a mark to their glory is left
That too will perish; the ground is untrue to every mortal creature
The glamour of life is libertine, though it is no more than a jest

Heaped upon mortal eyes to entertain, nay to deceive
The very substance that this worldly kingdom lacks
So we bear the vices as the phantom draws to take our hand
Though we deny it, we say the chains are broken, the seeds unplanted
Death can never take away the things that live on, so we believe in this
Praying we are not mistaken, praying we will not pay for our errors
That our comfort will not be refused in some unseen heaven
The darkness falls, we pose against the unknown once more
The clouds scatter overhead; the countenance is subdued in the seizure of finality
With all these afflictions sent, dispirited, we suffer to be banished again
The forward gaze leads to nowhere, we wrestle to flourish,
Though the rituals keep us down
One circumstance alone is afforded us, we stare out to the endless brink
Of love and death and fame that none are denied and must bow to
So we fall in, we fall away, muted, eternal, together, sans word, sans speech
In united peace and everlasting disbelief we fall away content.

Forsooth

Oh forsooth, forsooth, forsooth
Grievous lover, do not be disdained
Let not those mountains bear their full weight
Or the tears of sorrow to carry like streams away
The sadness, the strife and the long agony
For the mask of troubles exempts no face
No countenance, no expression at all can hide
From fortune's hard and wailing thrust
In this scenic gamble of life there are many musts
Many triumphs, defeats and soft farewells
It is the departures that wound the breast the most
It is those cosmic throes of pain
Which paint the stellar landscape of easeless pains
With portraits red and white and ever blind
With limber relics so ungraced and thorned
That it inclines one to drink the ripe potion
And bid this uncordial world and its harsh decorum away
To flee from the staff of conceit and the smiles of vice
Whose trespass is a scandal to a happy being
Whose blazes are allied to prosperity's sweet eyes
Oh but the draught of injury has no end
Revolt hoists itself only to be galled and bereaved
The saps of bitterness linger at the lips like darling kin
Until the orb of prophesy is made a vassal to the night
And turpitude does not leave the bounty of hope's citadel
The garland of custom melds with the towers of rebuke
As then the lamp with dolorous rays shines out
The charity is gone, gentleness has no host
Tyranny is the thief that thrives and conquers all heights, all
Fellowship is no more, warmth no more, tomorrow no more

Time is nothing, dream nothing, breath nothing
But if the wrath of all these nothings is nothing
Then love mocks me to the bone, spurns the flesh to feel no more
To bear affection nothing, devotion nothing, the fame of esteem nothing
Passion is adored no longer, emotion dies of its soft tenderness
Innocence is the touch that burns the agile pinions away
Thus we are left scanted, the pageants leave and rive and obey
The command of bitterness that bears this whole mortal stage
Without pardon, with all mutiny we are led to our barren graves
There to crown the monuments with laurels of disbelief
There the palate to taste the unending bounty of scorn
And be forever forsworn, forsworn, forsworn.

The Rain Fall

The rain, it falls, the sounds hit hard
The silence of the hour, all is spoken within
Like a courageous word whose power is unheard
Like a burning love that blazes down the night
Making a brilliant pyre out of those purest stars
That have no ease inside their sinful selves
But my heart rests in a soft innocence
Half conscious, half pierced by the summer grief
That the ripe fields of blossomed buds must die
That nothing young and free can ever survive
But can hope's seclusion last? The sun declines in elegy
In hapless gratitude of the life that awakes with the morn
Blessed and kissed by those wider plains of beauty
A beauty that must perish, a fairness that protests
Against the unrighteous wrongs of this unkind world
The violins of yesterday play, the meads unfold their past
A thousand songs beseech my tender imploring brain
They run and chase and pulse ever wildly
But never can they touch my spirit, it so thrives
In a realm untouched, ungrasped, unknown by all
Thievish time cannot wield it, religion cannot condemn
The halcyon mutiny that the lonely mind affords
What idle peace, what pious contentment, what awe, what infamy
What bliss, what charm, what warmth, what vast enchantment
This scope of life is like a brink of a precipice
Whose farthest point does vanish beyond the ledge
So I take my hand and trace the sky with it
Balanced between fate's tension and gravity
The leas of heaven open, I stand poised at the verge
As the symbols of destiny dance all around, taunting fiercely

The skylark fades, the songs are gone; the pain, it withers with time's anthem
And once again the rain tumbles hard against the ground
I hear it, I die too with its constant and eternal sound.

Every Emptiness

Sadness fills the every emptiness of my bones
As I think on times past, on what used to be
On the great power of love that is no more
On all the fond memories and sweet remembrances
Of friendships strong, of brotherhoods unified
Of a wide fraternity that brings soft tears to the eyes
And drags the soul of youth to its kindred knees
Of years too quickly lapsed, of minds in solitude drowned
So the scapes of the sky take the breath away
Leaving recollection to burn upon the brink
Of deeds undone, of whole enterprises unfinished
Of the maddest of passionate realms unpursued
So the heart slips away, the pain is too deep
The grief is burden, all comfort of life is lost
Hope offers no solace to the wading thought
Of desire and strength and mortal eternity
So nevermore can the hairs of the ageless time regain their hue
Never can the shades of tomorrow cast their fair gleam again
Oh that golden ray, it too must die like a soldier
Thrust upon the open sky of a bright multitude
Oh how the fair art of this show must blindly end
Such uncivil affairs, how cruel! The anthem fades
The song of bitter solitude retains its joy
As the force of the living pulse abruptly ceases
And seeks the kiss of the world yet unseen, yet undreamt
Oh what a paradise awaits these proud dusty bones
As the scene of the grave opens, as the crypts stare wide
Calling out our names with cheerless mirth
Oh what soft redolence, what sighs, what mournful cries
The happiness of the unheld invites us in, the star shines

The moon descends; the angel takes the scythe to the majestic throne
As all at once from the wakeless dream we arise unknown
Only to fall before the alter of night
And then to recline back into the unreal realm of restless nothingness
There again to dream, to sleep, to be born once more, once more, once more.

Greatness Is Greatness

I conjure to believe that greatness is greatness
Just as love is love and truth is truth
Nay, rescind that last thought regarding truth
Absolve it from the very depth of muse
Truth is no more than a common absurdity
Nothing at all but a play of words
That the people of this earth use for their own intents and abuse
For their own desires of greed, that is human nature
Spread out against the fabric that makes us of one kind
That pervades our thread of unity, it corrodes and wears
The common bond that makes us appear the same
Yet separates further and further out from its own grasp
Oh what a dream it is, after all? Who can make claim to reckon truth?
Who can true discern between one substance of being and the next?
For if something is divine, can something exceed it?
Can the attribute of greatness ever be superseded?
Or can one prophet be holier than the next
Or a word or vision more inspiring than its peers
Can one profound wisdom be less profound
Or something graceful to be less graceful
Or a thing of beauty to be less supreme
Or a song less melodious or an art less cultured
Can the quality of genius ever be of second rate
Or glory of lesser glory or a triumph less prevailed
Can all these things of the world be scaled in magnitude?
Or rather do they dwell in a plane that no hierarchy can contain
Nor can expression ever suffice to explain or describe
Do all these things exist on their own accord or do they require the mind
To beset proof to an insubstantial reality

Oh what falsehood, what dubious webs we weave
When the orb of fraternity is shattered and the strings are loosened
How can we reclaim the strength conquered and lost?
When constantly we cast ourselves to what brings ruin and despair
Oh what tragedy, to the drape of darkness it will flee
And there find comfort amid the lack of difference
Amid the serenity, there my hope will reside in place
Waiting for the morrow to rise, the thrust of inequality never to be felt
again.

Hard Tasted and Sweet

How now that life is both hard tasted and sweet
The lot of some is to suffer, others are free
To suckle the privilege that destiny confers
With the fate that their happy fortune bequeaths
It is an all-pervading game of disparity
That this world is made with and by its nature cannot rid
Nor can she endeavour to break apart the yoke or noose
It is too intrinsic to its fame, so shall it forever stay
Imparting its reign unto the helplessly unawares
It is a babe of cruelty that seeds out each day more and more
Until the equal fields of truth are consumed
Until its cankered weeds reach to the end
That every mortal tomb is encrusted with
So these are the parts we play, each one to death resigns
Until the light declines and we are fled with it
With what constancy this swift drama sways!
The lease too quick expires, gone is the faith and life's fidelity
Some are to starve, others on the plate of richness feed
Some with the chalice frolic wild, others their dry bones remit
To the solace of the ground that takes earth for earth
And considers it his due, requires it to be restored
Upon the plain where no marks of prospect breed
As some are to love, some in scoreless hatred churn
Some grow old, other eyes meet the constant face of youth
Some are beggars to their core, some take on the peddler's trade
Some are born with argent spoons, others with clay smiles
Some men are free—indeed aren't all men enslaved?
To the restless finality that never dies absolved
To the unspoken ministry that summons up the saddest beliefs
The stars blind their brace, the sky seals its womb

Woe to the riots of this blackened fading
As everything mounts its worth upon a bedecked throne
Only to be overturned by the tides of time's indifference
Yet the seas of human pulse rage forever on
Until the casks are drawn and the everlasting hours cease
Until the glow of heaven strays from its languid seal
Each of woman born must face this wide defeat"
"None of us from birth are equal or the same
"Yet upon the drapes of death, our lusts assume an equal fame."

The Coldest Hours

When upon the coldest hours I lapse to sleep
And fame wakes back to show its hand
The world reveals its truth, its yesterday
And comforts me with the dream of nothing
Oh how lovely that fonder youth was
When I would peer to the white angel's sky
Believing that their souls existed
And mine was only part of theirs
Experience makes one both the wiser and the fool
Age is the prickly blade that drives sweet ignorance
Away from tender eyes, its pain still thrusts
And lives everlasting, the heart is informed
With the promise of tomorrow, with what must fade
With the ceaseless chronicles that over and over are played
Still the colour never leaves and we pursue on
To the greater of the widest and unknown
Yonder our own beings and this unpleasing writ
Blessing peace to our efforts, aware that peace is contrary
To these quiet lives led, it is more than desperation
A solitude and emptiness altogether pervades
And we are slaves to the machines of our own control
Our own fates, we call it fabled destiny
Winning steps each day to a far, far bleaker end
The music begins, its loudness lacks clarity
And we are prey to each indifferent note heard
The daisies grow, the sun wanes upon its throne
The violets press to the ground, there is no tomorrow to sing of
As all of life escapes as the freest dream of love and liberty

And nothing remains to stand clear upon the night
Nothing save the sweet rose of hope that never was.

The Tempest

How life sits and tortures itself away
And we let it pass and think nothing
Though in pain it writhes, still we forget it
Even as humankind bites human kindness with grief
We dismiss the fangs and call the venom nature's craft
Which self-embraces all that wrought evil breeds
It is a despised art that the wretched mind conceives
To be an unbeloved fiend in a world of madness
We journey from post to post and moon to moon
From one side of the earth to where no earth remains
From one palsy shake of the sky to the starless scape
And still the mortal heart is base and cruel and sinister
Its control is corrupt; its grasp of goodness is decayed
Vile has become the way of wealth and majesty
While all around a creed suffers with hungered need
We are deaf and blind to it; they are the fated to fade
And much untied to our destiny of self-importance
The tides and drama sways, the darkness gains
And we become the scorn of woe and suffering
The worth of happiness upon its power is impeached
The virtue of reward stands no more
If all we do is strive and take no leisure back
If compassion and truth resort to hated vice and villainy
What are we but machines of our own defeat?
Surrendering the sanctity of all that shines endeared and sweet
So then we must lapse to let the soul die unseen
Than to give in to the putrid impulse that toils inside
It is a game of fantasy, so let us flee and fly
To where the whiter heavens reveal a brighter glimpse
Of the wide argent trace of truce

Untestified of its visioned grace
So we are the players resigned unto our throne of peace and half misery
The dawn will rise again, the shame cannot hide
The evening dims, nothing is as it was before
And altogether we are never free as we believe
Yet tomorrow arrives and we are set free
Unto the palace of death and mystery
Never will it leave until the illustrious eyes darken
And all of hope is consumed on the altar of mortal dust.

Beauty

Beauty
It dwells alone, it lives alone, and it thrives thereon
Inside the sheepish mind that burns for love
Upon the external is in flames and nothing more
Is the quality of a most divine nature
That imbues the mark of every glorious and breathing thing
Like a rose in its April shroud or the sun in its morning skin
These attributes shine like a blush that does not die
Oh never to escape or flee or perish from the tender night
Nay, fairness shall always remain inscribed as thus
In immortal art that no foul spirit can disdain
No demon can rob, no war-like god can make fall from grace
Which misery cannot cloud or darkness overtake
In any hour that the universal sentiment persists
As that tepid power pulses and teems internal
The spirit will strive on before the mirror of Beauty.

Man's Cry

Man cries the day he is born
Unto this unjust globe of sorrow and despair
Of pain and wounds of a thousand bleeding ends
The lips are answerless, the torment is so great
That it would be more easeful for some merciful seraph
To tear my heart out from above and wrestle with it
Thus blindly end this wicked and unpurposed game
Oh uncompassionate fate! Wage the stars against yourself
And see how hard their burden of fortune weighs
How fast and swift their tortures hit this stage
Of life and tragedy and the blare of uncivil hopes
The contempt dissolves within an unbound sea
The edges of the earth are fledged against eternity
So I take to the conclave of dust and find my happiness therein
Away from the cares and woes of the unsolaced world
Undejected I resign, within this vast expanse I expire indifferently
Dreaming on nothing save that cold lack of tomorrow
That shall turn to betray all with its brutish signs
No, I ponder upon your eyes, and all is soft and sweet and calm again
Without regrets my essence flees, nothing gold can stay
Thus I dream of you and love and warmly leave all away.

These Days Spent in Vain

All these days may seem spent in vain
All these hours, I confess, appear as play
But my love, with your beauty shining on and on
This cruel tyrant of life is suppressed
Warmth thrives upon the every mortal plain
That desires everything true, kind and righteous
That truth is you, that kindness is your soul
The colour of your dream exceeds the holy mind
That strives to know what a perfect love is
What the unblemished heart of passion can achieve
Which a thousand stars hung upon a gentle night can never
Believe me, my love, you are the fairest glow born yet
Which the power of these feeble skies cannot understand
I struggle in pain, agony wrecks my strength
Hope only makes me weak again, the torment is undying
A unfulfilled yearning brings ruin to the living blood
Ambition rends in agony, all moral is lost and forsaken
Time is left to remain as the lone unscarred monument
As a reminder of the forgotten woes of yesteryear
Of all the ages gone that cannot be captured again
How can one continue on with aim against this bleak scene
Or stride further on this vast and ultimate stage
When wanting lacks cause and death's darkness is not unseen
How can I forge on against the burning scapes of infinity
When the human will wills no more than for one sake alone
That sake being you, my all, thus do not deny me your touch
Embrace me with the soft disdain of a happiness that must fade
Alas, unite our fates as one, call it no other
Other than the eternal fortune that alongside you and me belongs
By the sweet persuasion of your love, bring to me a fairest bliss

And I shall redeem you with the crown and kingdom of all I have
My all, be kind and true and we shall fondly survive
This harsh and wicked game that to nowhere leads
This stage of bitter paradise, from it we shall flee
Taking flight to where the heavens are all bleached before our eyes
There we will be far from the pangs and throes of longing
Unto the shore of the unknown, hand in hand, arm within beloved arm
There to be free, there together be, there never to be born at all.

Day, Night, Day

Day, night, day then night again
This scheme of life burns on and on
But as your beauty shines clear through time, my all
I see no impasse to what we can achieve
This love can transcend above the highest star
The moon, the sun—they are cool and heated just the same
Your heart is one pulse, one million flames ahead of everything
Dreams are but a slave that obey you
Desires heed your kempt fairness and majestic graces
The seasons are but a tempo to your sole worship
Sleep is nothing but a delusion that will not fade
Affection is the stir that keeps the soul alive with hope
Thus as that desire is sustained in me
The whole of being shall be devoted to you
To your gravity, your cheer, your hungered smile
I lament the fate of the heaven's a hundred times over
If suffers much, the kindest of this world are often the fairest
And as your light beams, all wounds are healed
The beaten pangs of the unknown grief subside
The cold warmth of death softly pales away
The thirst of justice, it is given due reward
The elder gown of age, youth's vibrancy
The peril of loveliness, the patience of strong admired eyes
Sirrah, Sirrah—all will be settled in peace
Wickedness will not befall us, happiness shall embrace
This muse of existence that presses to never die
Hark, so let us flee together upon a lone united hold
Our hands to touch, love's eternity to never release
Until the treasures of the hours are won as ours again
And we conquer the vision of the immortal stare once more

Our spirits against each other to prevail
This everlasting feeling nevermore to be lost.

Where Goes the Time

Oh where goes this time?
Does is simply fly away with wings?
My love, when I am with you I feel nothing
Nothing of the cold grasp of death or the draping curtains
Or the sad fall of the sun, the finality
But isn't that how it should be?
When I stare into your eyes, the skies are held dreamy
Oh so every lofty, a lightness that no word can describe
The bluest clouds, the serenest scape
The whitest paradise, it is your face
My love, it is your fair eminence
Or should I call it brilliance—oh I am a demon
A shameful, shameful devil, my soul has no rest
My spirit can abide nowhere, it does not deserve to
Except besides your hearts or shared between our minds
After all, it is one love we dream—forsworn!
One passion, one romance, one amorous ecstasy
Of you and I forever to remain
The two brilliant angels across the night
Upon the meadow, the greenest fields, the summer leas
Upon every plain of pure and purest happiness
That is where our comfort remains wide and free
The stars rain down their dewy lights
And still your glory is the crown of them all
Your kiss, your blush is the wildest prize
Your complexion, how it is the jewel of everything
So never depart from me, my love
And this soft and slow promise I will make
That I shall love you forever, for all of time
Until pleasant time itself ends and our hopes are as one

Until we are together unified for all the hours that are to come
They shall serve as flowers blossomed between you and me
So love, where indeed does this time go?
I do not care, as I have it and am with you
As long as it is owned by these two beings that are as one
Against all heart and love and soul
My all, I share it with you, letting all things else to flee
Thinking of nothing more that you and love and destiny!

Old Loves Spoken

These old loves spoken all fade
Nothing remains of their bones within the vault
The daises twist about, the violets curl in their multitude
And we are the mortals that praise their drink
The cups lift up, the concords spread
The midnight holds out in solitude, dark and fled
The poems play, the parles whisper out
By the moon's fairness I am reminded of your love
The impulse burns, the fevers rage, the yearnings endure
And I only think about you more
Ponder upon you, the madness swells within
And it comforts me to some place kind
To a destiny that is blind, a fate that is aged
Oh never to see despair wage its hands again
The wars, the cries, the sorrows of tomorrow
The breath, the hand, the throbless heart
The soul that rests within a restless vein
My affection you sustain, my adoration is yours
The dividing strength, the healing power
The every quality that is true and weak
The embers untouched, the gestures unlived
They shroud me, calling up your fame
As the most beautiful thing that can be called on
The goddess of pulchritude ever to be born
Your clouds, your sky, your gloried stars
Your meads, your eternal fields of fire
The angel's wing, the sweet paradise
The wondering eye that only gazes to you
Only reveres you, you are its cause of praise
The virtue that lends being worth

The quietness that is embossed, its relishing
The fondness that testifies to immortal time
You are the burden and brilliance of it all
Your light survives on, I am bruised by its shade
Forever to be alive by your warm desire
Or else to be engraved by death, nevermore to think
Upon your face or love or the hope that keeps worlds upright
And thrusts to nothingness all that is without
Of you or the one power of romance
The impeachment, the blame of love, the embers of life never to be lit again
Never to be felt or shared, the earth blackens as you are gone
The work of breath decays when you are no longer near to be held
With the last strength of man to resign to the universe of heaven
And there to splendour in your shine that within me everlasting swells.

To Bid Farewell

How can I bid farewell?
It is not well with me to say goodbye
Or to part with you. I would rather plead
For you to remain strong along my side
Beloved, you are graceful, I crave you
Beyond man's burning or his greed
I desire you as much as saints their piety
Or as much as happy beggars their indigent state
A rich man's treasury, that you are and more
The glow that thrives, the light that keeps me enthralled
For a thousand ages, I testify your love to be
The greatest accord of miracle, none can exceed
Or be called lovely by a lovelier word, you bruise
The madman's adoration, his addled sense
His night and day, his reason and rhyme
All that he holds high pride to
As your peerless stream shall forever shine
The rays of glory shall not decline to the smallest degree
Our hearts are free, our passion is steadfast
Idle pulses retreat to softest sleep
To the perfection that never was, the embellished dream
To the beauty of yesterday, its pitied fire
They never wane; emotions burden the candle of the night
Yet amid the mist one sweetness burns
My love, I stare into your face and think of nothing else
No tomorrow, no good-bye, no forever—we are born eternal,
immortal to die.

Substance of Life

How can life endure or be called the substance of life?
If you, my love, are vacant from its throne
Tormenting me with compounded despair
Like the moon upon the sun, the stars upon their sable pall
And by the low tune of sorrow, I am denied you
By nothingness, my eyes are forsaken, my soul surrendered
The privilege, the perfection of your face
Or the sweet thrum of your voice that carries long
The birds are but slaves to yesterday
But with your light cast, madness is new found
Yearning plagues what from the fever cannot leave
Rather the world to be renounced and to die alone
And for a tender hour leave away from your heart
To think upon the kinder thoughts that exist
Purpose has no fashion, dreams are frail
Desire has no charity, hope is not sincere
Vows are but thieves of the desperate brain
The oracle is banished, the tincture of the night is obscured
The starlight flounders, the orb shines no more
And all of life in the wildest infamy drifts
Sans the passion of tomorrow, romance ministers like a pawn
To the hold of death, the ornaments show the way
There can never be a day that I can contently live
As there hides longing within my frame, my being
My love, I shall never rest, between life and this breathing death
I will forever stand until the mercy of your love empowers me.

No Justice

There is no justice in the world, none at all
Not as long as my heart falls before the ground and bleeds
In senseless desperation of the love it feels
Of the pain that affects its innocent depths
How has it wronged, how has the mind of passion sinned?
For the story of love is so broken and wrought
That the human pulse lacks the invention of praise
For that affection that is so deserving of exultation
The laurels are fled, the angels have cried, the heavens have perished
And all around not even the loneliest sound is heard
The desolation sinks in and gives the soul to madness
The cruelty, the fret, the blind disobedience of reason
All leave the mortal strength to grope in darkness
Oh human nature has always been the foe to liberty
We are not the children of men, but the infants of gods
Who in fierce idleness wage a siege against fair and tender beauty
Time is their instrument, they decree perfection to fade
In silence, that perfection resigns to the abodes of the unknown
The call of tomorrow as well expires with the unshaken wind
The seraph's sigh at the sight of the morning star
Whose gilded grace is profane and wicked in its form
O' the moon appears as a mere and tiny orb of dismay
Before these long and scattered shores of eternity
The rose then falls upon the gentle grass of the night
I lift my eyes, I peer out to that infinite sky
Upon my fleeting pulse I desire nothing more
Than the justice of love unshorn.

She Rests There

See how she rests there, so ever beautifully
Like the balm of midnight smeared upon the summer air
Like angel-light spread upon the infinite courts of heaven
Hope is like a wading dream, a fruitless vacancy
When glory as hers is seen as pure and true
See how she leans there, against the hawthorn sill of night
The moon prostrates down, it kneels in greatest humility
Before the alter of her grace, it bends down its noble head
And thinks not on rank or fame, for she exceeds it
Oh my love, how life is an absent void, worth not a thing
With no colour, no stars, no innocence anywhere
When your brilliance is denied to the holy dreams of thought
When nothing righteous of this world survives at all
Upon the round spheres that from the inside burn to be free
Free, free—oh yes free unlike my imprisoned heart
That feels constrained by what the bounds of youth allow
What majesty! If only that old and wisest skylark
Knew of this talk of romance, the bonds would then relate
A divine and happy story that has no need for ending
So then this sorrow shall be forever retold
In wailing sadness, it shall be sung from the brinks of these sobbing lips
In memorial to you, a vestal token to all that your beauty stands for
What fair excellence, my soul resigns in peace, to a gentler comfort
Though still it is sensing of the bitter pangs of unhappiness
Of what can never be—what absurd scenes; so my vision decays
Never to dream with optimistic hope in this life again
Still I hold you in my arms, within the depths of my lapsing brain

Though in truth the cold dust of death welcomes me
Once more I am free, my love, united with you, free again, most free.

Rehearsing Your Name

Rehearsing your name like an oath or vow or promise to the holy forged hour
With the signs of heaven sealed, kept under the open warmth of the tepid day
The fundament opens its veldts; I see one truth across its infinite fields
Upon its plains and realms and untainted kingdom
One virtue stands to bright love and its wide purity
And that is all that you are, all that you will be, all that ever
Was the fondest trace of gentle yesterday
What loveliness, what charm, what a brilliant glow
The angel rests to its side and lets passion go unheard, silently pressed away
The gold-held hour of romance is fled, here subsides the music
There flees the harmony of my solitude, my deeper spirit with it is burst
A light shines down, it tells of a million volumes of unscored love
All prevailed above the love that can never die
As such for your love I am imperilled and speak a thousand words with addled tongue
The lips are impaled, the mouth is numbed and lacking proseful speech
The arms of hope retreat, the drape of death waits for them in silence
Waiting to conquer the force that must yield and surrender unbasked
Thus I stand for you, desire pressed against desire,
Warmth upon warmth my love released
Burning, yearning, longing for what is kept away from reach and is so pure
I think upon such dreams and let the world expire fast
I dream on what is true and you are it
Reciting your name, like a glorified religion most sanctified
Believing in you alone as in nothing lese I can believe in

Knowing you are the queen of my throne and love's sacrificing Realm
So I sink away and let the silence set in deep and strong and infinite
Braving the storm of rage, peace, oblivion and internal passing
Oh ever-lovely maiden let a script be written on the stars
And you to tame it, what glimpses catch your eyes
What wondrous looks do tease through that mind
What spirit, what flight, my thoughts take a thousand turns
All across the lattice where you are seen
Where your shadow is far, where the mortal touch is unheld
But the vision returns to you, the prophecy of fate is scribed
Inside the orb that shines out sweet summer's breath
And leaves dew and brooks and tearing streams to live on
To waver softly by and be long forgotten
Oh farewell to the remembered day of you
I kiss it with the touch of April's sweet unborn prime
The Elysium blends the sop of freedom's flaws
The moon buckles in the den, the angled shade of heaven resigns
The shimmering of the dusk trembles unimpeded
Melancholy passes over the roughest bough below the soft glistened night
The trees shake out their grief, the autumn bird sings out gentle song
And in it are contained the many rueful tales of love
I pine, I weep, I suffer to know the anguish and the misery
That afflicts and makes worn this intemperate heart
Oh what a show this life is, age is unprepared for the tide of woe
As the ready hand of time takes to its final place of destiny
As I bless the sacred beauty of your face a thousand times over
As I worship that form that deserves adoring
That greatness, that majesty released and thrown upon the open count of stars.

Day is Not Day

Day is not day, nor light is light
Nor does the sun gleam in full radiance
The moon is not the faithful moon
The heavens glitter dim and stark
The stars lack devotion, the sky glistens not
The whole world in a rearward darkness declines
As all of beauty is bound in your fair loveliness
The mind cannot conceive anything in glory
The soft rays of the lilac eve surrender unknown
The saffron blush of dawn trickles through unseen
The warmth of the moonshine dies untouched
And yet they are all but servants to your brilliant charm
They are enslaved to you in truest amity
A friendship that survives a thousand unlit ages
Oh holy is that sheen, may it forever thrive on and on
As I have strength, it shall be worshipped and caressed
It shall be redeemed by the pure fondness of youth
Its soul, its change, the full force of life
Stands behind the pristine grace that from you resigns
Long live the power of your ladyship
With admiration you shall be retained
Until this world from its suffering is released
And we are set free unto the wider bows of love's eternity.

The Human Mind

It is beyond the ken of the human mind to conceive
A love greater than ours, this shared dream
Holds at the very heart of what we can together aspire for
What the soul can bear ambition to achieve
For that does not end with the drawing scythe of the hour
No, the will is too iron-cast to ever repent such deeds
Or to atone for the heavy blades of time's great misfortune
Of eternity's disguise of bright and gentle levity
For as the rosebud has a life, so too does passion
As the lilac never frowns or declines, neither shall affection
Indeed sentiment shall outlive the raging sea of warmth
Hope shall set aflame the burning sun into a thousand stars
All the heavens shall be paved with some new diamond glow
With some unseen grace that is holy in its essence and its shine
I am like a lover reprobate, culled from the dressed plain of fate
Of yearnings and idols and the allegiance of ruin
Of the politic that lays upon and dulcet mead
Crest ever high upon the Lethe knoll of love's tragedy
Which is but a reviving censor to the dead and buried thought
Of youth's of nimble trophy and the million pallor that awaits
That is born in every sky full with feelings of togetherness
Two stars are crested over the moon, what vision do they signify
What righteous prophet must deconstruct their shape?
It does not matter now, the argent trace is fled
The aches dissolve, the constellations are no more the fiend
To the dateless journey of love that we must embark
The lamenting has lapsed, the rays show up kindly against the scapes
Forthright, the cradle of kindness is made ours again
The horizon fringes with something altogether divine
As it is your face, your form, I shall worship and adore them

Until the skies have left their sweet prodigious thrones
And no light remains to admire anything at all.

What Is Her Name?

What is her name?
Where does her beauty hide?
Where lies her true fairness, is she even woman born?
Or rather some goddess forged after the likes of queens?
Come now gentle queen, speak a little word
And reveal to me the complexion of your fame
Dearest child, it is your name that I seek…
Isabel! What sweetness from these soft lips ring
That never from my mind shall it be purged
What syllables, what verse, what a phrase of paradise
What comeliness, what divine air of pulchritude
What loftiness, what shine, what excellence!
Angel, that your blush glows redder than the demon's tail
Your face is whiter than the hawthorn clouds above
Your hands are softer than the dew upon the summer leaf
Your eyes are more magical than the skyward orbs of spring
Which sprout out every seasoned year in happy artistry
Oh how happy is that lit aerial scene
How splendid is your face, how brilliant is your soul
That keeps me alive over the thousand wings of human pain
The hour fades, to where is fled youth's blessed time!
Do for me the kindest grace of Eden, recite our name again
And I shall be at peace once more sans the regard of time
Release to me your heart of love in fullest embrace
I will surrender the constraints of life
My spirit shall be set free forever
Be my restless friend, tease me, what is your name?
Oh sacred Isabel, you are ever endeared!
That a thousand fortunes cannot redeem even a trace of you
A lonely ember, even that which is forsaken cannot compare

You are too precious to ever be made a token of
Too priceless, indeed too pure, unscarred and numberless
Oh how wondrous you are, oh what a lady!
Oh what a glorious dream your tenderness is
Thereafter I am mad for Isabel
I am in love with one whom the angels adore day and night
When they so softly worship, so deeply revere and esteem
For is she not like the morn that yields over the east
Spreading her youthful rays of delight like innocence
Is she not like the blue warmth of the crested moon
Whose silent platitude suspends upon the mortal everywhere
How fair and chaste that Isabel is
How serene and righteous her expression beams
More lively than a million unsung worlds reborn
But that I die in envy all the same
Knowing that your beauty is so alive and well
And still so vacant from these wanting arms of mine
My love, this lack cannot forever last
I too with bliss will be united; upon that fonder sight
Never to be left jealous for your blush or kiss again
Until I am restored and your love is mine by the honour of your name.

This Vow of Love

Faith pilgrim, you have breached this vow of love
Even though I am a slave to your temple
A servant to your grace, a thrall to your majesty
Be kind to me then, redeem me with your heart
And set us to where wicked time cannot chase
These summer orchards from our dream of levity
For one desire rages deep within me
And you are its cause that can also bring it truce
So then bind to me, lend to me your sweet warmth
Grant me your fairness, dare I call it heaven's piety
Or truth's own delightful son of prime
Oh how youth sways, hold onto me steadfast
Embrace me with your glow, our spirits shall lead out
Onto the plain where hopes rejoice with insolent tears
There we will ambulate, there we shall obey the clouds of praise
And call them gods of their own like, we are of a different creed
Who gives no worship to life's supreme eternity
For the days are truant of woe and unhappiness
Yet a sadness sweeps over the brooks and fills the ponds
It passes over the streams with so mild a tenderness
That it reprieves innocence of its full-throated mirth
Oh grant me the counsel of our love, perchance I'll hear the bird
Warble out in the midnight air the treasons of vanity
Oh what fond pursuits, the soul spies on tormented pride
But casts it far away, it is too impure
Love is a gift best left untouched, unsavoured
For it burns and pains those who hunger for it
As for me, it is better left forsaken
Deserted, I turn to your face and find the comfort of peace
And pray to the god of the world to die, to die, to die

To perish and to pass under the fairness of your shine
As a sacrifice, oh my love, spare me, I can speak nothing more
But minister to me your love and I shall live forever after again
Suddenly to wake, to never tire, to be the heir of all this earth
And then to resign in peace, aside the patience of your wide loveliness
Then to desire nothing more, to be troubled no more, to speak never again.

Upon Her Face

Can you note the beauty upon her face?
The tenderness upon her smile
That ruddy glow that shines from cheek to cheek
Or the fairness of her eye, dare I call it charm?
Or the warmth that is crested upon her brow
Does it not drive you mad its essence to conceive?
The soul of its greatness for a moment to believe?
Oh she, she is like a demon of wild grace
Like one blazing—a star parted over the open heaven
Oh she is fire incarnate, she is love's own daughter, and love's truth
The sister to romance, she with the darker shade of passion burns
And nature with naught does crown her save loveliness
Oh she is a queen; she is the brightest ray of light
To have ever lived and flown upon this mortal sphere
Oh here are my wings, therefore I take flight
Out to the sky where pulchritude is young and free
That is where my soul shall always be
Upon the rosy scarlet head with thickets blue
The clouds and azure seas shall be born anew
To relish and savour her sweet embrace
To bow before the majesty of her face
Oh maiden how I am your eternal slave!
Your thrall, your worship, your servant of a million years
Your chained victim, my dear I am forever yours, your infinite subject
Yet by devotion I shall remain a virtue to your fame
My all, death spelled backwards is our babe of hope
Look at her beauty, cannot fate be so cruel!
Look at her lips, that chin, her shoulders meek, her everything
Her hands, her form, that ray which shines on and on
Oh farewell unkind world, I escape from your rule

All to die and transcend to where she is a dream no more
And nothing but her pure beauty ever again is seen.

Contrived Words

Neither pen, paper nor contrived words
Can never know you as well as your beauty's truth
Nor pleasant rhymes scribed on the woody leaves of day
Can preserve the essence of you who is so fair
For the ink takes not to its rightful place
Nor scholars to their high-learned tongues of esteem
When the subject of your grace is discoursed
And lessons are read off from your pearly eyes
The poet stutters, poems flow not with easeful ink
When your hazel romance must be conceived
Your prized hand of loveliness considered to the ultimate
The wrestler grows weak at his joints
The mason draws from his work of fine masonry
When your gentle comeliness rises with the moon
And makes its coveted rays of night chariot away
Far into the cloudless realm that cannot be seen
Into the yesterday and not the vowed tomorrow of your light
The lyricist stops cold in his phrases of song
The banker ceases upon his act of lending
To contemplate on your complexion that is more prized
To admire you countenance that is lone upon the world
Upon this widest earth, you whose gentleness is unique
The seaman retires from his dewy trade
The astronaut from his sphere of starry void
All these look on you and admire in silent delight
The glory, the majesty that to you is lone
Unheld, unseen, undreamt within the mortal shade of the mind
Your complexion has a charm that does gratify
The untouched, the naked, the ill-believed prophecy
The truth, the meaning, the promise of fulfilment

All that the continent of words cannot suffice to explain
All that the heresy of writing cannot do justice for
Wordless I then stand before your wondrous glow
Sans the warm expression that still in me burns
Wrangling with the thoughts that fail to surrender out
While the tincture of you shines with swank occasion and sweet elegance
Indeed you are the divine maiden of timeless time
Of being, of all vast creation
Gleaming through the rhetoric of man's self-life and defeat
As your brightness fills my many voids of nothingness
Dark deceit declines, I fade with the grief
Until the undying hours lift from the dawn
And you are sensed upon all the air and land and love, my all.

Brink of Dawn

Upon this wider brink of dawn
When I think of you and nothing else
The gardens collapse, the summer falls
And you are the one standing dream that burns bright
High above the stars of this gentle sky
Crest upon the sliver of the moon that is fair
Perched upon holy heaven's loveliness
And my visions pulse for no one, nothing pulses
Save my heart that longs for you
For your fame, your grace, your greatness
As the morning flame blazes again
Yet my soul appears to die if you are not with it
If you, my angel, are not with me
If not all your love to give
Then in death's shade to forever live
Never to see the light without your face, never to survive.

Every Hour

Every hour that I breathe
Every hour that I dream, I dream of you
Every strength skulked within my bones
Every power of my soul's life
Is the tribute, nay the deeper token, the endless gesture
My dear, a symbol that I shall always love you
Until the stars close upon their realm
And the phantom of the eternal night
Dies away, the true warmth is kept within our breast
Regret and sorrow cannot claim our soft society
Golden youth is a shield to such shackles of despair
So let your eyes take flight from this racked madness
The cape of sadness, it too must flee
Oh maiden, the midnight is but an hour of prime
For us to rejoice in these old tears shed
For the flower to revive upon its lush estate
To leave the unforgiven harvest on its field
Together this better year of romance
Shall retrieve our hands so tightly clasped together
Our hearts melted upon the one purest blush of hope
One brilliant admiration, your face is the light
That exceeds the burning of a million days enflamed
All of fairness is ablaze against the whiteness of your hands
Before your beauty, thoughts are subservient
To the loveliness that in heaven is supreme
For having forged a creature as you are forged
A creation that has no equal among the untold score
Your pulchritude, its soars higher than the undreamt sky
Forever to fancy it until I die
Until this world crowns me with its marks of esteem

With your grace, my love, the rarest of all things
The grants truest peace and tender calm into my life

Hereafter I Live

Hereafter I live
For the mercy that from you shines
The night is but a night
The day is a passing day
Is a flower no more than petals and a stem?
The stars are faintness, rocky worlds are worth nothing
The seas are but pools of tears
The harmony of Nature is found elsewhere
In solitude perfection is whole
But in the quality of public fairness
Nothing can outlive you
Nothing can be called better love
Than the purest beauty that from the teems!
The brilliance, the glow, the emanating fire
Thy clear loveliness, the desire of my heart
It is you, your hand is what I call heaven
Truth is the brilliance lit beneath your eyes
Your compassion, your warmth, the world is young
And in it hides the gentlest of deeds
Above the list, a thousand workers scribe your name
And call your touch divine, it is holiness
Your kiss my dear, is prized over a million things
A million lives lived and dead
Cannot hold attribute to a moment you are near
Your warmth, your hold, your tenderest fame
Impales the infinite hours of rueful time
Your eternal features, they outlast the oldest things in life
Of inward being, of wildest nothingness
Of inbred strife, you are the stuff of paradise that rescinds the pain
Forever the pleasures gain and inside the substance of the mind

Is found you again, praise you my love, you shall never die
The immortal privilege, the ivory moon waxes sans yesterday
The cheerful larks, their happiness, their rays of song
The stories of fate that play out long, oh sweetest destiny!
The moments that promise to never resign from tomorrow's scene
The drink of levity, the ocean of bliss, the unborn dream
The youth that rebels itself in the fondest of cloudy ways
The slow restless vein, the softest pulsings of need
The untamed lip, the tongue that is forsworn to lasting rhyme
The carmine light of eternity, the blaze that conquers on and on
The greenest sward, the thickest rose, the bluest stream
The amber sky of a million trickled brightness
The everlasting gaze, the stare unto impartial beatitude
They all burn and shall forever
Mere worships to your name,
To your love, my all, that shall never fade.

Long Days and Eternal Years

Brief hours and long days and eternal years
Melodious birds and gentle flowers and richest meads
All of the sweet things of happy happiness
Are combined in you, you comprise it all
Your lips, your kiss, the light of your eyes
Your purest holiness, it warms my soul
And sends me away to the softer clouds of the sky
Lends me the brighter rays of the moon and star
But can the spirit of the sun be far
When you burn so brightly next to it
When your beauty shines with such brilliance
My heart is brave, therefore I call you fair
My dream is pure, you are the source of it
And all the visions of the mind are pristine
So ever glad I am for your love
Of your loveliness, only few words I can speak
And even those are mute before the glory of your face
Your reflection, your tender embrace
It is perfection, an endeared queen upon its own
A greatness that has no equal, oh I am your slave
My love, I am the mad fool that lone waits for you
And counts the passing nights in innocence
Until you are returned and lady justice is restored
As a figure into my arms though she means nothing
How can she, when something as great as you already lives
Already stands high upon the kingdom of my hope
So then to the music of your voice I resign
Until the happy thoughts of yesterday revive
Of all the clean yesterdays and tomorrows to ever be

To ever come about, so come away my love
And there we shall together rest.

The Dream That Burns

The lamp that shines, the dream that burns
The form that breathes, the soul that desires
They all sustain their virtue for one sake alone
The world revolves around its gyrated spin
Life holds to a supreme purpose
As long as passion is not denied the strength of love
And yearnings are not refused the sweet cries of hope
As long as tender affection retains its grace
As long as the hours of loneliness do live no more
As long as winter is barren of its frosty shades
The warmth of your hands, your glowing blush
Shall keep the sky lit with most famed stars
They shall keep the heaven of dear existence alive
Long after the sad thoughts of death have faded and decayed
Your vision shall restore the undying sights of peace
The unceasing shares of brotherhood and arrested time
Shall ebb against the sands of yesterday's defeat
New crowns will greet our heads, never light our eyes
The whole of tomorrow will seem something pristine
Oh all those joys I shall then share with you
I will take you by the hand and lead you to my heart
Whose nimble happiness can never be by mortal things betrayed
Thus I take solace where your beauty is divine in constancy
Never letting the supernal truth to pass our way with sombre effect
Nay, we shall prove blind to it,
I shall never let tragedy fall into these bracing arms
To make the play of fools out of what is so endeared,
Yet fleeting and there again to see the light of your face no more
Oh beloved, I grasp you by your lapsing trace and my spirit flies
I bow humbled before your beauty and let it reign

Oh these tears, let them rain—the dominion of love rules the world
Sorrow to wield the everlasting realm to whom all must submit
Oh nightingale, exhale your songs in less doleful ease
Let them pass untried, untried, unredeemed
For in gentleness we all must take our turn of sleep
Thus I close my eyes, thus I shut my soul in death
And sleep the millionth sleep of loving, of forever having you.

Tears of Silence

I am left in the tears of silence and disbelief
The arrow of this world is much hard cast
And my face is no more than a pale ghost
Which tries to retain its warmth through the reflection of thought
That falls upon your shine and calls it heaven
Oh am I worth the injustice of memory
To be treated with such blind contempt and scorn
For when the trace of fairness I conceive
The world's despair is gone, eternally fled
And nothing but loveliness takes the crown of hope
The pensive sacrifice dies; there is no weeping to be done
Yearning redeems the loveliest of hours
And makes kings and queens out of our dreams again
Thus like a flower, I look to your unfolding grace
I breathe in the rarest fragrance of your skin
And escape to paradise soft and forever free
Your elegance, it lights up the flame of adoration
And sends the esteem of beauty to its lofty court
Of sweet Elysium sans the sentiment of hated time
Or the ruin of Providence that makes resplendence dim
For when fate lacks will, life has no ardour
Emotion ceases like dry streams against the sands of desire
When that desire burns alone, the plains of existence are parched
And the deliverance of tomorrow is no more found
Thus the allurement of the sun resigns its delicacy
The state of brilliance as well reclines into the shades
And finds the relief of solace within the moon
Whose splendid features are immune to immortal pangs
The strides of deformity rage against the tender heart
And drive the blades of passion into the core of the devoted soul

Starved, the spirit flees to the crest fallen realm
Of truce and sadness and the kind brotherhood of attachment
Yet undiminished, the rays of solitude endure
Carrying out the command of the fortune's destitute
Until the farewells and departures break away
And lead us to our undiscovered country of love's promised liberty
There to be free,
There to never feel the resentment of mortals who must die alone.

The Plainest Truth

The plainest truth of heaven is written here
It is spoken as thus: you are the fairest among them all
Maiden, you are the loveliest beauty ever born in this starry scene
The gentlest creature ever to walk this world
Your ease, your grace, your brightness
Sets the earth to flames along with my soul
Now tell me, should I think anything less
On the rays of your glory that shine like the delicate sun
With the eminent glow of all the skies and paradise revealed
Reflected within your eyes, the hues of summer gain
The colour of the garden rose, its envious state
Declines unseen, you are a vision above all of them
That pervades the stark embers of this proud life
Of this warm spirit and love and unheld eternity
Shame on me! Oh beloved do me some harm
Afflict a serving of that tender pain that youth so wildly desires
And old age is covetous of; my veins inflame wildly
My face does blush, your hands, your breast, your calm cools it well
So give it to me again and round about this song shall go
Until the dark times of what the plaintive man must bring
Upon such an hour, our hopes shall be united, our vision as one
Your prettiness shall serve as the centre of it all
Your soft smile, the pleasured openness of your arms
Invites me in again, so I shall everlasting enjoin
This immemorial union that calls our names as one
As a single dream, is not this immortal fame already won?
The star blazes, the moon of destiny prods far
And we shall be perceived forever under its darling light
So take my hand, my yearning shall take us to tomorrow's fortune

As then we shall be free, as now are hearts are ever free, forevermore unbound
We fly, we flee—relishing love's remembrance is sweet
There, here, I take out my promise and place it before you
Are we not the freest to be born upon this page of eternity?
Oh indeed we are my love, take my hand and let us together run
Let us fade far away—oh our love to never die again.

Drowsily I Sleep

So drowsily I sleep, my love
Uncertain of what the yonder bays may bring
What the fresh tides of the sea hold in store
None do ever know, so let them stream into this open shore
Let them stream like tears that like brooklets flow
Along the sinuous curves of the mountains and the glens
Along the sweet silence of the untold summer brink
Where all the birds and flowers loll dankly in the air
In remembrance to saviours lost and fortunes forgone
Of light madness escaped over the tipped pinions of thought
Of the amorous mind that can never let go of perfection
Can never release the scene that with tender harmony filled
What joys, what sad solitude, what cries
The brain is forsaken and untouched by yearning
The vein is left vacant of its warmth, the softer pulse dies
With it the dream, the hope, the kinder reverie
They all sink away into the dark depths of oblivion
So I look out to the sky, turning to those delicate stars
Somehow believing that they are corporal, through I know better
Though all seems void, still I embrace my own-scarred reality
Before the dust shatters that too and the earth flows back
To carry me away to a realm more pleasant than this
To a dominion more graceful, to consume the soul that has not yet lived
So come away, my love, let us fleet together, together crested, together free
Under this united scape of bliss and amorous destiny
There under the moonlight, our happiness can be garnered full
Regained forever, never to perish or to be condemned again
The heaven takes us, the rays of dawn open wide their hold

And inside its crimson arms we fall, we flee
Oh once again this world is ours and love so ever free.

A Thousand Things

A thousand things may come and go, my love
The spring bears its fruits, the summer revives its light
The meads carry on with a lovely glow
The becks, the streams, the leas of tender paradise
Though bathed in splendour
Cannot compare the least with your soft glimmering
As you are like an angel endowed with beauty's complexion
With love's own divine and ever secret graceful fortitude
Whose brightness can never escape this blue-lit sky
Or ever leave the palm or touch of passion's artistry
Indeed my love you restore the pleasantness, the peace, the calm
The kindled breeze, the stoked fire of a queenly love
These features hide within the depth of you
And can never flee; let my soul be lost in yours
With tears of fondness we will be carried away
And the fear of tomorrow will be far from us
To find us, to darkly seek, nay its reach cannot penetrate
For as our bond of love is pure and everlasting
For as truth takes to our side and swears to never resign
So dear beloved, the substance of the undying dream is ours
Nor will the sun or moon shy away from the blossomed trees
Above which the stars hang and desire is warm and alive
Where from the verdant meadow the lark's tunes are quietly hummed
Oh what an exalting song, how my spirit sighs unburdened
Taking solace where your beatitude shines forthright
There my being is at one with the hourglass of fate
As the night descends, the black sphere restores the hands of darkness
Your lips remain as the only thing seen, immortal and worthy

Of human suffering; the pain uplifts from its darkest shades of fame
As I devoted kiss them tight and bid the world a long goodbye.

That I Feel

Hold strong my love, every power that I feel
Pierces like the wayward dagger
When I consider the worship of you
My heart is enfeebled, my eyes feel wounds
The whole of yesterday departs onto the sky
Where the holy dream of you is seen
Where your divine power is intensified
Spread across those free stars of night
How all those divine embers of the air
Scatter wide with the effulgence
Much like the crown of your fleeting glow
That climbs high onto the heaven of your light
Where love is consonant with emotion
Enshrined forever, that is how your beauty is portrayed
As all of life dissolves in the realm of sophistry.

Cannot Love You Dearer

This I must profess, I cannot love you dearer
Nor can my lips dare to deny nature its right of beauty
For as the lot of stars brought my soul to be born
I thank the blessing of the sky for having put you near
For me to worship, to understand what is divine
And yet how I adore you more than the soft summer bud
That brings back the tenure of hope to all that lives
Reinstates colour into the tokens of warmest blush
Oh how that reddest shade belongs to nothing else but you
You who is the garland of life's triumphs and life's victories
For you are like the sunrise whose rays glow faithfully
You are like the moon rays that tether aloft in peace, so ever calm
And like the darling air upon the sweet gentle eve, you are it
The fires, the touch, the graceful desire of Eden—all of them are you
Manifest in a glory that from you softly teems
Ah that you are like the gift of paradise itself
And as the world is the world, thus you shall remain
The eternal song within the depth of my heart
Forever true until this earth flees in mutiny
And nothing remains save you and love and innocence
Oh what bliss awaits my spirit then?
So let me confess once more that I love you the greatest
As I leave, I leave believing in your modesty
Never looking back until this troubled globe is spared its pain
Remembering your face, begging nothing from that kindred sky
Save the tender dream that in you thrives and swears to never die
Or else I to die forlorn and you to be ministered to the throne
Whereby the power of one strength our minds are one
By the occasion of unity, we yield to each other

And then defend the righteous hours that are left
So late into the night when you and I are the heirs to time's immortal touch.

More Beautiful Than Beauty

Can I say that you are more beautiful than beauty?
Herself being the lovely child of you
More lovely than when loveliness is supreme
You are the crown of them all, the perfected state
The sheer esteem by which fairness holds steadfast
Is gathered in your eyes, your face, your delight
The pleasure of your warm depth, the cheerful candles of your countenance
Shines through the stars implanted in your grace
Sealed and pursed upon your fairy sweetness
Upon the midnight of your glistened brow
Your delicateness, your soft embrace
The glow of your temperate soul, your brilliant spirit burns on
It hangs higher than the rose in the dew-pressed garden
Loftier than the heaven plains of paradise
As a famed bliss is found within your arms
At its core new wings of love unfold ever unbruised
Untouched by every mortal who knows what pain is
For sweet is the music of the weightless bird
And as my mind feels gentle void, I relate to it
I ponder back to your reticent beauty, its disguise
That is so scarce and unblemished within my thoughts
Oft I consider you the heir of the world
The angel of holiness, the undepicted art of life
The sole bride of greatness, the daughter of youth's hope
I hold high to your truth, my all
Though in truth you are better than modest truth
More pious, more pure, more magnificent
More radiant, more lucid than the tides of scoreless seas
More constant than the sun that spreads its inconstant grief

And lays sadness on the fainter shades of time's reward clock
Nay, fie to that, death and age take all away
I am left with nothing but the admiration of you
Your hands, your lips, your nimble trace, your unresigned glory
My heart races with an unknown faith, an abortive mutiny
A nameless protest, a debate, a plural majesty
But when I see you my ruinous veins turn calm
The wreckage, the decay, the cold darkness within me fades
Forbear, I seek the pardon of your love again
Until the eastern sign departs from the sky
Until the undying moon itself surrenders its charm and perishes
And the black night is all that we have left to know
Sans its glow or the reflection of the pretty hours
O' I will worship what you are cast on
For lady heaven is but a playful dream of the day
My eyes are only set on you
Forevermore, never to be released until we are far and together, my love.

So Sacred Met

The halo of your face, it is so sacred met
That the eye of man cannot conceive it
Nor the heart to report what substance it is
Nor has the tongue strength to express
What the mind is at fault to never believe
Oh what glorious perfection inheres in you
What gems, what pious crowns of holy affection
What graceful majesty, it is like a proud leopard
That preys on the skilful hawk when her back is turned
When she is blinded by the halos of sophistry
Off that verse of flattery I feed
And adore the wailing shimmer of the night
Who is in pain for not concealing your brightness
Your mien of infinity, it is stealth to this material world
It passes like a muse whose sacred glow cannot be touched
That fairness is disjoined, it rifts most every heart
That dares to look on you and not be delivered to traitorous death
Or imbrued by the ransom of sweetened joy
That revels in your pure eyes, it is apothecary
Love is a fund to men of robes and gowns
Who rail against time's sanctity, but still obey its strength
The lance of fate, it is the accuser, it draws to preach
The misdeed of having surrendered to your breathless warmth
Oh how riotous, my pinions are minced and breached
Thus I fly away like a centaur with a broken stride
Like a ruined beggar, to wander the roads of life and dream
Of the promises of tomorrow's hope that all betrays
Thus I fade, never to think back on that dismay
Musing the imponderable, it is your beauty

The soul cannot be constrained for dreaming that
Upon that glowing sky I shall be free never, never, never…

Arman Nabatiyan

Lineaments of Your Face

Those fleeting lineaments of your face
Do persuade me to such strong felt love
That I tell the world I will go mad
If you continue to enforce refusal
My heart will drown in the wit of sadness
And will leave the thoughts of tomorrow unborn
So be the lesser stranger to my cause
And I will hold you up, I will laud you
Praising that pure and white heaven from which you came
How the light of that tender glow glistens warmly
Sprawling out its gentle rays of paradise
For my eyes to behold under the shade and bless over again
How you are the truth by which my softer hope survives
Be the kinder of our two souls and grant me your grace
Make the courts and thrones of your fairness decree
For us to be the heirs of its profited union
Maiden let your beauty shine all over the seas
And the calls of love will echo back
A laughter dignified in the hour of youth and passion's prime
Devotion begs its strength out from these veins
Yield to it, surrender your darling pride
And we will be the masters and the conquerors above ungentle time
Extend to me your hold of brotherhood
And we will flee away unscathed from the nettled wounds of life
The shades of darkness fall, solitude expires fast and far
We are the champions of this triumph sung low, yet glorified
The happy stars return their power into our hands
Destiny obeys the kinder fate implored by our hearts
As dreams do scatter with the wind of the untouched

As against this sandy shore we return to the dust
As we are together alone against the banks of love and eternity.

So Untrue To Love

These hours live on, they are so untrue to love
That I seek the solace of your heart
And consider sacredness all that lies within it
Your pose is blessedness, a dream indisposed
To the wider wakes of this abusing night
Along the silent crests of the sea
Along the craggy shores of your unprotected fame
The moonlight shines as a warm blanket
Lighting up your face, darkening the rest
Blackening the world to some unreal delusion
Still I cannot accept the solitude, the clouds drift back
They are all rebuked away by one loveliness
One outstanding shine, one beauty supreme
One fashion that outlives what true glory is
And you are the pureness that I think of
When the music plays and placid is the soul
It is you, my dear that I conceive inside
And relish all over like a young evening star
You are more delicate than that wild amber twining
More precious than scarlet blush that never dies
Warmer than the cheeks upon which that blush reclines
More fragrant than the kiss of spring's newborn rose
Hail my maiden, whiter than those wings that you behold
Fairer than the shadows of dawn or its pale mystery
Ever true and sweet, one word cannot convey it
One devotion cannot express the strength I store
In eternal memory of your vibrant glow, your light shall never surpass
The history of your name, the full kindness of your depth
Against the peril of a thousand anguished deaths
Shall never resign, such speech is heresy

As these lips breathe their song, I forbid it all
And only remember back to your fonder look and touch
Oh forever my angel, I remain alive with that
And as long as life retains life, I will need nothing more.

Power of My Soul

You are my destiny; the power of my soul
Excels in the depths where you're true, my beloved
O' this unity shall aid to carry us far
Far into the horizons and bright cloudy scenes
Where no one can perceive the amber vision of tomorrow
No one can ascribe darling colours to the unfled rainbow
Or a name to the wide temple of glorious love
Or to your beauty pristine, to your thrived vitality
The bourns of the ken do open wide
The brooks, the glades the amorous valleys
All touch that fairest brink, the blazing sphere
The flamed pinnacle of summer
The climax of wondrous youth lives through your azure eyes
That golden bud girths the unshed tree
As it must fade with the daisies of spring, the weak daffodils
All blow away in their prime, leaving the raw dust to parch the ground
The lilacs and the poppies recline in abeyant peace
The easeful breeze makes all the happy flowers sway
Robbing them of their sorrows of old, though oblivion fills in strongly
Stealing that fonder blush of innocence
That is inclined to remain among the unknown fields
The callow bliss, the soothing lyre, the melodious joys of the season play on
And each song of a great enchantment tells
A story of lucid seas and sorrel shares and high mysteries of romance
Of delights perched within the gentle plains of sweetest mirth
Within the hawthorn orchards of warm paradise
Oh the Elysian soil, the dew of the soft-tickled stream flows vast
The garden and the grave, the verdant climbs of restless passion
The tender earth of remembrance, life's dream and levity

Its bright aspirations, its formative stars, their most graceful solitude
The esteemed fate of love's great and flourished artistry
The blessed crowns, the cheers, the auspicious ages of ethereality
The sound of earnest prose, the musical scores and untold volumes of light
The scroll, the parchment, the grateful tongue of the solemn bard
The lips of praise, all of them combine in worship of you
To give service to your adoring comeliness that must be extolled
Oh how alongside your beauty I stand, adoring your long-lived majesty
Everlastingly, undying, it shall remain immortal in me, immortally preserved
Those holy rays of dawn, those raw shades and casts of night
They are but sacred prophesies to your forever-lit fame
To the calling of your cry, your name, your breathless pulchritude
And so I sigh away, and so I die, without a pulse left within my heart
Without the love-mortal beat pressed against my frame,
It too has perished from the bones
Oh the lonely mind aches, so I suffer in quiet darkness
Under the silent and still court of the high jealous moon
Praying that this tale through the throat of the nightingale will be played
Every time the eve is warm, the skies are dear and hope is peerless and abound
Humankind shall fancy your perfection and expire consoled
Only to borrow a trace of your goodness and then to perish in righteous peace
Nay with your pious love regained—my all—forever after to survive.

The Comfort of Youth

So there flees the comfort of youth
But as I have you hung as a star
The darkest skies cannot be dark
The drowning ocean has no depth, it is not black
And the moon holds vigil over you beauty
Over your glory, none can conquer there
The richness of your eyes, the sweetness of you breath
Your vision, it carries over a thousand unseen lands
And still I peer farther yet, my angel
In innocent hope that your source can somewhere be found
That your warmth, your heart can be materialized
The hour to me is but a thievish ruse
Prose is the falser friend of nimble time
But as you live above these million ceaseless clouds
Oh beloved, the complexion of eternity will fade to death
The hard labour of joy will be flattered in the mind
And the strivings of this savage life
Will meet ruination, longing will not remain within us
The songs of paradise will deliver us away
We will heed its call, we will transcend to the heaven throne
Forever to love, to marvel in your pageant face
The throbs will slay the unforgiving sorrow
There can be no woe to survive, we are the freer spirits born
Always to be pardoned by the pulse of destiny
My quiet love, the birds cry their tears loudly
Listen closely, within their little cheers and silent agony
My dear, you will find me crest within your soul.

The Gentlest Rose

Upon the night only the gentlest rose is seen
That flower, its sweetness, it is most heavenly
It is you my love, my all, it is your face
That cries to me the thousand tales of untold sorrow
Of yearning, of loss, of dear-felt misery
So rest upon my shoulder and cry no more beloved
That need for pain, let it flee, let it perish, watch it die
As there remains hours to time and strength to my soul
I shall comfort you, I shall uphold you
Keeping you the queen of my mind's amorous reign
I shall retain you near my warm and pounding heart
Never to let you go, never to let anything hurt you again
Nothing to threaten that tender thought of yours at all
That hand of passion, that sight,
That glimmered scene of romance shall not be impaled
Fear nothing my love, the scythe of death, the cold pang of the dust
Can never torment us as breast to breast we live together
In the higher realms of immortality, there nothing can ever reach
The golden hold of our desire. The belonging of our shared spirit
Begs the world to be united in the forever peace of youth
In gravid warmth, in kindness to what fate can bring, that blazon of levity
Upon the morrow I shall bow down and worship your supreme beauty
Without dispute, I take to the rare course of your eyes
And fall deep, deep into the loveliness that gleams
And I adore them, claiming all other fairness as treason
A mad deceit, a serial fashion of nothingness
Oh I devour them, the streams and silver brooks trumpet loud.
The divine grace excels only in you, in you it is perfect
From you it shines so immaculate and unbruised

Like some paragon of nature, vesper-like in form
With timorous hands and awesome skyward reflection
Like the ancient moon, its lone mutiny, its dark rhetoric
Playing with the instrument of stars, so they are not immortal yet
The minions of the skies, their vast glorious orbs
They are but humble thralls to your tresses and your brow
The wide dream of hope, its profitless escape
Is assailed, profaned before the summit of your pulchritude
So thrive my love, thrive! Against the moistened kiss of death we shall revolt!
The will of fate is at ease, its sings of happiness, of the fond unrequited love
Ye who read this, as these words hang from your lips
Know that though mortals die, love shall not
Those these bones and flesh are fled, my love for her is not
It cannot die, no never can it die—time bears the art to make all decay
Save those who love, they to an eternal heaven fly away.

Your Beauty Is

Beloved, your beauty is to me
Luminous, kind, brightly expressive without compare
Statue-like and twin born to fair Venus herself,
Which although of goddess birth, holds to higher envy
Of your unwearied name, the treasure of your heart,
The perfume of your youthful nape
That sorrel blush that shines Elysium forth
And grants Psyche the wings of an unbound decree
To fly forth, to be dazed and in ceaseless vertigo
Standing bare before the searchlight of truth
Drunk in the vast Ocean of Love
And yet thirsting for that yon light
That keeps to the shoreless sea of hope
As I drown in the desire of your soul.

Fondest Love

Fondest love,
I melt away and think of nothing else
Save of you, of your face sincere
Of your heart that is pure, your lips that are burning
Ablaze, flames are the centres of your eyes
The core of you, your sweet blessed soul
Everything that is lone to your features, your touch
Your cradled hands, your sentiments
Your divine innocence, a brilliant thing on its own
I worship your youth, your flowered smile
The blossom upon you that grows brighter and brighter yet
Is retained within my mind and can never leave
It is locked up, kept with the darkest seas
With the blackest nights that shows one moon
One star, one crown, one feeling of yesterday
And all three are you fair maid, shining like a beacon upon its height
Like a saint, the host of heaven, the holiest angel
And that is why I revere you alone, oh lady, oh queen
Oh goddess of a thousand undreamt dreams
Along my side, above this open sepulchre
Your brain with my brain
Your life with my own shall drift
Together unbanished, enthralled and boasted
As these wide worlds and skies melt away
As the blush of the great hour is no more
But as the universe of your beauty stands
I shall never die, only to cry, wanting of your sweet eye, my love.

Dearest Love

Dearest love,
How I will not forget you after all is gone
As this world winds away and breathes its last
Still you shall be enshrined upon my brain
Within the depth of this unending universe
I shall keep your image clear as the azure sky
Brilliant as the sun, as colourful as the dew-fallen night
That sets sweet roses on the garden floor
To be plucked like blossoms of the fragrant spring
So shall you amber locks be endeared
For all of time, for all that time cannot embrace
I shall retain your glow, your tender vibrancy
The lips are open but absent of speech
Lacking is the prose of elegance
That can hold truth to the beauty that you bear
The seasons fall and father age tumbles dead
Fled are the seeds of the hourglass
In perfection all the horizons stand
In admiration of your light and gentle grace
Oh how tender is the music of your voice
It tames and quells and resigns to silent sleep
The soft tiger that nests with my heart
How you shall always be looked upon with highest esteem
Until envy from the world halts its curse
And your faith anoints the blessedness of the night
Forever my love, in the warm peace of your sight to be.

Holiest Love

Holiest love,
This pen flees with yesterday
With your former touch, your former hands
Those widest meads of youth
Those tranquil gardens, those white clouds
Dissipate unto a fonder ray
And all that remains is your grace
Your summer, your flowered innocence
Your tender rose, your quiet solitude
It means the world to me; so never fade
My soul will cry, my being cannot stay
If not to be comforted by your love
By your sweetness, by your fairness that is renowned
By your everything, oh my darling
Your shades, your embrace of night
They do soothe me so, let us leave
And stay where our hearts rest with our minds
And there we will forever find
The feeling that is whole and true
Oh my all, you are it, that and more
As I recline to where your gentleness wakes
As we together close our eyes
And dream the starless dream of eternity
Of hope, of us—never to look back, my love
As we are together, let the whole world turn black
For nothing shall burn brighter than this vision that we share
Peace, my love, I will return again one day
After the birth and death and afterlife we shall be free
United, my dear, our souls forever unified.

Untamed Love

You untamed love
Oh dearest, oh beloved of mine
Tell the world that it does not matter
Tell the night it is not boldly dark
Look to the face of the moon, say it is not bright
Mercy, not as long as you own my soul
Our wanting minds shall burn higher than all the stars
Oh indeed, tell beauty that she is not fair at all
Or life that it cannot be life in the least
Tell hope and dream they are just a peasant's game
Which old men play with when their beards of youth are gone
Tell Psyche that she is a mere nomad slave
Of the orchards and plains and fields of truth's own prime
Oh one cannot hold comfort in time
So tell it strongly, that Father Time is as well a ruse
A deception, a yawned belief, a desire unfulfilled
But tell love that she is indeed everything
That no fortune can be a queen above our happy crowns
Our smiles, our bliss, our tenderest joy
Tell the white rays of the hour that they must die
That strength cannot stand against the warmth of insanity
And yet how you drive me mad my dear, you drive me to the verge
Where the horizon can be seen with the gleam of the untold
The unknown, the untouched, the fondly yearned
That is the essence of nature, so let us unite
And sing a cheerful song upon the bough of the lonely lark
We can make it there; our wings shall embrace away tomorrow
As nothing remains but this beating clock of the dust
Tell my heart that you surrender mine, submit your grace
As then mine to yours shall soft relate

All the affections I have felt since birth
And have all returned for you; now welcome me as death draws nigh
Rescind the sadness, compassion is still new
Kiss it farewell, kiss me and bid life a long adieu
Oh passionate slave, romance's self-made thrall
How my blush wanes forever without you
Counting all these precious moments lost
There flies the stars, the signs are briefly shown for us alone
Let us flee further yet and think nothing more on this waiting
Fate stumbles, unto our knees we must resign
As I take your hand and carry my world with your sway.

Daughter of Love

Fair daughter of love,
Upon the silent night the mandolin plays
The stars spread their light wider and wider
The music flows over the fountains and the seas
And still the mind is speechless, it cannot begin to express
The glory, the beauty, the grace that is manifest in you
The days take to the road like a nomad traveller
A wanderer of fate that knows not where he goes
But seeks the blind allies of despair with steadfast heart
He is blind to passion; therefore fame will not follow him
He shuns away romance; his soul will die with him
Fortune weaves no fashion for such unfeeling men
Where is the emotive pulse, where are these brighter visions held
For in them the scope of happiness is found and sorrow is lost
In those vast fields of hope and dream and brotherhood
The eager breath reserves an abode where it can thrive
Where the aspirations of the mind are supreme and pure
But then the song of sadness plays again, my spirit is grieved
As it is aware that its righteous essence dwells with you
That its brightness lives through your eyes
Through your blush, your cheek
Not by those hands that are desirous of your sweet and tender love
Its brilliance is released unto this great world of lunacy
Thus it shall survive forever, as forever keeps to its word
As the blazon of the dawn maintains its holy excellence
With a promise unspoken, life resigns to you
Crowning you the guardian and keeper of its long cherished eternity
The temples fill with bliss, the summer swells to and fro
The doors of heaven open, the citadel is overturned from its place
The seat of paradise, its fairness exchanges with your immortal own

In everywhere the thoughts of love stand unassailed
The tepid patience of the rose, the glint of the quiet pond
Impress themselves upon the look of perfection that cannot die
As we embrace that perfection, giving no tribute to stately death
The black robes of tomorrow, let them draw upon the balmy eve
As time is the defender of youth, this sunset shall never fade
As under its bathing glow we sink,
We expire sans questioning its endless strength
Against its fiercer brink we rage, never before its ultimate darkness to fall
And there once more we shall love, we shall be
The star unto fate that from this amorous sky shall never leave, my all.

Dearest Queen

Dearest queen, oh beloved
The trust of words escape from my soul
How can lips hold onto sweet utterance?
When every answer of beauty with our breaths resides
When every dreaming that the mind can compose
As instilled in you, there is no comfort to summer
Not warmth to the April bud or wind of May
Nor is there colour to the June-lit evening sky
Nor does the heaven or the world regret these faults
Oh angel as you embody what is supreme
How can there be room for more or less?
As upon this plain of infinitude you reign
With such wielding strength, I know not a power of nature
That masters the art of grace and glory as you
Of majesty of virtues vast and unseen
Of love and fairness and a soft admired heart
Of worshiped eyes that stare through the pane of night
In search of the star that above all else burns
Yet that celestial orb is you, my dear
You who conquers the silent emptiness of me
Thus I shall remain a servant to your loveliness
Until all the truths fall out from the darkness
And we are revealed held together under a single light
Forever clenched, forever awaiting the hour to break free
Together released as an eternal spirit that has never died
Oh love, how I wish for that time to be everlastingly.

Oh Fair Rose of Mine

Oh fair rose of mine
These hours of youth are too cruel
Too uncivil, too unkind, too savage for this world
That would let a beauty as fair as yours to fade
Would allow the dark rains to scatter and fall upon your face
Blackening all that is divine and supreme
All that is magnificent against a white peerless sky
How your innocence, your soul is all of that and more
How the dew of your cheeks are loveliness unto themselves
That time can neither mar nor make pass away
My, you are the proof to this immortal ground's strength
That issues forth endless heat, zeal, feelings, idolatry
A worship as severe that it wrecks the mind that dreams it
Full blinds the soul, wounds the heart to a slow and betraying death
That heart that tried to be a patron to some eternal business
Whose affairs from birth were marked with suffering and waging pains
Man has no right to entreat such inspiring strengths
So its fortune is to die, a slave to passion, everlastingly so
The odious censure of romance shall ravish like unpitied vice
The emotion that is moved to embrace it, to adore its despair
It first shall decay into a silence unheard, unseen by all
So gaze on, ye mortals, its fangs shall outlive you
Until the rapture of the hands tears down the light of heaven
Until death consumes the hold that is tightest held
And love remains as the shield to all that must be destroyed.

Oh Princess Dear

Oh princess dear,
Oh beloved of such precious love
Guardian to kindness, angel of sweet joy
Those words of yesterday are not recanted
For as they proclaimed you supreme, they were and still are true
When they declared you as this world's fairness, they did not lie
So how can the heart's grace be denied worship?
Or glorious affection ever be turned away from your sight
For your two eyes light up heaven with so strong of flame
A diadem so bright that sages mistake it for a nightly orb
Whose rays shine with the promise of eternal perfection
A supernal wholeness majestic as it is divine
That is your slender form, spoken softly about
For you are like the gentle agent of dream
Who paints the scope of slumbered eyes with becoming scenes
Your voice is like a passage from discord to harmony
The notes upon your lips, they are the alms on which true spirits rely
Which noble souls will unworthy die in the absence of
Oh what vain burials, what shapeless zeal
What a corrosive bale lady fortune besets
It is wicked enough to drive the sane insane
But one look towards you and all harms are allayed
The wine of living is the taste of your kiss
The feast of existence is your merciful touch
Thus resign with me to the yester fields of redolence
There our hands shall play against the philtre of innocence
Like little tribes of warmth within the shades of winter
We shall find our bliss through sport
We shall lace pleasure across our burning palms
The isles of paradise our passions shall surround

Eden itself shall crown us with its gilded crown
Love born kings and queens of hope we'll be
Happy thralls to unknown and earnest jollity
With an ancient hold across all life we'll fly
Until the eternal realms of joy do set us free
And thereon we are retained on time's forever platitude.

Oh Glorious Angel

Oh glorious angel
I watch you from a distance
And burn and burn and burn!
For your beauty shatters all
It is nothing short of divine eminence
How you breathe new light into the staggered world
That is otherwise dark and lonely, lacking all grace
But with you in it, existence merrily thrives
Your eye catches sight of my eye, your glimpse, my glimpse
Thus I shall stare deep, forever transfixed
Upon the glory that your soft skin emanates
Upon the gentleness that your sweet voice thrives
Across the air of verdant tepidness
The sun but pales in inadequacy
Before the full and lavish crown of your loveliness
Before the staunch hold of your shapely countenance
For all other complexions decline in compare
I sit in the corner, skulked below the hedge
Crested beneath the shade of the willow, aside the darling rose
While little brooks and streams of summer carry on around me
Quietly I am perched, observing the splendour of Nature
Adoring every attribute of its cradled perfection
Wondering how the fashion of beauty is so rare and flourished alike
These questions baffle the mind and addle reason
So I turn my eyes away and place them on something more wise
Upon your tender face that requires adoring and not the worship of thought
Thus I am contented, my mind is set at ease and free
And I desire nothing more from the scape of living
Than the eternal portrait of loving you

So I resign behind the becks and brambled edge
Never uttering a word, stealing only the sight of immemorial time
There are no regrets, no yesterdays, no looking back
Never to burn again or to feel passion, but to only understand it
I die, the streams endure, nature carries on as before
But oh love, to be around your beauty for that brief instance of life
The whole world blazes and is set alight
Free unto the skies of heaven where no one can touch
Those true stars of fate and hope and dream that forever shall rest with me

Oh Gentlest Grace

Oh gentlest grace
The morning sky falls away
The veils of sunrise die upon the unlived throne
Of youth and hope and amourility
Of all the sweet perchances that cannot be
So I embrace your glory and feel the world's comfort
Eden's pleasure unfolds into my palm
The fragrance of eternity fills up my breath with strength
Upon the white horse I fly around life's dreaming track
And see you seated beneath the tree of majesty
Hail Queen, hail, my soul resides with you
On angel as you own the essence of my being
Take hold of these possessions and fly bright
Take height to where every being can gaze on you
And in their depth of passion can admire those attributes supreme
The hours drift away like tides, the days are gone
Affection eases the seconds like summer rain
Like warm streams that curve along the meadow's edge
Like brooks of tears that water the leas
Like the limpid ponds gathered around the verdant banks
Of time and loss and fair beauty's defeat
The resignation of love is as thus most eminent in death
The conclave of the night transforms us into beasts again
Passion becomes the dark metaphor of tragedy
The stellar lights wrongly depict the hand of fate
All the while the mind wrestles with the grasp of what is true
In the servitude of yearning which all does betray
The clouds and summer foison grow restlessly
And then vanish; these are the chronic spurns of life
Against all belief, I resign to where your love is most dignified

Across the winter of distress, I find my patron of eternal spring
As you are that patron of my soul's deepest longing
That soft voice woos me with its melody
This score of love, let in play, our souls need its notes
Let this fable of romance be rehearsed through our lips
Though words need no persuasion as there thrives such devotion
The tenure of eternity is forever posed within our arms
As we take each other's hand against the scene of fury
Never letting go of the hold until the whole world expires
Still upon that bleak height, you shall be mine
As I keep you always and together faithfully, my all.

Oh Dearest Darling

Oh dearest darling
I let my hands run wildly over you
I let my lips hunt for their feral feast
Of divine amourility and riotous grace
Which is so warmly pressed upon you
Oh angel, I burn, burn, burn
For the gentle taste of your nape
And dream the million dreams a thousand times over
I fall away into the arms of deep-seated bliss
Of joyful contemplation and pleasing strides
It makes me content, it satisfies me vast
The glorious aches of paradise I shall embrace
Oh grant it to me and I will take it all
Yield up your strength, together we will cry in delight
And make erotic laughter our crown of life
The voluptuary's smile shall never be wiped from our face
Caroused, the cradle of affection shall not abandon our playful repertoire
Our enrapture, our desires shall not be relied with pain
Until the seas erupt and the carnal tempests cease their thirst
Still in secret store I shall thirst for you
Heeding every word of Cupid's tender word
I thrive on it; your moaning sounds are my harmony
The winsome accord of passion takes to my heart
Compelling sweet fantasies to fly their errant ways
Chiding ardour to take its full share of divine liberty
Believe me maid, all of divinity is you
Eden's yield is the paradise of your immortal frame
My eyes turn in worship, adoring the cordial fairness
Oh what supreme merriment; it condemns the soul for wanting more

But I shall persist to yearn until the relics of youth smite me down
And fate bears the agent of decorum no more
The record of purity, slander trespasses it with treachery
Yet still I brace around those forbidden fruits again
Resting on the holy comfort of your spheres
Until time nettles mortality and all these cheers perish away
Thereon our throats to cry no more, your voice to soothe me
As I hold to your lips, sealing the undying kiss
And lapsing far, far into the undreamt night.

Oh Sweetest Love

Oh sweetest love
Those faraway isles of yesterday
Carry with them a dream that is past
A desire, an affection that never more can be
Thus I resign to the gentleness of your face
And bless this holy world a million times over
Exalt a thousand burning instances within my heart
Without the exhaustion that passion lends to toil
Oh the free mind is something incorporeal
Yet all things that look on you are brought down to earth again
To taste the rains of mortality, the pain of sadness
Which always must accompany the final scene
To which we are the centre-staged player of defeat
The colours of strife, they blare, ever blinding
The rays are too callous, the sky too cold, the ends too bleak
Oh the eternal brinks are always like spheres of tragedy
That offer no succour, no solace, no relief
To youth's imbued breast of nativity
This earth shall always breed kindness with the blade of cruelty
So I take to the golden hour of fame
And climb atop the argent spheres of cloudy shape
Allowing my spirit to fall free, man is born ever free
But conscience is the heir of slavery
As like traitors we plunder on, pride does spur us boldly
The oracle turns to naught, the tempest dies afar
Without censure, vexation derides humanity
The thorns are ripe to press against the bruise
Within the darkness every virtue is trespassed
As then the Flowers of Albion expire away
Leaving no honest trace but the Poems of Love and Yore

To remind the soul of the once happy Hours of Youth
The verdantly sways in an easeful nothingness
In the arms of your oblivion I sense the dream again
As I fall away into your sacred warmth unheard, unheard, unheard.

Oh Angel

Oh angel
The time has come to face the agony
And shed the mortal coil of music
Which floods the youthful mind and makes it believe
In the most fanciful of artful passions
The fame of death, its barren wilderness pervades
In every place where the dolorous torch burns against the grave
Of silence, memory and nothingness
The monuments fade against the stylus of destiny
Brazen pride cannot stand long nor can love conquer
The thousand cloudy pains of life's affection
The sorrows and the tragedies, the wide dismays
They rive against the very force of prospect
Which grants gracious light to the vesper stars and skies
To the orphan orbs that have no brother or friend
Except the prayer that the lonely mind to them affords
So the last suffering is writ, its scores are outnumbered by the silence
The flame of solitude is the hardest hit of all
It is the piercing bruise that never lets go
After all the wounds are exposed and left to bleed
Oh this world is the hazard to gentle dreams
Whose aspirations are no more glorious or exulted
Than the sweetest sleeps that beggars indulge and wise men die with
Thus let me be the sage, the elder priest of mutiny
And siege the scarce rays of love's fair prophecy
Which lights forth these peaceful swards of Elysian gentleness
I relinquish nothing but the commission of defeat
Which forces to weakness the will that falsehood obeys
But as the soul is not custom to yield its strength
The riots endure until the hands take up the vantage of fate

Leading to the fields where thoughts elope unburdened and free
Leaving the attire of tomorrow to dress the unruffled plains
Of love's pageant and retreat sans time and sophistry.

Oh Beloved of Mine

Oh beloved of mine
These many wide and stretching roads of life
Are but scattered with dry and bitter dust
Foul grains that blind the eyes in cruelty
In the schemed tragedy of fate that is not to become
Anything but a dark and distant scene of nothingness
Hail, among all of this your beauty shines forth and bright
With a prestigious gleam that nothing else can bear
The pastures, the meads, the leas of paradise
They all have their gentle faults; your soul is not among them
Instead it dwells in some higher realm of Apollonian form
Where his rays shamelessly spurn the lover's plight
Pegasus cannot wield the sea, Venus is his matron
Nor can the mortal hand suppress the reins of the lover's yearn
Be this known to you, the cry of passion shall never die
As we are its children, as you and I are borne from its womb
As we are nursed in its palms of silence and slow time
There is no change, no place at all for antique vows
For as togetherness keeps our blood warm and raging
Death shall not make cold the thriving pulse of these wilted veins
The mask of eternity shall unveil its grace to us in kindness
United, we shall hold this precious crown of happiness
And claim it as our brother, as our friend, our everything
Those shores, those scalding sands, those waves of the unknown
Harbour affection within an all-encroaching depth
Upon the crust of this earth, there can be one dream
And that dream is the franchise of your glory, oh sweetest maid
As we are fashioned from its dust, it is your worship
Whose virtue of substance is so great it is something altogether divine
One look, one stare, one eye only!

Cast upon you and all the saddest hardship is fast absolved
The world is but a czar and we are its privileged servants
Thus I am martyred by the pale dawn that lifts its argent head
I believe in nothing else, no sport, no stage, no amorous trophy
Save the vision of love that from your countenance teems
The sun shines forward, the stars scatter back, before the ground I fall to die
Holding onto your hand, oh angel, as a memory to what might have been…

Oh Charming Angel

Oh charming angel
There is no study of life, no book, no proof, no wisdom
No page out of the chronicles of eternal time
That can furnish the answer that my heart is in quest of
That my soul seeks, that my dreaming mind requires
For all the glories of the world, they rest in you
All the promise, all the fire and the scapes of wide eternity
All the wars, all the strife, all the conflict of want
Share one underlying cause; it is you—you who addle reason
Who sends madness to take its throne upon my seat of life
To replace the sanity that once swelled through this breast
And then to let truth fondly drift away from innocence
As the warmth of the sky with a thousand colours is dressed
The face of heaven is disguised in so many unnumbered ways
That I love them all, I beg the stars to shine as faithfully
I implore the moon to shed its rays more bright
Oh if it could only dare to surpass your hawthorn majesty
That light fairness, it has no counterpart, no living compare at all
Neither fashioned of rock nor dew, nor rose, nor warm fleshy thing
Indeed in its whole the universe is unparalleled before your grace
The oceans become a pond, life appears as sweet delirium
In everywhere the potion shall never lie dead
Nor will the garden fester, nor the daisy swoon, nor the summer pale
The whole scape shall exhale relief abolished of sadness
The license of time is restricted from its dark and merciless hands
No night descends after the dusk, happiness teems in copious sheaves
The angels rest in their place, yet all sways in gravid ease
The pent up wings of romance unfold
Passion embraces the dwelling hours
Hope caresses the lasting whispers of the eve

As the orchard of elation fills the unlived eyes
And we return to the Elysium where we are forever free
Oh in our soft heaven united, where our fevered touch of love shall never die.

Oh Dearest Heart

Oh dearest heart
Deepest desire of mine
I shall grieve these scores of misfortune forever
Life appears to be some scheme of tragedy
Continued against our love, devised against our hold of tenderness
But the rays of innocence shall not be quick to fade
Not from your eyes, nor face, nor glimmered tears of night
The industry of the stars shall burn to keep our souls alive
To maintain our passion, the truest affection can never die
Not from the angel wing upon which it was born
Or upon the winds of heaven that thrust colour to the sky
To that molten sun of yesterday, the dream of its glorious shade
The whole universe of magnificence that cannot cease to awe
Which dwells within the chamber where love is pure and unforgotten
Oh that vanity rebels upon the bright midnight glow
Along the throne of man's mortal spirit
Lies a shattered sanity whose rifting pieces
Cannot be mended save by the warm touch of hope
Save by the guiding light of zeal and brotherhood
A memory for the things whose essence is undying
Immutable like the every unbroken feeling that we share
What power, what dispute, what emboldened sobriety
What serenades, what songs, what beauties, what virtues rare
To the scene of darkness our ritual leads, there we flourish
There the garden is green and the seizure of time is gold
Youth is unburdened, glory stands undismayed
The whole world in a quiet stillness sways
Nothing suffers, nothing resigns to those seedless clouds of day
Luminous and lit, we all rock back and forth endlessly

Believing in eternity, in hope, in prime, in the things that lend happiness
In the thought that love can wound, oh so we are the creed to quickest fall
Out from these scattered heights of life never to turn back again
Believing in, holding unto that madness love until the very end
Then to be released, then to be free, oh in our mind to die but be
Happy once more, beloved.

Oh Most Precious Angel

Oh most precious angel
You are the heart of me, the soul of me, my everything
The breath that stirs within this mortal frame
Does so on account of you and your supreme beauty
That warm glory, that soft and kindred majesty
It is unequalled to anything upon this joyful earth
Incomparable to all those white stars divine
Which hang up high, they are as ever soft and dear
They are ever sacred, ever immortalized within my mind
That adores you and worships you like a graceful god
Singular to this vast and wide and empty universe
Rare to all things made of earthly skin
But you shall survive past the wrath of worlds
And their lapsing years declining, decaying
Oh fair angel, oh maiden of undying pulchritude
Your beauty shall thrive, those delicate eyes shall not cease
To look into our sky of love and dare to fade
Those lips, that brow, no, our peerless stars can never leave
Hope shall not perish, nor shall the dreams darken and decay
Time cannot lend ruin to what is eternal in its bond
Therefore hold on to me, embrace me
Keep this as your enduring strength
Go ahead my love, stare as long as you desire
Reach out your arm, press your tender heart to mine
I shall retain it true, persevered beyond the dateless scape of eternity
Far from the fists of anything that wields power to destroy
This great and perfect sentiment between us
I lead out, I turn to your mien, the ruin is gone
The holiest of lights takes the place of my soul
I am contented with the exchange, now the spirit can flee

And be free and fly to where the heavens do not siege the heart with scorn
Embattled I resign to those brighter clouds of paradise
Oh Eden—it is you, I am welcomed once again
Unforgiven, the robes of darkness pass away
Revealing you within the midst
Your vision before a starved and famined scene
I melt away; oh beloved I am yours, afraid to die never, never, nevermore.

Oh My Darling Hope

Oh my darling hope
How my world is lost every moment that you are away
How my veins feel drugged with a dark delirium
When the glory of your moon-like glow is kept afar
How you exceed all the ambitions that I aspired for
Nature's laws all collapse before your supreme beauty
Your praised loveliness, it eclipses the efforts of humankind
The seas of time, they are reduced to dry beds of dust
When your splendidness, your fairness is considered true
When the light of reason shines out upon your name
Enshrining the trace where you are most lovely
Desire is unsheltered, yearning does not decay
Not as long as you are perceived upon the lone seat of paradise
Incomparable, unequalled to anything that can live or die
To any mortal creation governed by the thrusts of pervasive destiny
The hands of fate scatter wide and bright
The grains of tomorrow settle upon the unfamed tryst
Of warmth and love and burning sophistry
Unabated, the ceremonial larks of night sing loud
Lauding the gentle grace that from you teems pure
What innocence, what flourished strides, what perfection
All the kindness of the world is manifest in you
As the pale drapes of the evening cover up the eyes
As the plaintive ditties are exhausted, their anthem then fades
As your face then regains, reviving the pleasant visions once again
Here I hold repose, here the rose must fall
For all the fair and simple things of the past are no more
As is madness I fall on my knees unto the grave
Thinking of you, dreaming of you—that thought is thus forever
perceived

I cry my final tears, the constellations hold eternal witness
To this, my undying vow, my love my soul belongs to you
Forevermore, the earth deserves its due of our life, our minds, our being
So let us resign our bones to it, a brighter day awaits
From this slumber to wake, our greater fortunes to take
Thereon with your eyes, my eyes, your soul, my soul
Never to look back upon this black world of grieving pain
Take my hand, receive this kiss, we fly to heaven
I beseech you we are one together free hereafter.

Oh Purest Child

Oh purest child
Those seductive eyes of white glimmering
Carry my soul into a world unknown, with delusions unheld
Into a vast dominion, a realm unseen
Though anything that resembles mortal eyes
You are the angel of paradise
That stands above my dream—wing to wing
Who looks over my hope's vision with undying unity
Oh what glory, what magnanimous strides we take
What conquerings we possess, what mad escapes
The redolent anthem fades, here gains the hue of spring
That lends resplendent colours to the gentle summer air
Envious is the tide of the wakened shore
That tosses to and fro its strength, its mercy
Its force of fate, destiny's lapsing enterprise
Warm is the rose that is born in freshest youth
But as life hardens every leaf, every petal of once perfection
The shapes and curves of tenderness are no longer what they used to be
So then faith declines, a new master takes the throne
That power is the feel of life, death, a being's indifference
The existence without cause, it dwells in void, in endless scapes
It wanders in the happier clime of nothingness
There upon the altar of human minds it was wildly born
So upon that selfsame mind it shall blindly decease
Until the hours draw out and the stars take their fixed place
Until the skies disappear into their higher crowns of dawn
The warmth blends in, it takes the more ambitious breath away
Leaving nothing in its place but the fairest dust of mankind
Such is the humble soot we gods are made of
Believing everything endures without belief

Deceiving the soul to believe the impossible
So the pursuits extend, though in truth all things must end
Even the poet of this pen, one day he too will never live again
Will never taste the touch of what seems everlasting and unbound
The softer pulse flees; the effort of eternities is wasted
Oh every poem must decay, so perishes the fonder day
As the reverent thoughts of tomorrow rest upon the unheard brink
Waiting for youth and love and time and you my child to wake once more
To fly to the kingdoms that have never existed at all
And there under the power of the shine, to resign, to die, forever free.

Oh Angel Dear

Oh angel dear
Oh sweet daughter of peace
I can profess nothing more
Other than I am enchanted and deeply in love
With every feature that from you brightly shines
You have two hands that lead the world astray
You are my queen, you are my love, nay you are my god
Fair creature, happy messenger of heaven
There is no hour of the day that I am not alone
As when your complexion labours not to be near
The whole of existence is like a blinded darkness
That shall fade and dissolve into the wan night
Woe to the dawn of misfortune, I shun its dim rays away
And hold the seething hand of hope to where your face burns radiant
Ah beautiful girl, oh gentle maiden of paradise
The evening is but Eden before your warm and graceful glow
As you are like some divine sculpt forged before my very eyes
That I love, that I adore, that I hotly hunger for
The remaining beauty of which I cannot begin to penetrate with words
Deep down inside a star's ambition lives
And it begs me to break the silence of the love I feel
Oh goddess of love, oh hail! Oh merciless beast
Oh drunken demon, how hard your rain of sorrow hits!
I am no more than the blood of youth and being
Forced to be the slave of passion and its soft dismay
Being hot-borne and fiery cheeked, the soul of longing never dies
Thus I retreat, thus I turn my eyes to a dream that is sweet
And hide myself under the scenes where passion cries

Oh what dewy streams, what drowsy sleeps, what gentle comfort
There I am contented with the brooks of love and starry lullabies.

Oh My Ever Darling

Oh my ever darling
The chains of this distempered world must fade
And all that shall remain is the mask of life
That bathes your skin in radiance and makes you supreme
Makes you the queen, all other praise can only flatter
The beauty of you that is perched ever high
Like an eagle in its proud nest of dawn
But then the altar breaks, the sacrifice is my soul
That flies to where your being is most pure
Is more brilliant, more true, more zealous
As if some divine vision was cast in the darling rays of hope
And so the mortal will survives, it endures, it teems
Wide across the fields where romance is spoken with one word
And that word is your name, voiced ever softly and pristine
So hearken to the sounds of summer that blow in their prime
Chanting our in a solemn cry, calling your grace mature
Ripe is the blossom that awaits the strike of the scythe
Oh with your trace departed I am no more, sorrow weighs heavy
I live and breathe and dream in a dark metaphor
In a calmness, a reserve, harshly taken from my hold
I am no more the being I used to be, no longer free
My essence declines; we are all but slaves to princely death
So its carnage rolls past, I trace its dusty hem unto tomorrow
Where tears fall upon the ground and expire unknown
I muse, I ponder, I contemplate desolation
When the vision of your lips appears before my haunted lips
I kiss the air; I drown in the blind storm of romance
And think no more on the unfolding times to come
The emptiness rages, loneliness consumes all former grief
Nothing can take a stance against that unseen night of carnage

Voided, I slip away, finding solace in the wide scape of nothingness
As these stars of our united fates revived unburdened
There we are both free, there the occasion of life can never die
I lapse away into the darkness,
Extending my reach as your brightness swiftly passes by
There to be revived, to your heaven to take flight
Extending our wings, warmth to warmth—shielding harm from ever
  falling again
As against your airy face and kiss and sleepless blush
I am whole once more, my all.

Oh My Loveliest Dear

Oh my loveliest dear
This world fails to survive in the shadow of excellence
It must perish, the musty colour of the rose
As well declines, it lacks the temperate shine of summer
That so generously fills your cheeks and makes them bright
I stare into the peaceful eyes of the soft violet eve
And see a reflection of a wraith so holy and fair
That I am apt to call it divine, indeed it is your soul
Which thrives through the ray of every born hour
Every dawn, every dusk, every uplifting morn again
The flowers of Elysium waver over their beechen floor
The sands of the dewy shore wane empty, the skies gleam white
The clouds do promenade in the most sacred of tranquillity
The plains of paradise are warmly open and at ease
The charity of the sun reclines upon the eastward hill
And you are lit under it, my darling, your glory rises
To a height that men are apt to call the heaven of dream
Whatever the name, I only know it as purest beauty
That permeates the fine sculpt of the mortal fashioned art
What beatitude, the petals fall over with the winter breeze
And in a silent whisper cry out your name unto the wind of eternity
The gates, the corridors, the long quarrels of time spread wide
They cannot compete with your beauty that is incapable of frailty
The shade, the night, the pleasant tempest of the unending season
Of the undying grave of life that we with humble fortitude call as home
And declared you as its queen, the everlasting guardian of this abode
That is softly revered as a throned homage to your grace
Oh take me to your arms, free me from the burdened chains
That the breath of man imposes on the lightest air of living

Through which the freest wings do spread against to fly from
To take flight and flee to where your gentleness is materialised
And is so ever real, held within my hands—
Embraced, adored, worshipped kindly
Deified as majesty; fairness suits it best
Oh my spirit never rests, not as long as the nymphs ascend
The ardent waters of youth and float about the pond of tenderness
Not as long as the brook espies the quiet rose along the stream
And the fountains beg to be the compass of cleanest moors
As you are the centre of life and fate and scoreless destiny
I seek solace in you and find my paradise therein
Inside your heart, gravity teems and scales like rogue climbers
Who have lost their pleasant way from the mountain that they devoutly seek
But as there lives only one treasure upon this honest earth
As you are it, all my looks shall turn to your face for all time
In admiration transfixed, in pure love unparalleled
As I gaze once more against the darkness of the calmest night
I resign in full to death, surrendered, knowing through it I shall find hope
Through its perpetual union, I shall be once again rejoined
With an immortal brilliance, oh with the temple,
The gladness and the smile of immortal love
That you alone provide, rescinding away all scorn to nothingness
Oh angel, I need you, I seek you—
My love, alongside your warmth I am forever restored.

Oh Precious Angel

Oh precious angel
The breeze of midnight falls
The fondness, the sweet reverence expires
All that is left is but a trace of the past
The wind of yesterday blows like a heated blast
Oh but how your beauty restores all that is gone
And can be no more again, the willow drowns against the river scene
The tears trace alongside the stream of the forgiven
The brooks etch their way across the pliant banks
The wings of the dove spread out unburdened
The summer blossoms return their glorious face
In renewed spirit to rejoice your tender love
To cast time against the infinite grainy shore
And then to turn away and think on life no longer
To go blind, to let the visions soar high
To have the desire of the unknown extend to golden heights
To reaches unbeheld, that is where you shall be remembered
Relished, cherished, endeared, kept sacred for all age
The things that cannot fade, your beauty is among them
So hold my hand and we shall together roam wild
Out to where the wandering of love shall take us
The wilderness of romance is set free
We are no one's slaves but our own
Our hearts belong to no being other than our soul
So unite, redeem me, let us escape
Under the morning sun we shall awake unbound
True my love, free to find our own immortal peace once more.

Oh My Sweetest Joy

Oh my sweetest joy
Every strength that abides within my bones
I save for you, the light of my eyes resigns
Softly upon the meadow where you are seen
And the sun is serene and the air is mild
There my bosom serves as a shield to thy blazing rays
That beat on and on, trying to forge their long way in
Within the chamber of my weakened heart that holds you in reserve
Within the vault of any truest soul, for you deserve it best
Thus deserts are given no rest as you frolic about
Toying with my inbred sentiments, how I worship you
And adore the glorious scene of the day on which you were born
I hear a little bird rest down on a lonely branch
Pining its woe to the bark that has an ear for sadness
Speaking of a lost love, of the story of a dream unfulfilled
Knowing that tale is of us, I cry my hopes away for it
And slip far into a slumber that dents the trace of fondness
Along the silent brooks, little reeds and grasses send cheers to me
Encouraging me to embrace and rejoice in some minor levity
To revel in the thought, hold bliss in the vision of you
Indeed it is true I relish the grace of all nature
But as you are not with me, all of that means nothing
I rather die as an unknown star upon the glimmered sky
That would be closer to bright heaven where you reside
Than to be a beggar to this darkened earth lacking love
Thus I shall confine myself to the barracks of time
Until the lust flees from my flesh and I am free
Until the pulse of the mind escapes and there is nothing left
Neither to the will nor strength of the human frame
So to never remind me of the warmth of your pleasant touch

Oh sacred rose, you shall be forever endeared to me
Thus is shall keep your blush and combine it with my own
Until colour from these haughty cheeks of mine do fade
The bondage will be broken then, the chains will disappear
Upon the lucid hour we will be left to romance love away
Passion comes to take us on its wing, the cloud of conflict decays
As glory fills the face that you alone have, that is yours ever and ever on
And patiently we fly—oh sister, oh queen, we fly, we fly together
To the realm where desires burn and we
Beneath its glow belong as one immortally united!

Oh Delicate Angel

Oh delicate angel
All that I feel through my heart is you
All that pulses through my soul
The fever, the fret, the ecstasy
All that my mind has sense to perceive
Is your beauty, your glory, your majesty
Your abounded colours of grace, your embellished throne
I sit alone with the lark rooted in his empty bough
And pine the fate of misfortune he cries
Oh how hard sweet sorrow hits this life
That I must love you, that I cannot have you, that you are lost
Forever surrendered to the grains of time that can be no more
My eyes bleed, my spirit sobs, my passion forever dies
How can it endure, how can it survive, how can emotion not perish?
When it must look upon the vision of you in memory
When it must release the hope of a perfect and most happy scene
Nay our mental stage is that of strife, I press my head to the darkness
And kiss the solemn grave of the world forever goodbye
What solace can it offer, what peace, what warmth of brotherhood?
To a mind as this so rendered in heavy pain
No, as long as men can breathe these lips shall not be silenced
These flames of want shall not be quieted the least
Though the burning zeal it lacks, love is not void
Nor shall the temptation of romance ever be resolved
To anything less than a wild and ambitious dream!
So thus I resign myself to the yonder scape of your beatitude
Dreaming what those brilliant stars to this lonely fate could bring
Dying below the tree, the brook, the stream, the love of summer melody

Oh my all, there I reach you, I feel no pain
There I happily die under the stars again and again and again…

Oh Unfled Love

Oh my unfled love
How the bowers and the golden tryst
Hang soft upon the bright azure sky
How gentle is the pulse by which we live
How sacred is the breath when it tries to leave
To expire all away, my love we will let it not
Your warmth, your true innocence
Is more cherished than the throne of the world
More than this blessed earth owned over and over
Oh how precious is your touch that can never die
And as the seasons come to age my face
To them it will surrender though my soul is forever free
So too shall your spirit remain with me
As the most endeared gesture of this mortal plain
Oh how kind is that vine of tomorrow
Its sweetest drink, your eyes are upon it flown
How I have the strength of every stride
When I look upon your beauty and a trace of it is drawn
When the little teary ember of stars
Reflects from your complexion, every heaven is calm
Every persisting doubt is warm satisfied
The enterprise of happy grace is restored
And runs against the faithless holds of thought
Your love is a religion, an adorned idolatry
A worship chronicled against love's born exile
So it will follow to where your clear fairness leads
To rest there for the smallest moment of time
And to call that moment the eternity that I believe in, my love.

Oh Flowing Love

Oh flowing love
How these notes play on and on
And I am a slave to your every chord
To every thrum that pulses from your frame
To your every vein, my dear, how very nuptial it is
Like the mild harp that never yields its pleasured cries
Whose gloried scale cannot be the least conceived
Your score is beyond the embodiment of music
It is beauty incarnate, dare I say perfection
Is embalmed within your bones, those gentle lips
Convey as much of life's harmony, love is a wide embrace
That does not cease when the silence carries on
Even so, you are the sweetest of that quietude
The sound by which every mortal wakes
Is forged by you, you are the writ of eternal song
That never shall be forgot upon time's slow remembrance
Your notes are kept as the most cherished things of all
Ever born to the mind of passion's lyre
No they shall not fade, never will these sounds decline
Until the tempest grows again and nature's wildest melody
Unites unto the world where no voice is heard
Where neither greatness is seen nor softness touched
Nor is sense ever needed for the higher soul
As your loveliness is clear perceived all around
And no one by the strength of music can question that fairness
Which is briefly grasped but then quickly melts away
Love will forever resign to the instrument of madness
And will find my inspiration's light within that speechless art
Forevermore to be your soft listened thrall

Until nothing of this heart's machinery remains
And your maiden hope is all that it can think of or believe.

Oh Dearest Angel

Oh dearest angel
Are not days but passing days
And years are years if they are merely drowsed in a dream
But it will not slumber so deep
Not as long as your fair beauty is near
Not as long as I am spurred on to your arms
Tush! No, I am nourished by your empress grace
And your shapely glory does all surround
How I do drown, still not forgetting you
You who is the queen and the saint of passion's crown
The fairy of the moon, the sweet maid of the pond
Around which my tender youth is shared and spoken of
Oh how your magic charms my feasting eyes
It sends me away, it carries me far
Thrusting me to flights that I so love to take
Remembering you on the fine clouds of the summer sky
On the gentle stars that hang beneath them
Oh how relished is your hair, that amber flow
Those delicate hands of ivory whiteness
Cherished is your finesse, your meek and gentle soul
The rose's brightness planted in your cheek
Makes the evening blush with warm desire of what it lacks
The night-time shines with a more jealous glow
The shades of darkness, the brief hours of nothingness
All before the dawn, they think on you
Wondering how your rays will clear the horizon's brink
The sable winds blow, the scape is ever pristine again
Is ever lucid, brilliant, vastly radiant, the tincture endures
Through the thousand moments of unbent time and sadness
Untamed and wild and magnificent

No, your soft voice will not perish today or ever
Never, never can the eternal lute dissipate
Not as your loveliness looms, beauty always speaks wordless
The silent drone is mine, unsolaced from this great world
From this being, from this exile that cannot be
As the midnight bud blossoms from the ground
And makes all calm and eased in tepidness
Allayed and beautiful, like all that resembles your beauty, my love

Oh Tenderest Maid

Oh tenderest maid
Oh damsel of grace, oh goddess
How I flee through the holds of a thousand nights
A thousand dark worlds, a million unlit days
All to see the captured beauty of your face
Its glory, its glow, its brightly arrayed majesty
I cannot speak of fairness for you are it
Heaping grief upon the lash of human eyes
On the shadow of fate that cannot have you
But I feel no sorrow, sadness is not with me
Not as long as your brilliance delivers true
And sets to fire all that I keep within my mind
My dear, all the things that are worth dreaming of
The finest things, you encompass them all
The bluest sea, the scarlet sky of wonder
The amber clouds, the white tracts of happiness
Your purity, your high-held esteem, your truce
Your loveliness is awesome above all else
Above the living touch, the blush of death awakes
And turns to the fragrance where you stand wild
Oh and is ever untamed, my heart is ravished
My orphan soul resigns its worth to you
It owns half the universe of rueful tears
Half the orb, half the oracle of lonely nothingness
The stylus of my love breaks again
Upon the unborn page, the raven worlds live on
And as they do, you and I take part in them
We shall reside upon the one perfect plain of heaven
That the stone of time shall not take away
The carriage of draws, let us together ride over the eve

And we shall be free, my love, let it carry us to its arms
There we shall forever remain
The boldest lovers in a realm that belongs to us
In memorial to a star that cannot die
In remembrance of our lives, of our destiny once more to be.

Oh Sorrowless Love

Oh sorrowless love
Let us together scuttle out of the dewless brook
And step upon the mead of summer shine
There we will be happy without grief
Without worry of the rueful rhyme of yore
Let us flee to where the sun dances wild
And we will prance sans commotion around it
Though amorously our love will be embraced
We will be tied together hand to hand
By the record of the nightingale and lone lark
We are destined for the heart shared by one pulse
Within one vein, one scoreless blush, one heat
One lifting dawn, one crowning promise of life
Amid the glades and streams and forest shades
Across the brakes we shall reveal the garden of our bliss
Our smile, our lip, our praise, our pleasure
Our united hope, our paradise of song
Seeing it through together across the softer leas of loneliness
Of emptiness, our love cannot leave us void
Heaven is drunk within the light of our eyes
And still we fly higher, higher to where the new cheer holds
Where louder joys unfold and sadness is no more
Oh the talk of love is pure inconstancy
My empress, then pardon this ruinous parle of man
That endures within the purity of shame
That still does not swoon to its hard defeat
Therefore I will look to the tincture of thy Eastern ray
Until the nimble walls of comfort tumble to the ground
And your beauty revives with unequalled fairness
Until it is not scarce and is seen everywhere that these cool stars meet

My love, always you will be mine within my arms
And we are the boldest lovers born upon this, our sky that never dies.

Oh Tender Babe

Oh sweet, tender babe of love
Newborn child of destiny and slow rhyme
The beatings of the hourglass pulse against the walls
The musk of the meadow thrums, the soft harmony plays on
And the eyes never turn back to look on yesterday
This quill writes for tomorrow, for all of seasonal time
That surpasses the thousand vales and holds and youth of summer
Exceeds the gold blossoms and harvests of prime
Which in easeful spirit claim to know what truth is
What sorrow is not, what love can forever be
Laden upon these heaven-set eyes of deeper longing
I see one light, one grace, one glory, it is your face
Your fame outshines all the rivers out of Eden
The white orchards, the gentle fields of poppies
They censor their musk with passionate indifference
But my heart being true, it holds to a constant vision
Where your loveliness brightly burns without respite
Without the suffering that the mortal veins are obliged to endure
So I will pursue them with sterling lust if you are the reward
That lies behind these secret scores of life and levity
Inside my mustered brain, a tortured thought resides
The muse that ponders your beauty over and over
But is never satisfied nor can it make any sense
Of how such divine perfection could embody the human form
You shatter all preceding sculpts, I am your slave
A thrall unto your endless rays of majesty
The wonder strikes me, I fall away unheard
And within the mutiny of silence, within the forlorn rage of death
I find your sweet love again, thus I resign before your precious feet
As a servant that is at will to do as you please

Have pity on me, as you are an angel bearing wings
Be kind and soft; be merciful in your delicate ways
Kill me softly so that I may never sleep again
Never be so bold as to dream a thing more supreme than you my all.

Oh Gentle Goddess

Oh gentle goddess, my divine love
The skies are sundered, the mind is broke in pieces
The chasms of the earth, they shatter wide
When your glory, your verve, your majesty
When the brilliance of your eyes must be considered
As the lone star against an enormous world
Whose worth is unknown, whose charm is endless
Undying as the breath of hope's eternity
The mind is no more than a mould of lust and fiery embers
A mask of piety, a prophet, a mutual thief
That rehearses the lines of love before a deaf sky
Of Phoenix's rage and siege and striking cruelty
That leaves the soul to revolt, the instrument of reason lays unredeemed
Like a banished slave surrendered to time's decay
Like the discourse of sorrow whose thousand accidents
Whisper silently into the wind of that which must fade
That nightly air, it is the idol of our dreams
Preaching of sweetness, compelling us to desperate arts
Though by itself it is no more than wild and savage nothingness
As we are pressed against the vast brink in pursuit of sense
To this mad game of rhetoric that we pray to and drown in
Sans hope, the blazon extends, the pains gall the soul of life
The suffering excels in everywhere that youth is prime
And emotion quarrels with desire's long infirmity
These are the hazards we prize, balmy, potent, diffident
These are the wishes we extol, though they vanish fast
Like the hot and ever burning sands in the earth's wildest regions
They, the golden traitors of fate that warmly bid farewell
In baseness, in wretchedness, in naive treason

Of all remembrance gone and tomorrow expired in despair
But the affection draws, ancient days gather together again
Amidst the light I see your face, I protest to the timorous raven,
To the ruddy arms of death
As the heavenly rays spy upon what destiny brings forth
Headstrong we lead away, in our own place a brighter light awaits
All the same we fall into the hands of death speechless and unheard
Yet by the essence we are still together and free, my love.

Oh Sweet Desire

Oh my love, oh sweet desire
Why carry on to play this game
This show, this stage, this drama of tragedy
What is it worth to continue on pretending?
When you have me, I have you, we hold together
Our hands are interlocked like the sunset in the palms of dusk
Enjoy the warm rays of bliss and if it so pleases you
Make believe that the end of this wide world is neigh
Then draw close, unite, let us be as one
Be as a single heart, a single soul, a single happiness
That can never be withdrawn or torn away
Can never be made to fade unto the unrighteous dust
The sky is ours; its freedom is our dominion
Its air is our shared breath, its light—your eyes
Its youth, its innocence, oh that is the fair everything of you
Its tenderness, that is your face, supreme and divine
Your complexion, your soul, you kind glory
The music inside your gentle dreaming mind
They are all as paradise, thus I desire them more and more
Until I burn away and nothing is left of me
A flame of sacrifice devoted to your lovely cause alone
I shall expire, but to perish will not come about
For as your truth lives, my essence can never die
My being would be restless, awaiting your beauty's touch
To lift me up to the brightness that speaks nothing of the past
Forget the yesterday, the mad yesteryear of time declines
With the brilliance of tomorrow, all fulfilment will be brought
So cast your vision unto the ascending sunrise of hope
There we will be seen unbridled; there we will be together sworn

Until the scenes of darkness come to decay from our sight
And nothing remains but you and I born upon the eternal memory of life.

Oh Loving Maiden

Oh beloved of mine, my loving maiden
Dear damsel of a thousand untold nights
The stars rebel, they hold not to the attachment of the sky
The summer buds as well divorce from the warm ground
In which their roots are drunk with something holy, an everlasting dream
Whose embers never decrease from the sweet loving brain
That sleeps and sleeps and dreams of feral things divine
Faces whose shadows neither darken nor dim before the sun
But retain the stalwart hold of airy kindness
Elysium then cries, the brooks of elation are spread far and wide
Across the purple plains of the country sans constraint
Where angels fly in their nakedness and cherubs flee
In joyous glee of their human-like freedom endowed
The nymphs and dryads by the willow tree wake
And dance around the fountain of soft spouted youth
There the stories are all tame, their lips inebriated
With the enamoured tonic of youth and purity
Of rings and pearls and gentle unseen crowns
Cast upon the throne of desire's scattered peace
The elixir flows through the veins, once more all is forgotten
Oblivion settles in, lust holds at the brink of the human pulse
All strength follows from that dubious sill of beauty's madness
All obsession, all rapture, all the scores of mawkish levity
Lonely sentiment walks up to where the halos burn bright
The stars turn into gods and then die within our arms
Oh ye gods, die no more, our pleasures need you
Our yearnings ache for the fancy that your wilderness affords
The balm covers the eve, I am blind once more
My heart is assailed; love is the hazard, the prize, the infinity

That all require, both lusting and afraid of its searing blush
But damsel as we both breathe and are together alive
I still long for you like nothing else of this world
Until the seas from these crusted lands expire
And nothing but the blazon of our hold excels against the sky
To that course I adhere, waiting until the chimes of death summon up the bones
Devouring everything save our love and truth, save all that is pure
Through these splendid eyes of romantic innocence.

Oh Delicate Being

Oh love, oh darling, oh delicate being
Friend to eternity, idyllic flower of summer
The memory of your love I commit to the mind
In silent worship and admiration
Of all that glory and grace have passion to admire
The hour of readiness for my heart is come
It calls on you, oh sacred patron of life
To set free these bourns of want and loneliness
Oh pilgrim of innocence, comely child of hope
The laurel of dreams, they but creep twist the grave of romance
Like a glowing rose that desires to be pretentious
Like the garden of perfection whose name is not wrought to decline
With the wicked thorns of vengeful time
Thoughts are riotous and lend license to famine
If the brain shall be disjoined from your vision, the skull shall twain
Lamenting the peerless sky of base and wretched stars
Who are too cold, too blind, too burning to understand these pent feelings
The soul shall not thrive in any region where you are void
For without your dotage, life has no boon at all
Without you as the ransom, the joy, the art, the deliverance
The purpose of this flesh would flee far and unworthy
Oh for it is that light of yours that makes existence sweet
The glow of that countenance makes me endure the suffering
Of the thousand deathless pangs of fate
I cannot boast of its joke, but only yearn to divorce it
I cannot embark on any bold journey of youth
However much I admire and with heart commend it
Thus embrace me, redeem me, rescind away the dulcet pain
Ally these cosmos as my partner and not my hated enemy

Counsel my ears with a soft and embellished word
Against the shroud, I shall forever be contented
Oh angel, tomorrow shall not stand fierce with its woe stricken rage
Oh maiden, the dreams lead out to somewhere bright
The force of fate draws us together and forever strong
Through the argent clouds we chase the rays of fortune and fly
We fly and fly and fly until we are united and cast free
Under the court of heaven, there to share this love for eternity.

Oh Great Goddess

Oh great goddess chanced upon my sight
Fortune's symbol of high grace and gentleness
That angelic beauty, that glorious eminence
Drives the will to madness and unsettled rage
Oh it is a restless burning that can never die
When peering into your beauty one is left wanting more
Still thirsting for that fairest perfection
Which in you, my dear, is holy and eminent
Beyond the glow of the waking star out yonder
Which in its infantile reach of life
Slips to death and is thus most dispirited
For the sways of chance are libertine
Such is the nature of living; the soul would not deny its due
Though existence is harsh and blind and unjustly giving
So we must endure the aches and bereave the pain
Still we must look up to that greater attribute of the world's embrace
That makes the time we have on this earth forgivable
So I look to your face and see how it is divine
I note the agile loveliness that in all is rare
Save those of free spirit, patience and pure mind
I thus release my essence to yours
And feel the universe as calm as a million edacious births
It is your kindness that sustains me, your sweet love
Shines long after the night has died of its lone rose
Long after the moon has surrendered its crown to the orb of the day
Your brightness shall remain with me
Your embers will kindle the lavender drape of the sky
Heaven to be unchained upon that hour forevermore
The dream of paradise upon that moment will cease to be
For thereon it shall be shared within our two hearts

Unless the drawing scapes of fate sunder unknown
Tearing our hold apart, rending fortune, leaving hope unsung
Resigning the brakes of time as immortally dead
Still against this waged and forlorn scene
I turn to you, your light, your love—and am eternally contented.

Oh Rosaline

Oh Rosaline, my love
How the whole world shines in darkest envy
The moon with its jealous glow, the sun with its brightness
The sea with its blue dream, the player with his part
Romance itself dies untouched upon the brain
When the loveliness of you must be conceived
When the grace of your beauty is conjured up
Within the sunken depth of the mortal heart
It swears to never flee, love is undying and restless
When the art of your eye, is seen
Oh queen of tenderness, oh goddess, oh lady divine
How the sunshine blackens and the evening falls
When your brilliance breaks through the thickest clouds
Your beams guide the way of my forgotten soul
Oh Rosaline, Oh Rosaline
When in the centre of your blue windows I stare
Pain is forgotten, time is the lost entity
By which the seasons fade, youth has no savage end
The harvest of this prime earth, its reaping pace
With the clock turns back, hope is regaled with your voice
For you are as ever, ever lovely
That a single glimpse of you is the curative to madness
Espied, the opium of desire, warmth's remedy
And all these starless sleeps that echo through the night
Are void of a substance, the wide universe lacks
The untamed flow of love that burns in you
The fire of paradise that lives and dwells forever
Is contained within the chamber of your gentlest hold
Oh how splendid thy soft comeliness is!
I shall leave to tomorrow, keeping nothing but your fame

Nothing than your true name that is truer than truth
Oh Rosaline, the state of nature is no more
As your impression fills, no vision but one remains
Save thy lone charm and light that to humankind are left
As the immortal embers to all that this eternal life can ever be.

Oh Grief

Oh grief, oh grief, oh loss again
Cries cannot bring back what is beyond grief
But darling as I long you and consider your beauty supreme
It far surpasses the delicate sadness of the night
Or the tincture of the star whose shine is jealousy
My burning heart rests before the altar of worship
Ready and at will to leap against the pure
And by expiring prove as the sacrifice to your love
By self-treachery to demonstrate the virtues of grace
That casualty of hope that all free men does betray
And sets them in thrones of chains all over again
My gentlest angel, I hold conference with the holy sky
Whose continent abode gave birth to the swank richness
With which your fair countenance now teems
Only a god could see such sweet piety
A loveliness whose features are like lullabies
Of the most nursing and soft favoured kind
To the nursing ears of affection's mind
What winsome joy, what sprightly felicity
What hours of love's history and treason
Within the sessions of stellar dreams
I hold belief in the rebellion of destiny
I cast away fortune's veil and let the riots begin
Hearts are but traitors if they enjoin the siege
Souls are but cowards if they implore heaven for deliverance
Nay, I am bolder yet; I will chase fortune's whips away
And rest below the shade of your bright and visionary face
Finding the eternal comfort when all the world is naught but dismay.

Oh Fair Pilgrim of Youth

Oh fair pilgrim of youth
These sheaves of autumn all gently stand
Like grains of gold for your beauty to garner
Your loveliness to gather the bounty of life's richness
Oh how supreme, the harvest of sadness draws
And unloads its burden of dismay into our hands
Doles the bitterness, the staggered cry into our muted souls
It then leaves; the vision fades far into the yonder brink
Where the horizon is black and grief teems abound
The spirit with woe is laden, the emptiness is too steep
Your love flees faster than what these swollen eyes can comprehend
So I resign to the mortal part of my nature's birth
For the dust to consume in hunger, for the stars to sport within play
The music thrums low, solitude gains with the blessed rose
Comfort is lost; all tears of happiness are shed into the ground
The petals of the marigold lapse with the dewy summer pond
Truth awakens from deepest dream; sleep overtakes its lucid hold
again
And all that remains staunch against the faithful night
Is the hope of our shared passion's survival
Of our endeared love to forever endure the bleak wilderness
Of time and pain, the sky's harmony long desires discord
And so the feelings perish, gone is the verve of the once pulsed vein
The fiery blood of romance dies, a holy power takes its place
That drives all of humankind into the perfection of immortal silence
Oh that quiet ease I behold, yet am most fearful of it
For when will the desperation of such awkward yearnings end?
Oh never indeed will that majestic sun relent
To release the sandy rays of its excellence upon the earth
Madness besets the field, love is persuasion

Or some unknown sophistry that flourishes through ancient minds
Oh woe to fame, scorned is that soft artistry
Its kind fairness is but a pleasant ruse to the insubstantial heart
The climes of the constellations open wide once more
Under its brilliant sheen, we are unsheltered, ever born again
There rises the sigh of the tryst of love's glory
Its pale creation leaves a plaintive hue and musk censored everywhere
To settle upon the shores of unkempt tides, of vast indifference
Of pride, of praise, of reason devoid, of pagan thoughts
Of white palmistry, of crypts eternal in their end
Of bewilderment, of the lissom complexion of the silver eve
As so the ditties decline, the blush exhausts, the perfection of silence wanes
The repose, the weakness, the betrayed equanimity
The kindled coves, the star lit shine, they combine as one
The ardent stride, the bond of innocence dissolves
As I press my hand upon the ground under which you rest
Denying the bruising days of their steadfast misery
How serenely this whole scene of life is composed—though it must fade
The temple of heaven uplifts, a sweet carol from its court is heard
Crying nothing but "oh love, oh love, oh beloved true"
"Many worlds may die, it is their due"
"But as I dream and live, I think of one beauty, it alone is you"
And as I drown with this fever into the vault,
Thereafter before your magic scene I die most peacefully.

My Sweetest Hope

My sweetest hope
These petty griefs remain unsung
But as there is still sorrow left in the world
You are the cause of it
Your eyes, your soul, your breath
It drives me away further and further out
Until the dawn and dusk and civility
All rise up together, our leaps are one
Our fountains, our liberty—all that is yours and mine
We are free to savour up youth
And dream to the antique streams of yesterday
Oh forever to revere upon the fonder morrow
And never think back to what cannot be
What must progress with time, we are the foes to age
The haters of what must change, truth is a betrayer
Reality is the light least often seen, it is unmissed
Let us embrace and not look back
Forever upon these laced wings of romance to fly.

My Quiet Love

My quiet love
These hours pass in a blink
And we have gleaned the better moments of them
The brighter harvest of the sun
Lies before our feet, the world is kind
To us its sowers of sweet love
Of happiness and fair angel shades
Of the wide grandeur of this life
It's coloured view, its endless mountains
All the tomorrows that stand out
As we stand out with them as well
And do not think back to tomorrow
Its weaving drift, its pawn, its oracle
We shall look back to nothing but the ministered pain
To our sincere hand shared idly again
The peerless dawn, the news of millions
Shall not move us a bit, my empress
The dross fills, our rosy hearts thrive upon the night
As in silence the infamy blows
And we are left free in each other's hand forever.

My Truest Hope

My truest hope
My love, my darling
My sweetest heart of a million nights
Here, my soul rests
And it shall forever remain for you
For you who is the dearest creature born for me
Ever to be seen, my love
Oh yes my angel, my every wish is you
My every dream upon the hour
Upon the burning mind of yearning
Of loveliness, dare I say yours alone
Your fairness, oh my queen, daughter and bride to beauty
Faithful pilgrim, child of my worship
Clever saint, priestess of my joy
Oh beautiful, beautiful maiden
How I look on you and go mad
Have I yet mentioned that you are the prettiest woman ever beheld?
Ever perceived, ever to be coveted by mortal eyes
By my hands to be touched—oh I melt away!
No I won't say that, I am already perished, lapsed
Expired my love, I live no more
Dead, dead as the dark word of death implies
But there can be no darkness as there is the vision of your light
How can I live more, how can I not die
When you are seen upon the wide expanse
Of happy, happy living and the afterlife
Of teeming daylight and never setting suns
Oh glorious girl, that you are supreme
That you are kind, gentle and soft to the highest degree
To the utmost fashion, you embody every kind of goodness

Of some divinity, you are above the cloudless sky
Heaven itself you are, the warmest paradise
And as I hold on to your tender hand
My love, youth and time and I can never fade
Forever, oh yet to be forever my love
The stars and moon to crown above our heads
And I as the happiest man to die around your loveliness!

My Soul's Nectar

My soul's nectar
Let me tell you one simple thing
It is that I love you and always shall
As long as the earth remains the earth and the sky the sky
As long as the seas do crash with water and the ground with dust
I shall hold you endeared as a sweet beloved
Whose memory shall not perish with the curfew of the night
Nor will that face fade with the observance of others
Oh indeed your appearance shall forever own the sky
That soft complexion shall rule over the world
Like a million candles cast like stars in the heavens above
All the abodes of grace live by sake of your virtue
That virtue being strong, these beauteous dwellings can never die
Our hearts do share in them and wildly thrive
Like the portrait of sunset set against the mantle of eve
Our dreams shall survive the cloudless scapes of fate
Past those climes of fortune we shall fly to rule as kings
Upon the throne of togetherness nothing shall separate
This internal hold of paradise we feel through our eyes
Like loadstars I look up to your bright spheres
And feel satisfied with the full promise they afford
Of tomorrow, of glory, of warm eternity
Of all that is precious before the nimble sands of time
Of that unfailing patience that is the heir of the soul
Which as thus shall never let love drive the heart to madness
The gold complexion of youth leaps headstrong and fast
And strikes against these agile plains of happiness
Holding steadfast to its heat, nay it will never let go
Of all the soft treasures that romance provides
So as the worlds of this poet remain dignified

I shall retain you as dear, surrendering my liberty
Whispering soft phrases of love until our souls expire forever free.

My Ever Sweetest Rose

My ever-sweetest rose
How the day is reborn and life revived
When upon your eyes a memory is seen
A crown, a wish, a fond desire
And the soul is made peaceful again
When upon the childhood tears your cry is heard
A vision burns with such intensity
That the history of suffering is forgot
The mortal lot of pain is absolved
When fears, hopes and dreams are incident
You emerge from the dreams of all three
To make this beautiful life worth living for
Your face, your soul, the choir of your voice
Your steady pulse, that unbruised blush
Makes this globe of emptiness less faint
The throne of your heart, the temple of your being
Restores amity upon the unknown realm
Your warmth enshrines all that goodness is
So then my lonely spirit dissolves unto its rest
Never to wake to the sunshine of the unlived day
Unless your sight prevails the kingdom of the dawn
And all the stars gather under the shield of happiness
Oh until that marvellous day I will sleep
Until the embers of your love are made true
And I have no reason to ever perish, my love.

My Hope

My hope
The days of life are but a short lease
A play that must perish, all must meet ruin and decay
Save the anthem of your heart, it is everlasting
It is unconquered, unflawed, an unbridled art
That thrives against the darker manner of the world
My soul resides there, strength can never leave
Desire can never flee, longing can never die
Nor can a year be chained to the vault of fate
To the unlit chamber, never to be uplift again
But when the fiery gaze of your face turns up
The pale sky reddens, the violet evening fades
The sunshine declines only to be replaced by your complexion
The pride of morning sits and softly waits for your throne
For your time to ring through the valleys and the glades
The birds and the meadows, the mountains and the stars
The streams and brooks and silent riverbeds
Silently drift all to hear the story of your love
The nightingale upon its leafy cress
The lark upon its high-pitched dome and sphere
The rose upon its gravid ground, the fertile rocks along the craggy shore
Blend the song of admiration in soft tranquillity
In sole embrace of a dream sweet in awesome unity
In the lone worship of you, the hours sweetly chase away the tears
Times indifference falls upon the unnumbered tomb
As nature mends her work with a shade of majesty
Oh fair nature, how she is a queen of perfection

To have ever made a goddess, a beauty, a vision a truth
An angel like you that I love so dear.

My Truth

My truth, my joy, my forever love
The days will be long unforgiven
The hours and years will go unredeemed
And all of life will seem as perished
If your sweet love is not fair persevered
If your soft eyes, your hold, your perfection
Are not adored with vast and great reverence
The sky will decay, time itself will fade
Dreams and tomorrows will be no more
If your greatness is not brightly recognized
If your heart, your soul are not given full tribute to
The golden sphere of the moon will retreat to death
The stars will resign, the scarlet sun will dissipate
The shroud of darkness, the silence of loneliness
Will crowd below the blue immortal sky
The scopes will dim, the horizons will forever set
If your complexion is left against the ruins of the unseen
Nay, your love is immense, for soft are the whispers of the unknown
Blackened in the tide that threatens the world's turning
The earth traces a romance, you are its light
An ember of whiteness twinkles over the dusk
And is the hawthorn rose wakes from the gentle eve
All the creatures of living look to your grace
And exalt the perfect heaven from which you were borne
Oh my loved, so I will cry a song with them
Until my voice returns to calm and with my final call
We are restored unto our long waited vault of togetherness
My love, I shall be as blind until that brilliance comes
And we are cast free upon the vision of our lone embrace of eternity.

My Gentlest Love

My gentlest love
The azure skies are clear, the streams are ever fragrant
The meads are youthful, coloured, their dew is primed
With the sweetness of violets and dulcet fields of calm
The breeze is soft, the air most melodious
Indeed the whole world is perfectly serene
On account of you, the harshest pain is no more
The heart is quelled of its weeping cries
The woe, the sob, the sadness and the tears
All fade away; the picture of your beauty takes their place
The fairness of your eyes supplants all of restless solitude
The portrait of romance depicts one scene alone
And that is where you and I are together kept
That is where our wide store of love flies to an unseen height
Which none can touch, but surely dream of
The shores roam wild; let us cast ourselves to hope's refuge
And see where this intrepid stride of life will lead
To where the lonely pulse of this mind will wander to
Oh what majesty, your glory is like the eternal sun
Whose reign of brightness never leaves far from the mortal throne
So let us walk upon the plains and lawns of tender happiness
And behold what becomes of this desirous parle
Oh take my lips away—they are yours
The scented notes of the nightingale as well belong to you
The throat of paradise, the leas, the embers of lightest beatitude
Like golden rays of sand fall before our uncrowned feet
Tracing your loveliness with this deepest longing that I bear for you
So tenderly, oh these affections shall be preserved within my soul
Like an everlasting life that fails to recede away
Denies the rearward ebb the sequent flow of age

That all are fated to, each man borne must soon perish within his day
But this feeling that we share shall never decay, you and I to live by it
Else to swoon forever if it flees to dark hated death
Oh my love, yet upon the vision of my eyes the passion burns—
We are enjoined as one
Still, the triumph and the conquering plays on,
The united destiny remains as forever ours.

My Fairest Angel

My fairest angel
These skies serve as a hidden tryst
To which we can fly to and warmly share our love
That we can brightly thrust our hearts against
And think nothing on the pain of yesteryear
The coves of light, the clouds, the bluest wilderness
Gives its seclusion to the leisure of our souls
For us to play like a soft instrument of joy
And with our hands declare passion as the only bondage
Which we must oblige; our open desires to obey
The vision of passion that from the gentle heaven falls
Oh but the charms of darkness can never fall completely
For under its violet bruise, two lonely stars shine
Their brilliance collides, they are the prophet marks
That hold together the unknown signs and symbols of destiny
The earnest rays of the morning flood the plain
Our names are born by their gathering, spread within the air
Of eternal innocence and the untouched gold of youth
Oh what glory, my world is empty without you
With an undying longing, I reach for your grace
But fall short of the triumph to call mine own
The lark then holds the lute; I lend to it my cries
And sing the song of love's perfection that never was
Oh blemished is the wound, my voice with my pulse decays
Perhaps in another day, another year, another time it can be
In between the longest sorrow it shall drift away
As my slow breath resigns far, never to wake again
This shallow slumber of life's harsh ingratitude
That mocks me no more with the addled scenes that passion portrays
Until the shore of sadness takes me into its palm

And grants me with reserve, changes me with bravery's crime
Until the cocks of the hour all fall from their branch of peace
And nothing remains but the most unholy solitude
Until the days of yore give solace to the young and foolish minded
Robbing remembrance of its redolence and wide disdain
My spirit flies, I find relief where the shade of nothingness blends
Alongside the fountain and the vault of unkempt dreams
There you are beautiful, there you are mine
There this hope of love cannot make leave
Oh princess, oh divine angel of the court, I wait by heaven's immortal door
There we shall embrace, there our hearts can sing
My all, there we shall be free forevermore.

My Tenderest Joy

My tenderest joy
My sweet, my dear, my love, my all
The myrtle wraith of the sky is departed; its defeat hides in the dark
The amber rose restores its hardy strength again
The slumber expires of old; the warm heart fills in the wounds
And leaves no pain to be seen upon the pleasured eye of esteem
No tear, no bruise, no hated elegy
No hurting promise to linger on and on and on
The heaven spreads out against the wide universe of stars
The saffron flowers regain their quiet gentleness beneath the violet
scape
Oh what a blue abyss, what a tempered sigh, what a glowing kiss
Extends from your soft reach of amourility
Emanates from your touch, your hands, your innocence
Your smile of eternity, it survives relished and unbound
The grains of the field, the turning of the seasons
Speak of one love—winter is not winter
Nor are the sodden days of spring true spring
Heated summer reveals not its bank of wondrous prime
Callous autumn is unkind to the late budded harvest
But as your beauty thrives, the blossoms shall endure the extremes
From year to year, youth to age then youth again
You are holy in this way, a righteous angel in full composure
Whose divine trace shall never fade from this state of pious being
The compass draws to show the sun's glorious face of East
But as your comeliness burns bright, such arts are ornaments
They are wantonness, much abused and left unused by me
Left forlorn amid time's endless sea of undying night
Woe to such instruments of garish pride, the excellence dims
As what good are charts and signs and symbols of romance

When you are replete, most fair and ever graceful before me
For I see you, I sense you, my soul longs for you
And has no need for such shows to lead it to its prize
The prize is you alone
Thus it will strive with this last breath of remaining strength
To reach you, to keep you in these arms
To have you for this life that remains
Else before the happy paradise of your defied love forever die.

My Dream

My dream, my love, oh sweetest darling
The summer fountain shines its youth for you
The rose born upon the field of heaven blossoms wide
Residing in peace knowing that your majesty reigns above all
That your star is brightest upon this blazing scape
But my heart melts, it releases the tenderest sigh
A warm happy cry as you are near yet far
As you are everything, you are near
As not held in my arms, you are at infinity's length
Before the altar of hope I fall ever bruised
Praying that your greatness will be forever preserved
Just as they are kept within my eyes, the world shall prize them too
Shall cherish and retain this simple truth
That you are divine love incarnate, and nothing can transcend
The wondrous glory manifest in you, embodied in your nature
The gentleness, the temperance of your pristine calm
Compares with nothing else, is equal to nothing on this ancient earth
For that reason, without a word of reason I desire you the most
Oh I covet what from you teems, I long your brilliance
Nay that summer breeze of midnight would rather to die
Than to compare with the airy light borne above your wings
To such a luminous show, material wealth is a traitor
The toil and trade of life declines into an unresolved fame
My spirit flees, oh run away with it, let us labour
To take the being of love and possess it as our long lived god of amity
Capture it with your head, throw it before your feet
And I shall worship the ground on which you and I together stand
Everlastingly; can you not understand I am your servitor?
A thrall unto a kingdom where beauty rules alone
And you are its sister queen; May I call you the daughter of love?

That I shall and many more benisons shall follow for amourility's sake
Many more titles of praise, my shadow shall resign behind your nimble vibrancy
Contemplating on this most merciless power or love, its joyful countenance
I yield to it, I am a beggar, thus maiden I surrender full, I confess all weakness
Oh beloved I have no strength to carry on against the force of fate
Therefore I submit, unprotected, take me to your wing
And let us fly to where romance's vision below the sky-lit orb is seen
There our souls shall embrace under the day's white sheen
To recline back, return to that repose, soon we shall be free
Unified under the halo of one sacred state, our love enshrined
The sun and moon shall then crown us; the stars will be as our brotherhood of friends
Immortally, eternally until our last breath expires
And with a final touch we together perish from this world, my love.

My Sweetest Love

My sweetest love
Count me out of the multitude, I am not of them
I have eyes for only you and no one else
I inhere a heart, a soul, an inner being
But all of them are alive on account of you
By your virtue that gives me strongest pride
A burning substance, an existence all unkind
It dwells within me and loudly calls out your name
An angel from within my flesh reaches out to you
A song from within my depth serenades about
To memorialise my dear, to recall the fragrance
That your rosy skin, your blush, your grace do emanate
Your brow, your arms, your tender smile
Your lightest innocence, your true happiness
Enkindle my world for an unnumbered age
Your glow, your shine, your excellence
Pawns my hope of its dark despair and longing
Pondered misery is impeached, banished are the cries of sorrow
The truth is unspoken, our faith is speechless heard
A sacredness shall run between us
Your star will lead to where a thousand lovely gazes are spread
That is where my spirit with joy shall fall dead
Under the evening banner where your brilliance is the queen
And the clouds glitter with a gentle sheen of tears
Oh the moon to fall away and no one to believe
These hours that we have, my all—this love, this hold that can never disappear
Never, never as this song of love is forever
And our bones among the flowers and the ruins are together.

My Darling

My darling, my truest dear
What is there in tomorrow to look on? Naught!
Thus have trust in me; we shall be released to our sacred hold
To love each other, to have one another unconstrained
Unbound, embraced, unto time's eternity
Hope shall endear us, youth shall keep us alive
Devotion will be the force unseen by all
Save by you and I, the plains of life await us
The temples of joy, the smiles of felicity
The reverence, the fondness, the bliss, the purity
Oh your eyes, they are as holy mirth themselves
So then let us flee to where the sad tears cannot be felt
Let us fly to the scenes of heaven where we belong
The morn is lit for us, the evening shines
With a brilliance that is unspoken, untouched
With a remembrance that keeps us in everlasting promise
Of free warmth, fair spirit and truth's own levity
So look unto those horizons, our wings await
To carry the tale of our love forever after on
Forever is false, as unto that orchard of immortality they are poised
Where paradise is graced from your sight of kindness
Oh what glory from you teems my dear
Desert sands may feel loneliness
The empty wind is left to its destiny forlorn
The sun, the moon, they are both forsaken in their right
In turn the sea feels too departed from the earth
But you and I being as near
There is a power shared between us, a unique majesty
That cannot be forebode in this wide chronicle of life
So then let us be the master of this new born writ

And conquer once again this kingdom that is ours
Oh what do dreams matter, dear angel, I thirst for you now
And wait amid the pangs of death patient for you to come
To take to my side, to forever lie in gentleness
To taste love once more, to be as one.

My Dear

My dear
Can I say I love you even more?
That you mean more to one than what I can explain
More precious than the sun and its saffron rays
More glorious than the moon upon a peaceful night
Can I dare claim that a rose is not as lovely?
Nor is the stream gentle as your touch, your skin
Or the wing of the swan as soft as yours
Oh darling how you are my everything
How I cry thinking upon a moment that you might not be mine
Oh I choose to forget that such an hour can ever pass
For in you I find my gold, how can I want more?
In you I find paradise, the pleasure of sweet Eden herself
So then what can the bliss of greed afford?
When the sensation of all that is divine is with my arms
Kept and shielded forever, guarded from the harm that tomorrow brings
No, tomorrow shall not speak of anything unkind
For as your voice lives, all shall sway in harmony
Never, never dreaming of what envious time may take away
My angel, as your affection dwells within my soul
This deeper heart of truth shall not resign its life
And you are that truth, so crown me with your fairness
Call me your own; let us sit upon one kindred throne
United, governed by the star that to love's destiny leads
Let us gaze, let us peer, let us wander beneath that sky
Let us reside over what fortune lends provisionally to hope
Our flesh shall be as one, our desire as a single substance
As we are then set free to the yearning of fate untouched by mortal light

Unborn, undone, unseen to all eyes save these
And as these eyes survive, they reach out to you and passion's brightest wing
And call you the loveliest upon this brain conceived
As we together fly to our open scene of heaven—
That never, never can fall to black, my love

My Dearest Angel

My dearest angel
There are times when life itself appears as lost
And there is absent any reason to continue on
To battle against this wild and senseless scene of mortality
When the many shades of life have all but frayed
I look to you, I look up to you, I admire your grace
And all is brightly lit again, the void escapes
My soul is rekindled deep with an amorous flame
That neither the wind of season nor time can extinguish
Nay, the fire shall always burn, making you the fairest seen
Making your glory the imbued desire of my aspiration
Of what a yearning can ever want to achieve
Your beauty prospers in what dreams need the most
Then hearken these pleadings my love, I will lead us aright
Unto the kingdom where our songs and voices shall be heard alone
Against the emptiness of the night, our heart shall beat as one
Our eyes shall stare out with a single gaze
Our mind shall pulse with the same intense feeling
No, the wonder of innocence shall not be forsaken
Greatness will be found within your brilliant light
Love will be writ like a sad tale upon the stone of youth revived
The stylus shall break, the ink flows forward no more
The cries refuse to show themselves upon the eternal page
Of this life, hereafter and of all living breath
Heaven awaits a song—here, I hold it out unto the stars
Until all the shining spheres darken from the sky
And we are united as one under its sacred throne
Under its precious crown, we are held to its everlasting touch

Never to awake again until death comes
To take us to its realm and we are forever free.

My Beloved

My beloved, my truth, my dear, my all
Why care about tomorrow?
Why consider what with the moon will rise again?
Am I not like a million futures for you?
Am I not like a father who guards over his babe?
For life is only precious by your sake
Thus with all the strength I have it will strive to persevere
The peace and harmony with which our souls are alive
Under its glorious reign, oh how I am enslaved to that countenance
Under the soft beam, its glow, its warm majesty
All of paradise is ours and shall be for immortal time
A remembrance to this fond hope that we shall always share
Let the grapes ripen upon the tender vine
Let the yellow sun pour out its mellow blush
We shall be the king and queen of the lone untold destiny
That waits silently aside the hawthorn moon
Below the sky where the fairest star stands before me now
Calling out our names in the gentlest grace
Come my love, be shy no more, retreat out from your shade
Resign unto this scene of long-lived fame and happiness
Of mortal bliss and earth and sweet desire
Let us heed its starry cry and be burned away with it
Carried far away in its cradled wind of lovely rays
Oh in such a state all wishes will be liberated
So let us slowly flee to where the kingdom meets the shore
I to show my face and you to reveal your brightness
I to vow my faith, you my dearest, to listen and to hold
This hand and grasp this lip that shall never leave you, never, never to betray
Shall never surrender until all the world grows dark

And we are as a single dream upon the endless clouds of the undying night
Oh everlasting, my love, I will await you then
Seeking no more of life, my heart expires inside your own
My breath lapses without a tear, until tomorrow forever comes to us, my all.

My Truth

My truth, my dear, my love
After all the world has withered and frayed
I will still have you and time cannot crumble
Nor with its bitter grasp take away
The tear of yesterday, the light of tomorrow
It shall burn in you and me for all of forever
The coldness of winter, the drier spell of summer felt
Cannot threaten us into the darker shade of its fall
No, it will have you and your passionate touch
Your gracious hold, your warmth of remembrance
The flowers of your eyes, the lucid stream of your soul
Keeps me alive as forever is forever
As eternity is not a dream resigned in sleep
I retain the peril of this soft tryst
That wildly shines the eastern light in envy of you
In gesture of your unflawed perfection
How sweet is that ray which your visage leads
That brow, your hands of gentleness
Are so divine, void of life's fierce finality
It is beauty to the mind whose imagination flies
And never sees the ground again, your love is unrivalled
Oh angel, your fairness exceeds that which the stars engild
That which the sky can ever ponder on in true belief
All these days pass on; youth is a mockery to hope
Yet when your face is seen, heaven again is white
And the depthless heart is not without its path
So then let me turn away this blush from yours
Let my veins reverse their pulse in time
Until the clock is reborn and we are the babes and kings
Of a wide new paradise unseen

Oh darling, your words are the carol of its infinite night
And as the dulcet sway of the hour rhymes back and forth
I will look to you and the warm kindness of your arms
And think nothing of this cruel world that must darken upon its own defeat.

My Truly Beloved

My truly beloved
Within the greater of this heart's depth
You are kept ever sacred and revered
Your visage, your golden rays of youth
Will forever remain impressed upon my mind
Upon my feeling pulse, my tormented soul
You will stay lighted through all bitterness
Through the many horizons of tomorrow's hope
Of desire, of fame, of unlived destiny
Of all that burns alive within your eyes, my love
Within your truth, your trust, your gloried strength
Pain conquers all but the weak
Who sit on life's throne, letting the world to bruise them
Yet holding power by the inward warmth that you provide
It feeds the whole spirit, the spirit cannot die
When with the tender crown of you it is coronated
Poor father time, his arms are enfeebled
Your fairness is more nimble than ageless age
Your beauty is more supreme, your barest thought is more divine
The rose has less colour, the moon less brightness
The night endures in envy of weaker shades
The show of promise, the glow of remembrance
The mould of lean perfection itself does fade
When compared to your soft and gentle sweetness
Your name, your praise, your infamy
Your majesty that shines above everything
My love, I stare at you and am gratified
Your complexion nourishes all that is conceived as good
The pen surrenders, the seasons do not move on
The treason of the mind prevails; disbelief never leaves

Still along the tepidness of it all
I remember you and nothing else
And let the world escape, I flee with you my love.

My Prized Angel

My prized angel
Foreshame that these hours must be lost
And I denied the love of fate's favoured days
Yet these moments are not unhappy
As I look to you, as I worship your brightness
The whole world seems to gain a new shine
So I will relish life for the merits it bears
For all of its virtues and strengths, you are its lone treasure
The guiding light that glows in the heavens above
Does so in parallel of your warm ethereal face
Your delicate gestures, your sweet and supple gentleness
I hold it in esteem high above all the soul's kind attributes
Which blindly wander through the darkness of the night
Not knowing how to breathe or live or die
After your supreme grace is encountered by the inward sight
Which pristinely relates the sweet glory that the eyes perceive
What unequalled majesty, my twain heart roams restively
When the mind sends impulse of your darling dream
And lulls the spirit to long nothing but death
For in death is found perfection, thus in perfection we unite
With affection we stride against the fields of mortality
And with wings take flight to where the yonder bliss is set free
Free oh ever free to roam and wrestle against the thorns of time
Which nettle hope when hope is most aspiring
Which ring the scent of defeat over the freshly budded rose
Pressing shade over great conquests when ambition burns most fierce
Enforcing the scapes of tragedy when love deserves it not
When innocence is too young to understand fate's cruelty
When the heart is just too pure for the pangs of life's injustice
Thus the hand of the star fails to lift, impeached is destiny

In treason we are born, in treason we must flee
I take to your beautiful sight; it moves me far from this earth
Swiftly I fly, fly, fly—the wings are torn asunder!
Oh heaven, oh fate, oh life
I turn to you once more and die, die, die, die.

My Loving Bride

My loving bride
These limber aspect of the night
Are but the pale and wintered shades of tomorrow
Whose complexion is void, the lustre gone
No gleam, no shine, no happiness
No sentiment of joy is left to light up the world
To drive away the mad pulses of yearning misery
Of the agony that accompanies the honest heart
Of the pill that abrades the mind's bitterness
And drugs the rest of hope's disdain away
Oh time is a field, its wounds accost the soul
The wars of fortune's great accidents
Abolish the effort that man believes he can thrive with
The palliative of dream is false, abortive, unkind
Unshielded from the earth's carnal wreckage of decay
The falcon crests its scope upon the highest spire
And peers out from the zenith of drama
To see what crafty play is made of mortals flesh
The prey of worms that none can escape
The stylus and the hand that wields it, yields to death
Fortune silences all worlds, all
Triumph accedes to the victory of life's dismay
The tears and cries look through the ambit of nothingness
Adamant, abase, absconded
Regrets bail the former sweetness away
The warmth is abjured; gentleness is persuaded into bleak depths
Solitude regains and captures the heart's movement
Piercing the accords of the breast with hate
Rupturing the chords of solemn sanity
Slaying the commission of the endured will sans sympathy

The magic then destroys the harmony of yore
The secret stream of desire quenches the sands
The dear thoughts lapse into holds of emptiness
The world perishes, my essence flies to where your love is forever free
There our eyes to taste the scene of beauty and long eternity.

My Dear Child

My sweet, dear child and beloved
Let these hours pass, the brighter array of majesty
Stands at the foothold of tomorrow
When with true hope and gentlest ardour
We can redeem the future pleasures of our heart
None can rescind them, none can deny
This shine of bliss that grants halos to our heads
And makes the rank of passion something supreme
I wait upon the infinity of joy
That with your smile is given over and over
Surrendered in such soft sympathy
In such music and melodious rhyme
That the mind is sustained by the call of words
By the gift of speech that from your boundary flies
Oh perchance the jade of the moon does mock me
And beauty is no truer than it is to spurn
The patron of love whose tenure is distress
The mind of romance whose thoughts bear fruits of treachery
As belief is not contrived, so will thoughts not suffice?
To betray love with the weapons of dismay
To wrestle or hoist defeat with patient ire
No, the mist must fade; the oracle of desire is undying
The conclave of emotion streams out unto the brighter world
And takes your hand for its need of deliverance
The banner of perfection then sways to and fro
The palliative is your kiss; your soul is the remedy
Of this grieving winced from soft savage eyes
That declare your beauty the illuminate power
Which lends dignified light to the nepenthe of youth
A soft lamp fastened to the world's contempt

That pacifies the ills and makes life's winter bearable
Indeed the soul is found to the highest art of yours
And its threads strike the inner cords of me
I shall remain your admiring liege
Forever these affections to fill out the argent sky
And leave no token but silence of the unspoken word
As the lone tragedy of love unuttered—unfaithful, untrue to you, my all.

My Dear Angel

My dear angel
The world is torn asunder, it is not pure
That which rebukes your pulchritude
Is fated to die and scorn, most unworthy of fairness
Such gentleness, such kindness, hope is endearing of grace
If it must rely upon that dream of tomorrow
How can tomorrow exist when you are here now?
When you set all of life to flourish and teem
With a glory rare as it is bright
With a pleasing glow as well formed and delicate
That it sets the moon into a raging fire
Which anger itself can never recover from
How sad, how pitiable this lot of fortune is
Forcing the eyes to look on you while realising
That death entreats and cradles all in its importunate arms
It is the world's agony to be petitioned with such lamented hate
To be saluted with such blind and malicious deliverance
As to know the garden of your sweetness must also one day fade
There is no salve for such mental aches, so they are endured
Like a pandemonium without joy or colour or shade
Without all comforts of excellent art
That makes bold valour out of the hardest pains
How radiant, how shapely, how wondrous, how fine
We are born to act without the decorum of pride
As then the shine of loveliness leads me to the verge
Of the unbecoming world and the devoured existence
Of desires crushed and healed and left to cheerless demise
Of affections bled and commanded to the dark office of night
Of storms heaved and weathered and mutely decayed
Of desire unconquerable and never, never free

Thus the sun dissolves the chains of redemption
And thus the heart is left to grieve the unwaking soul
The muse consents with the swift powers of time
As then all is driven into the pitch of madness
Save your blush and form and love's unfleeting pulse of insanity.

My Gentlest Creature

My gentlest creature, my purest all
One embrace of your vision and I melt away
Far to where the amber clouds of tomorrow are not seen
Nor does the page retain the jet composure of this scribed ink
By which the quill of destiny is styled, so let it rage!
There is one bright ocean, one fair and darling sea
That holds open casts to tomorrow and the unknown
Let us flee to it, our peace shall be found there
Our unity shall endure anything made of mortal art
The cherubs are piqued, they hold up their wing with a tinge of strife
With the soft colour and blush of unbroken tranquillity
The streams of want flow fondly; the brink of amourility is not tested yet
Youth is not drunk; hope is not drowned nor desired poisoned
Through the spears of heaven are poised to thrust East of Eden
To plunge it deep within my heart, to send it into disjoined parts
To conquer the affection that with your warmth was staid
With your loveliness was burdened and so it my chamber ached
Until the inbred drugs of pain did quell then to rest
Only to revive the pulse again and rupture the swelling vein apart
Which burn and bleed at the sight of your purest touch
Which shed anguished tears of misery at the very splendid thought
That your blissful radiance can be restored into my arms again
Forever true, at least that is how I shall dream the score of fortune
Until the sunset against the white valleys decays
And under the halo of your light we are born free and whole and eternal
A slave to remembrances lost and past, no longer
A thrall to the fleeting symbols of the night—no more

Oh free my love, we fly together
So ever brave, so ever high, kept so ever near and free.

My Purest Angel

My purest angel
There you lie, along the meads
As all of gentleness like a paradise surrounds
The streams carry far my fondest thoughts
To the fountain that with lithe waters teems
There the pinions of tomorrow's hope are drugged away
There sweet remembrance serves as a light
To the fair world that is brightened by you alone
The leas, the ponds, the rivers and the bays
They all recline like an easeful instrument
Against the continent of needs and dewy springs
Of lands flourished with wet April's prime
What joy, what madness, what calm ecstasy
What wild repose, what motives to escape this lease of breath
To take high flight, to make the heavens as the lovely home
As the righteous abode where your lone beauty can dwell
As for I, I live in sadness, in tales of piled up sorrow and despondency
In widest scopes of thievish woe and uncertainty
In greatest disbelief of fate's thousand accidents
That can change the scape of mountains and the rule of kings
But nonetheless have resigned me to a forlorn fate
A fancy without shape, a yearning, a wildest dreaming
That leads to nowhere but protested grief, a most rueful shame
Against the ceremony of those cruel, inauspicious stars
That rebel against the levity of life and hold mutual alliance
To shrewdly rob happiness from these guiltless eyes
Of unbanished youth and want and freest touch
Oh but the malice of fortune never hearkens to the mortal pulse
As each thing, each human sentiment, once apprehended decays from the mind

So it is with love, so to is it with everything
With all else in the show of being that retains a most ephemeral fame
That fame must perish, life's vacancy replaces
This wide and unknown world whose charm alas fades
Yet amidst the inks and shades of intellect
I see one supreme vision, it redeems me
One pearl, one prophet, one diadem of love's discourse
All its words, the pleasures of this preached earth exceeds
Brighter than the glow of the Phoenix flames in its own progeny
That is how my heart feels for you, the restraints die
As with a final calling I cry out your precious name
And there before the cloudy rays of the moon and sun
I fall, I lapse, I expire unto your darling soul, the dust takes me
In worship, in adoration of all that your glory embraces
As your warmth, your sight, your scene all hover above me like a goddess shine
Oh my all, I die as your most faithful servant, your forever thrall
Thereafter the favoured orbs of the sky blaze on no more
The darkness claims us, upon that infinite night I am eternally yours, my love.

My Solace

My solace,
I bear no arms, no shield, I wield no defence
Against these crazed wars of affection that rage internal
That stir inside and wage me against the siege
Of love's yoked blood of amourility
I dream, I have a right to dream
Therefore I see visions of you and nothing else
I behold you like the night's rare and brightest star
Freed against the skies and endless oceans of nothingness
Even within that scape of void, something holy burns
It is my heart; it longs vastly for your righteous glory
For those eyes of pearls, that azure soul of paradise
How can my spirit otherwise exclaim its pain, its torture, its misery?
Its hardened hurt, its wound, its tinge of wantonness?
You tempt the soul without need to reason—reason being youth incarnate
I shall yearn you until this world lies aged
Long ripe and ready to bid a silent farewell to its matron sun
Yet hold on to me and there can never be that dark escape
No vibrant hours will be fled, no precious time decayed
The sword of hope and levity will be within our hands alone
Moved by our loving arms, no fortitude of strength can breach
This glory of gentleness that we feel for each other, eternal
And shall forever keep alive until this surrounding earth frays
Thereon we shall be freed from the cries, our essence shall fly
To the supreme height of heaven where nothing can reach or confiscate
This firm refuge of love that is forever ours
So caress me in your palms, call me eternally yours
It shall all one day come to be true I swear, my love,

Upon that day it shall pass as truth
The skies will be blue everlastingly; the gleam of the sun will not be dark
The swans will not cry, the ivies will not vex the entwined lovers
The whole of existence will be engulfed by your bright sheen of loveliness
Before that coming scene of fairness, I fall, I bow, I kneel, I resign
And ask to never wake from this harsh and wayward sleep
Unless thereafter I am given the soft and sweetest promise
That you shall never leave, that you shall remain immortally by my side, my all.

My Sweetest Angel

My sweetest angel
Oh bride, you are the dearest thing of life
That has ever fallen into my arms, I adore you
And hold as faith your passion of youth
How bright, how soft, how tender it is
How darling are your eyes, the rhetoric of your breath
Tells me of the thousand perfumed ballads sad and wise
Of a million verse whose every etch is the pulse of the heart
Relating of the scoreless yearnings unfulfilled
Treasured, they are your holy lips, your heart is gilded
Your soul is paradise, your touch is divine
Therefore brace me, release me unto heaven again
I desire to be free, by your gentle warmth to be set at ease
Oh what fondness this platitude is
I look to the stars, I see folded cloudy dreams
Of bliss and hope and forever unheld nights
I turn to you again, all fears are fast dispelled
This mind, my mind, it is condemned with aching want
The want of the palsy hour that your vision exhales
After having perceived it, only darkness entails
A bold and silent madness that none can understand
Save those whose souls are pure with lofty innocence
Oh what winsome injuries, your beauty is like a beacon
That lights the unsung paths of deft consciousness
I resign in seclusion, yet find your picture, your lone gravity
Hung everywhere that eyes have strength to see
Oh what liberty your soft glory is!
It can never vanish though my own composure fades
I will pursue, profitless, I will chase the treason of time
Lo! Till it surrenders mine and malice is served shrewd justice

Until this slow practice of love is denied us no more
And you are no longer taken from these supple hands of mine
Until we are together seated upon that thriving throne of united
  amourility
I will think of you, I will remember you, my all
As the timorous shades of evening fall
And nothing remains but our wraiths entwined together
You and I, under the kingly sun of redemption to be as one
Sans prayer, sans need, sans thoughts of death's eternity
I blow you a kiss as there you sleep, I leave, I leave, I flee away free.

My Loveliest Dear

My loveliest dear,
These flowers of spring pass away, nothing remains at all
This life on earth is temporary and dreamlike
Without defence, it is not here where the truth is to be found
But must be sought further on, beyond the visible and tangible
In that bright and lofty place that lies yonder
In the region of the dead, the gods, and the holy sacrifice
There my heart beats upon the altar for you
Waiting for tomorrow to drown with the heavy sun
For the laden pinions of hope to tear away free
To liberate the mind that dwells in hesitation
Of affection unspoken and forever left unheard
Of desires uncloven from the depth of the twinging tongue
That longs for one true star, one pure sight
To cast upon these scapes of madness and redeem
The azure heaven of dreams that has not sinned at all
Oh beloved, the golden dawn then trickles through the olive tree
Seducing the soul with its glorious streaks of rebirth
Compelling the moon, oh that jaded votary
To take up the wintered shade and be a patron to the night
Which looks down from its zenith, smiting us with bolts of distress
Against the plumes of the oracle, its weapon is contempt
The fates work fast to seal the covenant of doom
Binding it to this vein of youth which is so earnest with pride
That it rather perish for your love and leave the world unsung
Than to bear the thousand hurtful aches of living
Which would dare impose even the slenderest trace of an hour without you
Or the passing grain of sand without having you forever close to me
Oh I strongly die at the thought of these and more

Which dare threaten a day of existence with your absence
Time is both the impostor and the fool if it believes
That I accept these deceits and surrender life on its account
Never, never, never—nothing shall keep me apart
Knowing what you are, I shall hold that dear memory
Until time with hope decays, carrying me and your love far away.

My Dearest Love

My dearest love,
Nothing of this white hope remains
All has perished and scattered far away
The internal peace of the mind is shattered hard
Into a million broken fragments of pain
Into a thousand cloudy pangs and piercing wounds
Unembellished, the heart declines and fades eternal
Thinking nothing on this world of misery
Of cold blindness and inhuman trusts.
The skies, its gods, all of fate has betrayed
This tender heart that has wronged no mortal at all
Has neither afflicted nor abused the privilege of life
That only the sullen fools of this game flout proudly
The rest, they hang their heads in base despondency
In disputed anguish of the triumphs lost and cried
Of all the angers waged in vain and needless strides
Reason is barren to make sense of such tragedy
The commission of the mind is surrendered to something altogether unknown
The internal wars carry on unabated, undismayed
The suffering has no end, so I darken with the shade
Of the fallen night sans dream or liberty
I turn back my eyes; I stare into the depth of you
In kindness and truth I need nothing else to live
So I die, taking you aside my soul as it flees
As the mind flies and speeds and is forever free, my love
These dreams die just to live again
Sometimes I wonder why they rearward recede
In the minds of aspiring men
Who forfeit their lives, letting ambition bleed

What purpose or cause is apparent in this great scape?
Which affords will to live onward without end?
All these dark pursuits that lack escape
What will become of them, what fortunes will mend?
What stride is worth to forgo eternal sleep?
To let the light of the stars to muster and burn
What blind advantage is there for lifting up from the deep?
Showing passions for life then letting them die in turn
None there are, none do I think there to be
Any worthy purpose to this stage, let us thus resign in mutiny.

My Love I

My love,
If all the grounds were as parchment
And all the oceans as ink
If every tree in every forest stood as a quill
Still all of these would be insufficient
To scribe the love I feel, to portray the warmth
That pulses through me and is so ever true
With righteous zeal I attend to one worship alone
It is your face, your hands, your brow, your cheeks
Your glowing eyes of paradise, your mystery
The beauty that from you shines is glory itself
Born incarnate, manifested in a fashion divine
Your beauty, your fairness, your tender loveliness
Are qualities that have no equal in this world
They are virtues that only angels can aspire for
Oh how I wish I were a heavenly god
To be close to you, to be near, to never die
To feel your love, your breast and then to expire
Unto eternity and never have regrets at all
My love, upon that scene of eternity I await
With immortal affections, to feel your hand, to dream, to never die
Oh forever you shall be the burning star upon this endless life
Thereafter our hearts to share their innocence
Our souls to fly, to never die, oh to never die, my all.

My Love II

My love,
Do not leave these sweet hours broken
Or the chambers of my heart mended in their place
For if indeed the colours of Avalon are pale
I shall forsake this proud and contemptuous world
And flee where I shall find your soul as true
There I shall find my true happiness and self
Far departed from this universe of material being
My dream shall fly to where the essence of yours is pure
Untainted by the harshness of this blind and enduring fate
Oh heaven is much kind to gentle virtues
And as I am pure and simple in my love
Its grace shall not be denied me the least
Oh stars, show me your passion, I shall be your love
And thus be forever enthralled to your mercy's fortitude
Show me the brightness of your eyes and I shall thrive
Beyond the million endless lives that mortals suffer
And die to live again in that dark dream of the unknown
With tenderness my flame is set to burn again
Like the unceasing blaze of hope's bright togetherness
Let me to the brink of time and desire takes flight
Where the colours of the mind are softened with your sight
Oh destiny, take hold of me by the pleasured chords of life
Press me to the arms of my sweet love
And never let those chains of liberty break free, break free, break free!

My Love III

My love,
Let us lose ourselves
And think no more on the time that awaits
That holds out to take away youth
For as youth is in us none can deprive that magic
Nor can they dream to, it is ours everlastingly
My dear it can never flee from your hand or mine
Nor can it darken from the moonless sky above
Or be denied to our ears and muteless tongues
That pray to be embraced warmly
As we live, life shall forever seek the light of tomorrow
The glow of yesterday shall be forever fond
Forever unforgotten, how can it be lost at all?
It burns within my mind, it dwells within your heart
It is the eternal keepsake of our souls
Of our freedom and long lived happiness
Of our spirits that reside high upon the brink of heaven
No, this piety cannot leave from us
The halo shall always keep the fire lit
The whiteness does not fade the least
And as the music plays we shall dance to its lyre
Forever and ever, my love, until we are free again.

My Love IV

My love,
My eyes search through the day and night
In quest to find the truest beauty
But hereafter as it stands before me
To nothing I shall look to, the senses are impeached
For you are the blessedness of the glowing sky
You are the slow beams of the jealous star
The envy of the moon, when the clouds obscure the admiring eyes
You are the lease of life, its sweetest sound
You are the release of a hundred hurtful pains
You are the arrow, time is the fiend
You, the glamour, death is the foe and enemy
You are the dream; hope is its direction that onward and forever leads
You are the voice of the nightingale when she sleeps
You are the song, the earth, the listless sea
You are the touch of the fleeting embrace
The art, the rhyme, the brush of mastery
You are the softness of the field, its gentle leisure
The pleasure, the bliss, the unbeaten paradise
The summer Eden, the autumn hold of remembrance
The imperishable rose, the unflagging hour of mystery
You are all the all in all, the eternal grace, the perfection
The undying face, the ceaseless breath, the immortality
You are the sunrise that shines upon the living breast
In the every moment I am awake and think of you.

My Love V

My love,
Often when the streams of thought call out death
I think of you and no pain remains
No pang can every endure such intolerant hurts
For when upon the fonder mind you are conceived
When your vision is pressed upon the more rabid brain
Happiness becomes the potion of the soul
Your cheek, your kiss become warm paradise
That can never lapse into the darker shade of infinity
No, glory as yours forever lives on and on
Higher and higher to where the open heart is free and unbound
There your beauty in its fullness is found
As if some sphere of heaven sundered in two
Shining upon the orbless work of day
That is your scope of majesty, my all
The every delicacy is your mark of grace
The every regent tenderness, the sovereignty
The cloak of madness, the bruise of the unfled star
All burn within my eye when your blessedness is seen
The brilliance, the aura, the gravity
The ruddy smile of the long eternal morn
The cask, the tears, the lone crown of emptiness
The dream, the sigh, the call of yesteryear
All of them are preserved in such perfection
Awaiting your touch, that sweet boldness
To make alive all that never was and will be
But a single token to all that your fair love is.

My Love VI

My love,
What if this is all a poet's dream?
And tomorrow we wake, and there is no rhyme
Nor world to speak, and we are not alone?
Are we not together pressed like the two loneliest souls?
That yearn for each other, that deserve each other's hand
Oh my sweet, I desire you, I worship your light as divine
I caress the pulse that from your heart breathes
That from your innocence teems brim and alive
How gentle that world of silence is
It carries a voice; you are the pilgrim and the shrine
That I adore with mastery, all visions fail
To describe you as your loveliness shines bright
Oh how tender is the gale of the adoring bird
Who sings about peace, knowing naught of cruelty
How fond it would be to let hatred resign
And fall against the shade of nothingness and the unknown
Still amid the darkness, we would be together found
Reciting the prayer of hope that cannot die
Rehearsing the want that often cries unfulfilled
Still we can transcend all that and flee away
Where the mountains glimmer with the brighter rays of dawn
And time disappears, the clouds wash away enfolded
The azure sheen regains its glow of innocence
And we are as one under its prose of life and recovery
Nay, this is no dream, so let us wander further by
And among the endless chronicles of undying love
Find the truth of writ wherein our love is found
These poems melt into the air, but my love, you are you still here

Or must we turn again to beauty's timeless grace
And there dwell in the gleam of this love's hold forevermore.

My Love VII

My love,
When the clouds and dark art of the sky
Are no longer faithful, I return to you
You are my friend, my truest liege
Who upon this remembrance shall not be forgot
How can I release your thought away?
When you warm instil everything I believe
Stone cannot be hard, nor time unending
The oceans as well must dry, the mountains move
When your fair loveliness is perceived
Birds fly from their nest, old fables are retold
The whole of the human stage is shaken stronger with the wind
Without a word, all of life sways with the tempest
The brooks shine on, the pleasures of summer sing
And happiness endures upon my peaceful soul
When your grace is seen, your face adored
Hatred cannot live on the mortal depth
The chamber of harmony pulses in reserve
When your beauty is near yet incomprehensible
When all the bright colours of your check
Slip away my love, so softly slip away
Never to be relished, save by the season of memory
I remain your thrall as these gardens open their eyes
As the sun and stars quarrel over your radiance
I will forever slide back in humble idolatry
In all the gifted features that you have, so unbridled
Prodigious is your heart, tender are your hands
That soothe my aches for all of cherished eternity
Oh how splendid is your love's charity
That sweetness, I shall hold it preciously

Until the nightly signs all expire
And upon the invited symbol of your arms
I resign, never from your hope to wake again, my love.

My Love VIII

My love,
There are not days as white as you
Nor stars as lovely nor dreams as supreme
As that which in my deeper mind is conceived
As mountains decay and proud seas erode away
But as there is breath to the pulse of every living being
My love, you are the fairer strength of them all
There is more power hid beneath your eyes
Than there is the brilliant will of life to all creation
There is more soft beauty kept below your skin
Than all the richest heavens can ever believe rests upon their scapes
My dear, you are the splendid grace of them all
Your fairness is the brightness that shines on
After a million ages have lived and died
Your hands, your soul, your righteousness
Your emanation, your clear and bright glory
Your glow which is the kindest of sweet light
Shall endure forever as a forever can be envisioned
Your face, your brow, the warm carol of your voice
The palace of your land, your red entreating lips
Imprison me against the scene of the night's fair idolatry
Your love is a siege, so then I resign away unpacified
And ponder loftily about the silver sphere upon the sky
So remote, I do not question its belonging
And surrender the sweet warmth that in me resides
Nay, the boldness of that silent song is embodied in you
Despite that the angels speak of a more delightful love
My all, I shall think of you until this vast truth fades
And I am left with nothing but your immortal memory.

My Love IX

My love,
Sans tomorrow's lust, we are still alive
We are but young children upon the meads
How sweet it is, this life, this breath, this hold
Your power, your glorious face
That through the thousand darkest eves cannot be forgot
Through the dreams of yesterday and the unborn moon
Can never fade, we are but pretty rays of light before its throne
Oh queen orb, your majesty is as divine
That eyes go blind, souls cannot feel a thing
The senses go mad within their care
The spirit is insane, the mind longs you alone
Oh love you plague my every inward thought
And as the triumphs shall testify to time
That we are the greatest lovers in the world
No brother can compare with equal passion
Sister Venus is not as free
The stars of romance hang upon their sky with burning envy
The withering heart is empty, their will is nothingness
Desire is the black space of sorrow that endures on
Still each day I long you even more, love is sustained
And pray with empty phrases for your looks to brilliant shine
The million band of mystery invents jives of grace, the old prophet
Cries in silence, the buds wake but again
And blossom out truth as beauty is to your face the lone fairness
The loveliest thing etched into the brain by your immortal love
Oh so I will then resign to pain
Not thinking back to the impulse of death or sleep
Or to the hazel night, to the debt of piety
To the untiring heaven, to the fond seamless air of destiny

Passion gives its due, the eyes their unflinching adoration
The lucid mind lends its impartial all
As I then hopeless fall where your tame beauty rests
The venom bleeds, the hour cleaves with misery
Remembrance shrouds about, the priest of comfort dies
My love, I turn to your harmony as the whole earth blackens around.

My Love X

My love,
My darling
A hundred undreamt nights—they fade
And I let them as your image gains
As your sweet face acquires renown
And you beget the fame of your heart in mine
Your fondness in my joy, your pleasure in my happiness
As the days and nights struggle without end
Jealous as your warm beauty passes them
The world is full alight; the stars shine without their secret
And you are the sister of fairness to them all
I am wont to be the brother of your innocence
Your warmth, your hand, your charity of touch
Your generous tenderness, your fine degree
Your shades, your marks, your scales of excellence
As the clouds drape the nightly sky
And I look upon your brilliance
To think of your love and nothing else
To dream of you and to be no more
Oh to conceive you alone as everything fades
Time is not the time of yesterday
Oh the crowning moon, the moon of tomorrow
My dear, the soft hour cradles our mind
And as you are left to its sight
I am a pagan to a god that has no end
To your beauty—I think no more,
I sleep no more, all is nothingness.

My Love XI

My love,
My all
I will leap to that highest scene of life
If only to capture a fragment of your embrace
The beauty of your face cannot be denied
Oh creature, you are the most glorious of them all
That shall outlive these little unfamed stars
You are the sun, the glow of paradise
Who shall endure through the score of gravid nights
The streams are lakes and bluest skies
Are but a humble tribute to what you encompass
My dear, to what you eternally signify
As sacred you shall be persevered
Unrestrained by any mortal stuff of this earth
Without any need on things that breathe or beat or understand
Yet my heart is yours and it shall be so forever
As a symbol to how a true soul can thrive
And be alive as your beauty is like a fabled queen
Whose warmest shows enrobe the sight of purity
Who englids the enterprise of the unseen grace
Faithless I am yours. Counsel me then with your amity
Your musk, your sport; woe, my doting is bruised
The steady voice is faint, the lips draw weak
As a kiss extends to your carnal cheek
And dies on the place where your blush is left unfulfilled
Oh love, forever and forever I am your slave.

My Love XII

My love,
My desire
Against the harsher day and dark dwelling night
Against the harder losses strewn across my life
And this pain that is cut with the thousand blades of loneliness
I desire you and you alone
I yearn you when against the brink of this ill-destined world
Nothing is seen to last save your beauty
Save your fairness, your glory that survives.
The million daggered clouds of ruination
So quickly will perish and clear up
When the halo of your fame on the brighter sea arrives
Wades against the more burning shore of love's eternity
She, your grace, nourishes the agony, the tortured wounds
These shrouds all tear away, the whiter truth dissolves
Along with the silvery moon and its pale compeers
The chains of fate, its dank spell of coldness
They dissipate; your cheeks replace what is gone and unreturnable
Unrestored, tomorrow is not gone, the story of yesterday has not past
The ageless hold of promise and the fonder privilege drunk
Is kept within your soft eyes, I savour them to the end
Far into the depth of unborn bliss
And wish happiness to every mortal who is blind to death
Who knows not of its timeless reign, of base extinction
Its affection shall lead all to the bleak end of dismay
No, righteousness saves not a thing, no scheme, no purpose
But as your wild beauty lives on through this vast place
I feel that I shall endure forever
Yet is not forever the kissed sweetness of your palms?
The fragrance of your lips, the light above your head?

This great worship that pervades alone the pageant sky?
I do not know but still I resign to them
Merely take me within your heart and soul and I shall never die.

My Love XIII

My love,
My all, my being
You are the deepest passion that runs through these veins of me
Whose power confers the scarlet strength to the pulse of life
I see only glory shine through the brilliance of your eyes
As if two of the brightest panes upon all of heaven
Had released themselves to the common ground below
Defying your name, making gentle your renown
By which all living things are animate
It is your grace, your complexion, your loveliness
That makes hope survive beyond the flow of reason
That makes innocence cower within the unsheltered frame
Of a weak and lonely heart that with desire is brim
Oh where has gone the serene portrait of the world
Wherein two swans can perch upon the hawthorn moon
And not offend the darling rays of the haloed stars
Scattered all around, dreaming no thoughts of jealousy.
My own prayers return to the vision where you were born
To where your sight spread a thousand flames upon the open fields
Of passion and romance's idyllic strides
The quiet tryst alongside the lilac plain awaits, let us run fast to it
And there hide our grief among the many fragrant summer buds
And tell stories of the lark whose sadness has faded from the lip
Of yore and antique age and reverent brotherhood
Of the devotion of youth that never dies with time
But burns stronger and stronger until the feel of love regains
Until its sky-lit stage is cast upon the white brinks of dawn
To forever rise with the constant hands of something eternal
An affection, a sentiment that all too commonly is void
And lacking from every depth where a truer heart is not true

But as we are righteous with our every touch, with our every way
Our immortal feeling cannot perish into the cloudless night
No, the darkness cannot take our warmth, time cannot betray
As I restore my hand to where it was before, upon your tender face
Woe! As with the thousand sweetest kiss,
I bid the world farewell with tears.

My Love XIV

My love,
My truth, my being, my all
Every atom of strength that stirs through me
Every ember of hope within the crucible of warmth
Burns for you, for you alone, oh azure fired god of mine
The flame that pulses through these yearning eyes
Are for your sake my dear, oh beloved for your sake alone
For while worlds may be born and worlds die
Through time is both fleeting and fled
Your heart, my love, your soul are meant for always
The immortal monument within my mind
Stands strong with your picture, with your portrait divine
Adoring every attribute and feature that is fair
Oh it is all fair, all unjust, tell me god where is one blemish
That I can point this scant finger to and say
This arm is not as slender or refined
The texture of this skin is not supremely defined
This complexion on this glow is not as glorious and rare
As the daintiest stars sprawled across the sapphire-gleaming sky
Show me one spot upon that gentle countenance
That would shame perfection of its exalted name
To wage such words would be a war against truth itself
For as I live, there is no equal in loveliness
In blend or mark or majesty that can compare
Or even hold compare to every angelic art and ethereal light as yours
Upon those wide and far and brilliant plains of paradise
There is no creature that can bear mortal parallel
To the every lissom virtue that you inhere
To the full agile wonder that in you is manifest
The splendid awe that from your essence emanates

It shall thrive forever; darkness shall conceal none of its rays
Just like a new born babe cosseted in the nurse's arm
I am rich fed by your beauty, shielded away from the world's hatred
So come nature, come cruel-fisted fiend
And tear my soul away, so I have no need for it
The darkness shall consume nothing; the hot tears shall not raze these eyes
As I have been kissed by the direct agent of heaven
The dateless oath has been signed
As those scarlet lips have sealed an eternal vow with me
I fear nothing at all, I am afraid of nothing!
I retain you within my mind, this scene then blackens
Setting me free to the higher realm where I am yours
Upon that infinite scape, we are together released everlastingly, my love.

My Love XV

My love,
Oh my lady, how I admire you so
With such strength, with such deep passion
That all the stars glow with a humble face
All the daydreams of the former year
Resign with such reverent envy
That they will never return again
They are not needed; your beauty dwells within my mind
The mortal soul pulses without faltering
Human strides cannot age nor conquerings be lost
To the dark throes of time, hope's innocence prevails
The light of beatitude, the warm hand of destiny
They both climb up through the wings of heaven
Decrying the song of love as the only madness
As the only lunacy that merits to ever live
That makes the little angels dance inside our heads
Romantic vibrancy is abound, your looks are radiant
They are pristine; they are pure as the cloudy cries
That falls upon the tomorrow that has never been
Nor will ever be as long as the sunshine of your face
Casts its rays with desire's constancy
So then the moonlight wanes, the amber trickle of the silent dusk
Drops into my ears, an eternal well is born
And from it flows the tender streams of paradise
That tone reflect your majesty and nothing else
I surrender in whole, my limbs decay
Upon death's scene there is no vision but of you

That is all I need, everything else softly fades away
My love, I am comforted by all that is warmly seen and unseen the same.

My Love XVI

My love,
This life plays on like a wondrous pageant
Whose chains of bondage are your bluest eyes
Oh how they bruise, how I need them most
How I cannot survive the nimble hour of living
Without your tame softness pressed against my own
Without the temple of your glory crowded on me forever
Oh my heart is yours; its modest state resides in silence
When pensively your kindness it considers
And crowns your charity above all that can ever be
So you are it, the fashion of loveliness thus shines forth
And gently speaks of the tender hold of your palm
Oh what artistry, what richness, what comely praise
What divine affection, your eyelids counsel me
On the advice of romance that to all other mortals is unknown
Perhaps better it is to perceive myself as dead
I am in the presence of an angel, my soul is fled
It seeks the arrant blush of your prayers to survive
It needs the orchard of your warmth to even breathe
To suckle the sweetness of your fair lineaments, the perfection therein
Oh how the nectar of desire is left undone, I relish it
And worship the diamonds that defend your charming face
That minister famed beauty to your shapely glow
Oh they persuade me, your whispers are as sophistry
That is spoken in the night against the white ancient moon
Before the vision lapses and the lissom song expires
But you shall always remain impressed on my mind
For as the evening sets, as the stars have esteem
As the host of heaven is sculpted in equanimity
In such borne amity, I shall woo you, oh brightest creature

And pray to the force that has found you in such thriving grace, my beloved
That had once instilled wide perfection within the veins
Oh my spirit flees to that kindled score of youthful time
And there among the grasses and the meads it finds a golden joy once more
That joy is your light, your love—I fly to it, I fly—I am most ever free.

My Love XVII

My love,
As destiny within me prides to live
Shall I do less than your beauty to worship?
Your glory to applaud, your fate to admire?
Nay, the work of the world is worth nothing!
Those prayers, those isles of lonesome paradise
That fragrant summer that will never be again
Shall I pine these many things of life lost?
And clear remembrance of its deft cry of despair?
And splendour in your righteousness until the dark hour's end?
So hold my hand, let us breathe together
As we behold the light that the newborn stars bring
Whatever the course of fate, you are its sovereign
Whatever its trade, its wind, you shall conquer above it
Whatever the shade of love, dearest, by you it is perfected
Then let us stand silent below the morning sun, our soul will prevail
In worshipped envy of the angel that flies high
His spirit owns the realm that our soul dreams of
The tower of majesty wedges between your bow and nothingness
Your grace, your zeal, your glistened elegance
As desires pile themselves upon the stone of grief
There is no doubt, the carrions are blown away
And we are left among the dust and songs of mortal peace
Forever to weave the tale of our hearts within the grave
As with gentle store we gaze out from the cask
And we dream of the unity that is ours everlastingly
And think on nothing more than time and time's eternity
Oh love, the unforgiven flower rises high to the moon
As the throne of our amity overtakes this ill-treasured world
The teeming musk, the ivy, the crown of yesterday shall be our friend

The whole Eastern scene resigns into a living shore
Your love and my love survive the raging siege of the mind
As we together play on within this fable that never ends
Against the riots and the strides and the vain embraces
Upon the stray thoughts of youth that glisten gold
Leading to and fro, love is the lord of this faithless piety
The fair vision sinks, the pulse of passion beats down
The rueful chords and the whiter rays of day
All fall incident upon this temple that must collapse
Unbroken, unfeeling—upon the worship of our togetherness that cannot fade
The mad dulcet air, the cradled touch, the trust, the finality
All recline backward in arrest, the swaggered counsel thrives
As we endure the madness of this short seen enterprise
Imperilling our lives for what cannot be restored
Imprisoning ourselves with swift descent, it too must perish
Until the martyrdom comes and we are released
Surrendered unto and Eden that is true ours
And by touch, my love, can never be forsaken again!

My Love XVIII

My love,
How can I ever be rid of hope's undying pain
Or this heart cured of its obsessive disease
As long lives your fairness, there also is one remedy
That I can conceive of, calling it your beauty
Your grace, your charm, your warmth which surpasses all else
Oh how the power of nothing can exceed your glow
Therefore I pound and ache in inner madness
Remembering all that you are, all that I cannot have
How you are the lone star above all the heavens
That governs the motions of the dark night thrown about
Oh how I am the fool, the slave, the simplest servant
Who gives no notice to the gentle pass of time
Though as it wades, I am aged more and more
By the eternal hours of death, I am separated from you
Yet by your perfection, my adoring soul is redeemed
Throned high upon the towers of your light's society
Where tender justice serves the restless yearning felt
Oh sadness can never flourish when the mind is true
Loneliness can never thrive when two hearts pulse as one
Therefore bow your innocence towards me
Swear that your devotion is saved for me alone
And no wickedness or sorrow's ruin shall befall us
We will be set free upon our own tranquil lands
Upon our own wide dominions of happiness
Never, never to be taken away, my all
Never revoked far from these honest loving hands
Nor withdrawn from the soft slumber of my longing dream
So spread your arms about and let the sun burn in envy
The brightest star of glory is immortally blessed before me

And you are it, forever to remain before my admiring sight
Staring deep at the paragon that you embrace
Entranced in a gaze, until my eyes grow tired of the impossible
Nay, that moment will never come, thus my soul is transfixed
Upon the glimpse of your pure truth of being
Waiting until the conquered shades of darkness fall
And the little rays all flee away to reveal your brightness
Long live your light, it shall never resign unto the kingdom of the draped
Until you take to my side and we are as one and infinite.

My Love XIX

My love,
All the feelings that I have, they are for you
I would naught deny even a sentiment
To your pervading beauty, you deserve them all
Thus descend upon me from your sky, take me away
Fly me to the palace where your tenderness reflects serenely
And the wild grasses sway in sincere loveliness
It is that sunshine, your fairest glow that I seek
Your face that I prize alone amongst all living things
Yet you surpass them all, your art exceeds
The labour of a thousand lifetimes spent in sacrifice
You fulfil what life on this earth can never
Your touch, your blush, your tepid eminence
Draws in the brink of madness, I thrust out from the imperilled verge
With a falling wish to land along your side
To gently die in your arms and think of nothing else
But of the night, the stars and your eyes of liberty
Under such a scene my soul will be set free
Forever after, owning nothing, having nothing but your hold
I am content now, let me fade away
To expire unto the sky where you and I are as one
Alone my love, alone together and eternally free
To perish brightly and dream that time is not wasted
Not as long as we are side by side, I await you there
Counting the precious hours until your glory lifts again
And makes a true worship of all that I ever need
My all, my spirit within this siege of pain can rest no more
I flee, I flee, and oh I yearn to be a part of you
Else death to take me, to whisper kind things into mine ear
To always remember all that you are, my angel

To never forget all that our great love can be
Oh I await you there, I flee, I flee
I await you there once more and forever, my love.

My Love XX

My love,
These hours pass; we can have no more of them
Life is but a short game of betrayal
But as I have you within my life
Our being shall endure for immortal days
Our unified spirit will be free
Upon that sky that no one can take from us
Our longings will be shared together
Our wings unified, our pulses as one
Our dreams, our minds, our innocence
Our hearts lapse, everything will be so kind
Everything will be a friend that cannot leave
Oh my dear how I will forever miss you
Days will seem as years, years as eternity
A moment lost, the greatest regret of all
As I press my frame to where yours lies
And let this whole scene decay until there is nothing left
Save where your beautiful face burns like a star
My love, I will forever rest with you there.

My Love XXI

My love,
Nothing lasts forever; we too are of mortal stuff
The flesh and its love are as well meant to decay
So let our hearts melt away unto the coming hour
And we will be so ever free
Oh my darling, my precious love
Time cannot bar us of tender strength
The rose, the glassy voice of the nightingale
Cannot dry our hands, our pulses still beat
And as they do, we own all of fondness
All of tomorrow, the sweeter part of yesterday
Oh beloved when I dream upon hope's lost friend
My mind returns to your gentle vision
Your sight, your eyes, your softened reverie
As all of the earth and skies may darken
But as I hold your love and hold it ever close
Tomorrow is sunshine; all of my being burns and is bright again
For your virtue and more loftier spirit
I make sacrifice to them and call it sweet paradise
It is prized heaven, your face is supreme
Your trace is holiness, I feel nothing more
Than the passion that races up and down my soul
My spirit, it resigns as your lonely servant
As the heart flies to where our love is bound
And there upon the endless sky, my all, we are forever free.

My Love XXII

My love,
This striking pain us more than can be endured
So I will resign as a wounded man
Into your arms of mercy, heal me
And the whole world will be righted again
Show me the path that your footsteps lead to
I will travel their for a million lives incarnated
If for a moment they will show your perfection
If for a fleeting hour your love can be revealed
I would scale the lengths of every untouched earth
I would praise the magic upon the boundless skies
All for the tender sake of your truest heart
All for the glowing aspects of your face
That outshine the humbled rays of night
That soar above all that is divine
So my hands crumble, my soul weakens away
I think of nothing else in this short life
Save you and love and dark eternity
Your eyes grant me the longest company
That I will ever need as I passage into your thoughts, my love
This time and forevermore, freed upon our embrace.

My Love XIII

My love,
Can words ever suffice to explain?
The worship that I hold for you
The kind pain that I trade with misery
So that you can be retained in graceful reverie
Oh what fondness, I leap away in joy
Like a summer leaf fallen out from verdant sleep
Or the swan awoken from its hawthorn shade of fantasy
I take the ruins of Pegasus and fly aloft
And fly up and up to where the stars are no longer seen
To where the flowers are looked down with gentleness
Oh what a paradise this sweet earth is
How majestic, knowing you are part of it
That dreams cannot escape the tender mind
Desire can never flee from the pure bosom depth
Not as long as angels remain hung upon the sky
And you are seen among them, the blushes gain in unnumbered fold
The eyelid softly falls again, hope is unspoken of
As the tepid meadow carries human thoughts away
My angel, through them all you are still mine
I still fancy you as the one vision supreme
I perceive life as nothing less than treason
If we are not coupled, arm within arm unto everlasting time
This havocked world would then be worth nothing
The music of the ears, they convey but naught
The earth shall stand in silence, defending nothing but the scene
Where you and I are taken together alive
Kept in the serenity that pure love affords

The darkness runs, let us chase its tail
And under the halo of time's eternity we shall find our happiness.

My Love XIV

My love,
This world is worth nothing
This life, this fleeting pulse of the sky
Is but a passing dream, a dream to be forgot
No hopes, no tomorrows to ever be remembered
No light upon the unlived day can even shine
All shall be absolved save our embrace
Nothing shall remain except the hold of our own hands
That keeps a vision to this bright eternity
The scythe of time runs free into our soul
Catching us in between the younger field of bliss
Of enchantment, of a vision that is so unreal
That only you and I share it, my love
All of these paintings, these fairer portraits of the hour
Will not fade as this sweet passion streams amorously
So come, come away my dear
And we will rest upon these finer plains of life
Until the autumn leaves and grey shades of winter
Do not deny the summer harvest that is ours
It belongs to us; we are the heirs of love's wide infinity
Immortally, as this fever swells within our fame
As romance's heat is sequestered within our gravid pulse
We shall claim it as a sign to our forever and forever love
Like a blazing star that burns as a memory to you and I, my all.

My Love XV

My love,
Where do I start to tell you of hope?
You came into my life; the world is not the same
Lo, it is surrendered, its seas are overturning
The nectar of spring is drawn elsewhere
The tides gather by the sun, the roses draw together
And you are the glory lived upon each
The power, the strength, the fairness of devotion
The truest happiness, the freest light
Grows along your trace, brightening the sky
Glowing with such strength, it flames me
As I step away to where the feelings burn wild
Where stillness is venom to the restless vein
The evening strikes, the stars tax the sweetness of the lips
The doctrine of prose cleaves in disquiet
No it cannot stand, solitude is shame
It is the cruel mist that bruises the soul
And leads me away to the unknown, oh beloved.
How I dream of you on the less fortunate day
And the clouds expire; the earth is no longer stark
The kindest scenes, oh ever unbruised!
Yet woe as dearest you are still not mine
The autumn knife, the blade of wilderness
The shield of mourning, my wont, my adoration
The physic that survives, the lottery of hours
They all lapse when the soft thrums play
Peril is renewed, the grief of old restored
Daughter, sister of beauty I search for you
And will not cease until this tame blood drains
Oh forever after, I am not worth your mercy

But as the heavens spin, I sense your gravity
I will blind my eyes with death until you are found
Oh love, thereon we will be as free!
Free, my love, ever free…

About the Author

Arman Nabatiyan was born in Tehran, Iran and has lived in the Middle East, Europe and the US. His style of poetry reflects inspiration from all three traditions but draws most heavily on the Persian repertoire of classics where an emphasis on lyricism, introspection and mysticism are unified into a single form. He currently lives in the UK where he is the Max Perutz Scholar at Magdalene College, Cambridge. His previous titles include *Poems: Love and Yore* and *The Hours of Youth*.

978-0-595-36356-8
0-595-36356-3

Printed in the United States
41677LVS00007B/145-147

9 780595 363568